D0558350

Innovation Theology

Innovation Theology

A Biblical Inquiry and Exploration

LANNY VINCENT

FOREWORD BY RON GAMMILL

WIPF & STOCK · Eugene, Oregon

INNOVATION THEOLOGY
A Biblical Inquiry and Exploration

Copyright © 2017 Lanny Vincent. All rights reserved. Except for brief quotations in critical publications or reviews, no part of this book may be reproduced in any manner without prior written permission from the publisher. Write: Permissions, Wipf and Stock Publishers, 199 W. 8th Ave., Suite 3, Eugene, OR 97401.

Wipf & Stock
An Imprint of Wipf and Stock Publishers
199 W. 8th Ave., Suite 3
Eugene, OR 97401

www.wipfandstock.com

PAPERBACK ISBN: 978-1-5326-0869-8
HARDCOVER ISBN: 978-1-5326-0871-1
EBOOK ISBN: 978-1-5326-0870-4

Manufactured in the U.S.A.   FEBRUARY 20, 2017

Unless otherwise noted, scriptural quotations and citations are from New Revised Standard Version Bible, copyright 1989, Division of Christian Education of the National Council of the Churches of Christ in the United States of America. Used by permission. All rights reserved.

Unless otherwise noted, dictionary quotations and citations are from Leslie Brown, ed., *The New Shorter Oxford English Dictionary*, 2 vols. (Clarendon, 1993).

Do not remember the former things, or consider the things of old.
I am about to do a new thing; now it springs forth, do you not perceive it?

Isaiah 43:18–19

Contents

The Company of God

Foreword

To CREATE IS TO make something from nothing. In this sense, only God creates. Innovators always make something from something else.

There are puzzles (when we have the pieces), and problems (when we do not) that will continue to evolve and change. The world will cry out for innovations that provide responses to these needs. Change is real. How innovators respond to this evolving reality will determine the scope of their actions, the paths they choose to explore, and the clarity, scale, and lasting value of their vision and work.

These essays explore a terrain seldom discussed, found at the intersection of innovation and theology. The terrain of this intersection provides good news for innovators. That good news could be characterized as "gospellian"—something that grows and develops from the gospels and the application of Jesus's teaching to a modern world. This intersection and what actually happens there is a perceptual space often ignored, seldom written about and difficult to describe. However, innovation and theology have interacted continually throughout history, regardless of our inattention or abilities to articulate. For the innovator, what happens at this intersection is perceived internally, more personal than public. Innovators don't talk about their faith, they talk about their innovations.

This zone of inquiry, of theology's meaningful link to innovation, has no boundaries. It expands and contracts at attempts to define it, control it, and put it to use. Yet, the innovative giants of history have done just that. Could Michelangelo have painted the Sistine Chapel without faith in and awareness of Scripture, and a personal vision of creation?

Could Lincoln have written the Gettysburg address on an envelope, traveling by train, under the weight and strain of an impossible responsibility, without the inspiring presence and power of Scripture? Could Martin Luther King Jr. have expressed "I have a dream" without knowledge of biblical poetry and prose?

Innovation abounds in Scripture. The nomadic tribes of Israel, wandering in the Sinai Desert, were instructed by God to build a prefabricated, transportable temple, one whose elements are described in vivid detail and whose scale is given in Egyptian cubits. And the story of Noah, who alone listened to the Spirit while all others mocked, . . . was this Innovating in the Company of God? How long has this been going on? What defines, and motivates this fuller aspect of work and walk?

These essays suggest that our conventional understanding of the roots of innovation is far too narrow and secular. For centuries, faith has influenced the work of all the arts: drawing, painting, sculpture, and architecture; and its focus has been to explore this crossing. Among mankind's great innovative efforts are these crossings of faith.

Experience tells that a maker's intent to innovate is an energy that is driven by a vast array of motivations—from the elements of being and character, to experience and education, to faith and belief in the value of work, as well as to the ability to dream, and the will to risk the journey that action demands. These essays remind us that some of our best work is good not because it meets our goals, but because it possesses qualities in addition to those we take for granted. Meaning and value are enhanced when our field of consideration includes "for others." Faith is not a limiting force, but an advantage for the innovator. Working with this awareness of the One (who desires the very evolution in our thinking and action that we seek) creates an engaged and motivating space as well as a Spiritual one. Innovative work will benefit from a measure of grace and devotion, and a mind made confident by the awareness that the Creator continues to create, and that this energizing force manifests in work, and that we can be, if not creators, at least partners in creation. For as the Apostle Paul said: "What do we have that we did not receive?"

As I read these essays I am reminded of who we are, and who we are ultimately working for, and that meaning and value are closely linked in what we do. I am also reminded that awareness of this matters, as the product of our work (seen and unseen) matters. These essays encourage us to cultivate, deepen, and actualize that awareness.

In faith itself there is encouragement, prayer, and promise. The prayer is the same as Paul's, "that you may abound in every good work." But the promise is no less than this: that if we do our innovating in the living space of awareness and service, then we are empowered by the promise that our work can be dedicated, led, inspired, deepened in meaning, and blessed by Grace. And as work abounds, the innovator will experience a transformation of meaning in this bounty. And in the wake of consequences following this effort, the innovator will capture new fulfillment, and a humility and wholeness in work.

In the cellar of our being there is a core motivator for innovation. It lies concealed under all the other reasons to invent: to make better the things that surround us, to improve and elevate our lot. This motivation grows from the seeds of new ideas, new visions, and there is magic in it. It is rooted in the soil of our knowledge and the accumulated wisdom we can access. It is a feeling driven by our will to know, to serve and to explore, and our desire to see the pieces fit together in wholeness and completion. It is the very foundation, the luminous ground of our source and core desire: to make and to see something never seen before.

Ron Gammill
Architect, Environmental Design
Berkeley, August 2016

Preface

The Brainstorm

TWO YEARS AGO I had what some might call a brainstorm. As with most storms, winds howl, rain pours and energy far exceeds visibility. Once the storm passes, the winds subside, the rain stops, and the air clears. Visibility improves.

Such was my experience with this brainstorm. When the storm passed I was left with a pesky vision. I was skeptical of my own thinking, remembering the observation of Peter Drucker that ideas born from brainstorms are the least reliable sources of innovation.[1] I was encouraged, however, realizing the vision was not an innovation, really. It was just an idea, one that wouldn't leave.

What I saw in my mind's eye were several conversational gatherings, each comprised of about a dozen people. Participants were those who don't normally talk to each other, partly because they live along parallel lines that seldom have the chance to meet, and partly because they may not know what to say to each other, how to say it, or even what questions to ask the other. Half the participants are theologically educated or educating. The other half are experienced innovators, entrepreneurs, economists and technologists, open to theological inquiry.

The gatherings were low profile, at least in my imagination; not a lot of promotion or glossy marketing brochures; just substantive conversations—lively, exploratory, engaging. Both halves of the room were

1. Drucker, *Innovation and Entrepreneurship*, 130.

having a lot of fun; serious, to be sure, but laughing a lot. Participants were having so much fun uncovering practical insights they decided to keep meeting, again and again.

Each participant was finding nourishment, encouragement, even inspiration from the others. It fed them all, intellectually and spiritually. The theologically educated found themselves delightfully engaged in a wider field of view than they had experienced before. The innovators found themselves encouraged, emboldened with deeper confidence, leaving each gathering with a greater clarity as to where innovations are needed and why. Others were intrigued, more than mildly. After a while, a common vocabulary began to emerge, not about doctrine or theology, really. More about value, hope and faith, and even, dare I say it, love and justice.

The initial conversations started in a few disparate parts of the country, like the Silicon Valley, Route 128 outside of Boston, Chicago, Seattle and even Vancouver. They typically took place in a vacant classroom, one with a pristine whiteboard, which by the end of each conversation was totally filled with lines drawn between boxes and circles cryptically labeled. There were even a few equations. Before leaving most everyone pulled out their iPhones to capture for themselves the images left on the whiteboard.

Initial gatherings lasted for only a couple of hours. Soon, however, some stretched into the evening or took up a whole day. Regardless of the time, participants in these gatherings wanted to continue, as each conversation generated an energy and momentum all its own.

That's the vision that stayed after the storm in my brain blew through.

In the immediate aftermath of this brainstorm I thought the leftover vision a bit fanciful, like a daydream. The only problem was that this one didn't go away. It hung around for several weeks. In hindsight, its stickiness probably made some sense. From 1978 to 1982 I was an ordained Presbyterian minister, and since 1982 I have been a consulting facilitator to large commercial corporations attempting to invent and innovate. Some refer to me as an "innovation midwife."[2] Regardless of the label, I have had the rare privilege of living and working between two domains that seldom interact: theology and innovation.[3] These two parallel domains rarely touch, listen or speak to each other, at least publically.

2. Vincent, "Innovation Midwives," *Research-Technology Management*, January-February 2005.

3. On the innovation side, mostly with STEM-intensive innovating efforts (STEM = Science, Technology, Engineering and Math) of commercial corporations; on the theology side, mostly in the context of a Reformed theological tradition as an active Presbyterian layperson.

The lack of interaction is not really surprising, at least from a conventional perspective. From a theological perspective, however, I sense both omission and opportunity, since both theology and innovation

- have much to say about responding to change,
- have to do with value and value creation,
- are ways people attempt to make sense, and
- shape human culture with positive or negative implications.[4]

Not knowing what to do with this pesky vision, I did what seemed like the obvious thing to do. I registered the domain name: innovation-theology.org. It didn't escape my notice that .net and .com were available also. I thought that would take care of it and I could go on to other things. Even such a small act as registering the domain name, however, seemed to make the vision stick even more. So, I gave in to it, which was when I realized the vision had a gaping hole in it.

Suppose these gatherings *did* occur.[5] What on earth would those gathered talk with each other about? The essays that follow represent an initial and possible answer.

4. Such implications are often long-lasting on both creatures and the creation.

5. See www.innovationtheology.org for current status of these gatherings and conversations.

Acknowledgments

MAKING SENSE IS NOT a solo activity. This is particularly the case when it comes to making sense of uncharted territories, like innovation theology. In fact, it may not be possible without acknowledging that most everything we know, or think we know, we have received.

Such grace came to me from a greater cloud of witnesses than I could possibly acknowledge. However, there are a few who have been in the foreground of this effort, without whom I would still be wandering in the wilderness. Their theological curiosity and practical support proved essential.

Fortunately I have been blessed in this endeavor by several generous and thoughtful souls who gave their time, attention and devotion to early drafts. Substantive suggestions came from Anne Badanes, Barry Brown, Rebecca Buckley, Greg Gudorf, Amy Hassinger, Austin Leininger, John McIntyre, Matthew McNeil, and Jennifer Whitten.

Subsequently Stuart Brown, Ron Gammill, Greg Gudorf, Marilyn McEntyre, and Jack Swearengen each gave later drafts much close examination for which I am deeply grateful. Their advice has been both invaluable and encouraging.

Kathy Bairey brought the fresh, critical eyes of an editor to uncover what I could not see in making this a more readable set of essays. (What remains less readable is a function of my blindness, not Kathy's editorial skill.)

This effort would have languished in the wishful thinking of my mind and never made it onto the page without the encouragement, friendship and prodding of these souls. I am deeply grateful for each and every one.

Introduction

Then I saw a new heaven and a new earth.[1]

ORGANIZATIONS RESPOND TO CHANGE in different ways and for different reasons. Individuals do, too. Certainly there are significant differences between what applies to an individual and what applies to an organization.[2] But what individuals do in response to change and what collectives do prove instructive to each other.

Of course *responding* to change is different than *reacting* to change. Without a space in between the stimulus of change and our response we simply react. When we respond, we have a choice and make it. When we react, we also have a choice, but don't make it.[3] The following essays speak to what we do in this space and how we think about it.

Responses to change can be located on a continuum. At one end are *absorption* responses. Here individuals and organizations have sufficient resources, momentum or clout to absorb change without adapting or adjusting to it, at least in the near term. Admittedly this is not much of a response. In fact it could appear as indifference. Near midpoint on the continuum are *defensive* responses. Preservation of the *status quo* and conservation of resources characterize these types of responses. At

---

1. Rev 21:1.

2. Niebuhr, *Moral Man and Immoral Society*, xxii–xxiii: "Our contemporary culture fails to realize the power, extent and persistence of group egoism in human relations."

3. Ackoff, *Differences That Make a Difference*, 108.

the other end of the continuum are *innovating* responses. These are conscious choices to respond to change in such ways as to create new value for others. In the case of a commercial enterprise, nonprofit or social service agency, such a response could be to try something truly new—a product or service innovation. In the case of an individual, the new value created for another might involve the risk of doing something extraordinary, both for the other and for the one taking the risk.

Financial or cost/benefit calculus rarely add up to anything but clear warnings *against* innovating even when the numbers are credible. Given the continuum of possible responses to change, why innovate at all? Why would anyone—organization or individual—take on the greater demands, uncertainties and risks that accompany innovating, particularly if there are other ways of responding in the "safer" middle, or even at the opposite end of the continuum? Why attempt to respond to change in such a way to create new value?

Numbers are only one of many considerations, including "the substance of things hoped for, the convictions of things unseen."[4] This capability to believe what is not seen is an essential trait of the entrepreneur and innovator. That entrepreneurs and innovators use more of this capability is arguably what distinguishes them from the rest of us.[5] But whether a defining characteristic or not, believing plays a central role in the experience of innovating.

If theology[6] at a minimum is defined as thoughtful reflection on believing experiences, particularly where God is believed to play a role, then the experience of innovators innovating is well within what can and should interest theologians. The role believing plays in innovating alone invites those with an interest in theology to take a closer look at what theology might have to bring to innovation. If only for this reason the following essays are offered.

However, there is another reason, especially now. The sheer number of recent publications on entrepreneurship and innovation is overwhelming. Even a cursory survey of this abundance reveals that more than enough has been written on *how* organizations should innovate. Little, however, has been said about *where* innovations are needed and *why*.

4. Heb 11:1.

5. Vincent, *Prisoners of Hope*, xi.

6. Unless otherwise stated, use of "theology" and its derivatives assumes biblical theology, of which more will be said in the essay "Innovating with Company Assets: Scripture and Spirit."

Some conversations related to where and why, however, are beginning. As I write this, the economies of the United States, Europe and Japan, along with many organizations and individuals within them, continue a seven-year drift in the doldrums.[7] Corporate sails droop, weighed down with unprecedented piles of cash, either uninvested or underinvested. Even the US Defense Department—a traditional sponsor of many major innovations—is expressing worry that its defense contractors are not innovating like they used to.[8]

The doldrums have remained since the gale-force winds blew through in September 2008. Some economists suggest we are in the quiet after another storm of "creative destruction."[9] However, there remains much anxious money on the sidelines. What may be even more troubling than all the sidelined money is the absence of vision, hinting at the relevance of the biblical proverb "where there is no vision, the people perish."[10]

Even before the events of 2008 the anxiety of society was building. The late Edwin Friedman spotted this anxiety among organizational leaders. According to Friedman, American civilization has reached a "threshold of anxiety such that reasonableness and honesty no longer defend against illusion." When this happens, "even the most learned ideas begin to function as superstitions."[11] Superstitions have infected responses to change and innovating as well.

It may seem a bit strange to deploy theology to immunize leaders of innovation from these superstitions. Some might suggest that theology itself is but rationalization for superstitions. If you agree with this latter view, these essays are likely not for you. But if you are interested in the twin questions of where innovations are needed and why, personally or

---

7. "Since 2008 corporate investment in America, the euro zone and Japan has fallen short of cashflow . . . making firms net savers rather than borrowers. This reflects both subdued expectations about near term sales and a more deep seated belief that, as populations age, markets will shrink and good opportunities for investment will become rare. Rising inequality may aggravate the process: the rich save more than the poor. Efforts by emerging markets to hold down their currencies and plough the resulting trade surpluses into rich-world bond markets do further harm" (Ip, "Dangers of Deflation").

8. Cameron and Barnes, "Pentagon Presses Contractors."

9. Also called "Schumpeter's Gale."

10. Prov 29:28 KJV.

11. Friedman, *Failure of Nerve*, 1.

professionally, and you have a modicum of theological curiosity, then you may want to read further.

Looking back on the past three decades as an "innovation midwife" gives me pause. Upon reflection we need more compelling answers to the questions of where to innovate and why, answers beyond the parochial interests of the innovating organization. The answers I imagine reflect more purposeful innovations that reside in the making of meaning more than money, the pursuit of substantive more than superficial value, the quest to contribute more than simply be different, the fostering of righteous more than merely efficient outcomes, the creation of just more than merely commercial success, the stewardship of common more than simply shareholders' interests, and the kind of growth that is faithful more than acquisitive.

Typically we define and confine innovation and entrepreneurship to commercial and economic endeavors. Recently, "social venturing" and "social investing" have extended innovation and entrepreneurship into noncommercial fields. Principles and experiences native to profit-making sectors are now being applied to opportunities for positive societal impact, not just financial gain. Many propose that one can do good while also doing well, challenging the notion that commercial success and societal contribution are separate and distinct.

Seldom, however, do we recognize that theology might have something to contribute to the principles and practice of innovation and entrepreneurship, whether defined traditionally, extended to social spheres, or both. But when we realize that the essence of innovation and entrepreneurship is *creating new value for others*, then it opens the prospect that this kind of activity may benefit from a theological perspective. In fact, creating new value for others may be essential to living a meaningful life—one that is not dependent upon getting so much as it is upon giving. Those of us who have tasted this experience know how gratifying, pure and purposeful such experiences are. Perhaps this is another way of describing the essence of what righteousness is—that state into which God persistently invites us.

A goal of these essays is invite theological inquiry into the field of innovating and its management. What motivates such an invitation is not simply intellectual curiosity, but practical utility. Responding to change is fraught with uncertainty and fear. Fear afflicts both the powerless and powerful, though in different ways. Neither is immune to the anxiety that comes with unsolicited change, especially when the response is aimed at creating new value. Such responses require courage. Theology suggests that faith and love are effective countermeasures to fear. "Perfect love drives out fear."[12]

From my own direct experiences—periods of success punctuated by dashed expectations and failed plans, personal and professional—I have learned what others have learned before me: there is no more reliable source of encouragement than the clarity of one person expressing the account of their hope to another. The Apostle Peter urged us to always be ready to give such an account for the hope that is within us.[13] These essays are such accounts, intended to catalyze the reader to clarify his or her own account and hope. From these experiences will grow, I believe, a conviction that unsought change is an envelope containing an invitation from a loving, caring God. In this envelope is not just any invitation. It is an invitation to create new value for others—in other words, to innovate.

CHARTING THE TERRITORY

What follows might be something like a scouting expedition. Innovation theology is an uncharted territory at this time. As a scout for the expedition my qualifications arise from firsthand experience with these two domains along with some published reflections to make some sense of it.[14] But the role and authority of a scout is limited. In this role I merely hope to point out where the more prominent peaks and valleys are on the innovation theology landscape. If you are looking for doctrinal precision or orthodox propositions you are not likely to find them here.

The cartography of *innovation theology*[15] will require conversational efforts that traverse boundaries seldom crossed. Economists, serial inventors, theologians, biblical exegetes, lay leaders, entrepreneurs, intrapreneurs and those who study entrepreneurship and corporate venturing will need to talk with each other, and perhaps more importantly, *listen* to each other. Common charts will need to be forged that cross the boundaries of previously uncommon territories, mind-sets, experiences and

---

12. 1 John 4:18.

13. 1 Pet 3:15.

14. See www.innovationsthatwork.com.

15. I could have called it a "theology of innovation" or even a "theology for innovation." I chose "innovation theology" because it has fewer words and is probably more a theology than a theory of innovation. It should not be confused with innovations for or in theology as that is what Reformed theology is already about.

vocabularies. However, despite such a daunting conversational challenge, results should lead to more substantive results for innovators, greater willingness to see change as purposeful not merely inevitable, and less reluctance to embrace innovation as an option. It could also prove enlivening to theology as well.

Normally innovation is viewed as a secular and largely economic phenomena even by those with a theological education; neither sacred nor spiritual. I am not sure why this is. The arc of the biblical saga moves from one divine intervention to another. It is filled with God intervening in the affairs of mankind to create new and unexpected events—possibilities that were unimagined and unimaginable before they happened. The interventions are many and varied. Take, for example,

- the birth of Isaac to a barren ninety-year-old mother;
- a burning bush that is not consumed in the burning;
- the parting of the Red Sea;
- David's inspired improvisation with five smooth stones;
- the surprise calling of Israel to be a suffering servant to all other nations;
- an exile and a return from exile;
- a messiah whose messianic character was not what most thought it would be;
- resurrections; and
- a dramatic conversion of a chief persecutor—Saul became Paul.

These are but a few of the more prominent ones, certainly not all of them. Could these divine interventions be called divine innovations? Many of these interventions *seem* like innovations—new embodiments of value that were thought impossible at first. Like many innovations they were unexpected. Still, it feels awkward to call them innovations.

If we prefer to keep divine interventions separate from human innovations, however, then reserving the latter as off limits to any considerations other than secular and economic still leaves a theological problem. It limits the scope and movement of God's presence and purpose. Imposing such a limit is *theo*logically difficult. It is contrary to one of the things typically included in the three-letter word "God": a divine freedom to show up wherever and whenever God chooses. "God does whatever God pleases."[16]

Given the few occurrences of the word "new" in theology's primary source perhaps it is no surprise that innovation has been ignored by theology. However, if we pause and consider the entire sweep of the biblical narrative, the cannon is filled with accounts of God doing remarkably new, unexpected and "disruptive" things—many of which were thought impossible before they became not only probable but actual. Rarely, however, is innovating considered from a theological perspective. Why should it be? What difference might such a perspective make, especially now?

One is the legacy this generation is rapidly creating for the next. If God's interests have something to do with intrinsic values like loving-kindness, doing justice and walking humbly with God[17] then how are our innovations manifesting these intrinsic values, if at all? Are medical technology innovations—arguably embodiments of loving-kindness—constrained by the need for a profitable return? Is the requirement of a profitable return a form of *not* walking humbly? Are social media innovations enabling us to do justice by creating more and faster exposure of hidden injustices? Are these innovations at risk because they might not create enough profit even as advertising platforms? Or are these platforms generating too much noise? Are we concerned that innovations producing economic growth—revenue, profits and jobs—are also eroding the fabric of communities and relationships?[18]

Putting aside for the moment whether divine interventions are synonymous with divine innovations, all of the interventions in the biblical saga manifest the purpose and presence of God, regardless of how well or poorly we understand them. Many of them God accomplishes through people, sometimes as individuals and sometimes as leaders of tribes and nations.

Companies or organizations have purpose and presence as well, and people are the means through which companies accomplish those purposes. People are never far from where companies and organizations show up. As a result, I have elected to use the phrase "in the company of God" in these essays not solely as a convenient means to convey the

16. Ps 115:3.

17. Mic 6:8.

18. Marglin, *Dismal Science*, ix.

presence and purpose of God. "In the company of God" also conveys God's apparent preference to involve people, even anonymously, to accomplish God's purposes.

"In the company of God" has some advantages. It suggests the presence and purpose of God. Being *in* the company of God implies that who we are and what we do and even who we do it with is either aligned with God's purpose or not. Likewise, being *in* the company of God implies that where we show up—literally, figuratively or virtually—is always relative to the position and presence of God. The phrase also implies that other people with whom we collaborate occupy positions relative to the presence of God as well. All of these implications are simply easier to express with the phrase "in the company of God," which is intended as a more vernacular surrogate for the kingdom of God on earth.

Innovation affects each of us, whether we realize it or not. Some of us are innovation victims: workers displaced by "advances" in information technology, small business owners put out of business by big-box retailers or Amazon, or consumers "forced" to upgrade our two-year-old smart phone made obsolete by the latest operating system update. Some of these victimizations are "first world" to be sure. Other dislocations and disruptions may be more than merely inconvenient.

Others of us are innovation beneficiaries: the curious with instant virtual libraries on our own desks; communicators with fast, cheap, easy and reliable ways to send messages to others elsewhere; city dwellers reliant upon fuel-efficient distribution methods to bring us food from distant agricultural regions.

Still others of us, especially knowledge workers, are innovation contributors, directly or indirectly engaged in developing the next new thing, whether laboring in a commercial R&D lab, testing a hypothesis or prototype in the field, or solving problems and creating solutions.

Whether we realize it or not, theology affects us as well. By "theology" in general I simply mean thinking about reality that considers the presence and activity of God.[19] Much of this thinking is implicit, even subconscious. To be sure, there are many who regard themselves as atheists—those who think about reality deliberately excluding the presence or activity of God. There are agnostics also—those who are not sure. But there are many who include God in their thinking about reality.

---

19. "Theology" in this instance does not necessarily imply biblical theology.

This is not to say that those who include God in their thinking do so in a way that satisfies them or others. There is likely a great deal of ill-conceived theology. Nor is it to say that these "believers" always adequately consider the divine purpose as often as they should. I simply mean to imply that theology—thinking about reality that includes God—is more widely practiced than we might otherwise acknowledge.

If there is even a smidgen of truth in the preceding paragraph, then it is a bit surprising that so little attention has been given to innovation theology. Theology, particularly biblical theology, has had much to say about transformation, liberation, reconciliation, redemption, and restoration. However, it has had little to say about innovation. This is not because it has little to say or contribute but more likely because it has not yet found ways to say it. Currently innovation is something confined to the next new thing, something that has to do with entrepreneurial activity or that which comes out of places like Silicon Valley—something subject to economic, technological and business perspectives, not theological ones. I hope what follows proves to be at least a start in helping biblical theology find a credible voice in matters related to innovation.

The essays are presented here in four sections, but each essay was originally written as a stand-alone thought piece. Therefore, each can be read in any order suggested by the reader's own interest, with the possible exception of the first three. Those should probably be read first.

Start with the essays that look more interesting to you. Since this set of essays attempts to "scout out" the territory of innovation theology in breadth more than depth, readers' interest is more relevant than the writer's sequence presented here. Some redundancy is a risk with this approach, for which I ask the reader's indulgence and forgiveness. The intended benefit, however, is the opportunity to investigate and enter the territory of innovation theology from different points of view. Such intention reflects the iterative and multilateral bias inherent in the practice of innovation itself.

The first section—Change, Innovation and Theology—has to do with where theology connects with innovation and why such connections matter in the grand scheme of things. The first essay addresses the reasons for innovating and how a theological perspective might alter and expand those reasons ("Why Innovate? Curves, Chasms and Crossings"). The second essay proposes a bare minimum of theological givens and makes the case for the practical importance of bringing theology into the field of innovation ("Theological Assumptions and Practical Purpose"). The third essay intends to invite innovators into the conversation

("Innovating Needs Theology"). It makes the case that innovating needs theology to help answer where innovations are needed and why.

The next three essays have to do with *accepting* change—how we think about change, how we feel about it, and what God might be up to in what is changing. The first essay in this section takes up the seductions of planning as it relates to change and innovating ("How Do You Make God Laugh?"). The second speaks to the loss-filled challenges change presents and the implications on our imaginations ("Change Wounds; Grieving Heals"). The third essay in this group proposes that change may be an envelope through which God invites us to respond ("Change as Invitation").

The next section—Making Sense of Change—is comprised of four essays, all of which recognize how both theology and innovation are inextricably engaged in sense-making. The first of these proposes that making sense makes more sense with God's help and God's lead ("Making Sense in the Company of God"). This is followed by an essay that proposes just what its title implies ("Make Meaning *Before* Money"), whereas the third one in this group speaks to the "elusive" character of God who invites our participation in making sense more than spoon feeding us with the sense God has already made ("Coincidences: God's Way of Staying Anonymous"). The fourth examines the quiet and often-ignored role humility plays in sense-making ("Humility: A Practical Necessity That Takes Practice").

The final three essays have to do with the practical challenges of *innovating in the company of God*. These practical challenges start with understanding what the company of God is and how it is different from other companies ("The Company of God Has No Exit Strategy"). The next essay examines the potential role and contribution of the church in contexts of change and innovation ("Church: Servant Subsidiary of the Company of God"). The last essay examines how Scripture and the Holy Spirit combine to contribute to our ability to innovate and how our attitudes about these two assets either help or get in the way ("Innovating with Company Assets: Scripture and Spirit").

Some may think I have gone off the deep end in proposing innovation theology. There may be an element of truth in this assessment. However, the simple combination of these two words point to essential yet unexplored realities. God is not only present and at work in changes occurring around us (not just within us). God is at work in our responses to change as well, especially those responses that aim to create new value for others.

In too many areas substantive innovating has been declining for years,[20] despite all the recent talk about entrepreneurship and innovation. Reasons for this are many, varied, speculative and worrisome. Might theology—that which helps us more articulately account for the hope that is within us—have an encouraging contribution to make, especially now? Continuing to look to economics—nicknamed by many the "dismal science"—may not be the best choice as a source of encouragement. Responses that broaden the field of view and invest in what's valuable to others might be better. This is what theology intends to do, or should.

In short, an underlying premise of the following essays is this: that God is engaged in change and that how we respond to change reflects our resistance to or alignment with God. To be sure, discernment in an accountable community is required to assess whether our responses are more opposed or aligned with God's purpose and presence in change.[21]

Certainly not all change expresses the purposes of God. Some changes may express the opposite. Likewise, not all responses to change are aligned with the purposes of God. Some are the opposite. And indeed, not all responses to change are aimed at creating new value. However, those so aimed and succeeding carry disproportionate influence on our lives and culture, for good or for ill. When they are not successful they waste an inordinate amount of energy, time and resources. As such, innovating is particularly worthy of theological consideration given the potential for contribution or waste.

Rarely will our responses to change line up with God's will, precisely. To assume so reflects a lack of requisite humility at the very least. Neither does resistance to change itself necessarily represent a resistance to God's will. It could be the opposite. Change and God's intentions are not synonymous. However, if we reframe change as an invitation from God, then to respond with love and faithfulness may represent the first steps in innovating. Innovation theology should help us recognize what those first and next steps are.

---

20. Wladawsky-Berger, "Some Advice."

21. Such discernment is best done in an explicit process with others in the context of a faith community (see the four essays in the section Making Sense of Change).

Change, Innovation
and Theology

1

Why Innovate?

Curves, Chasms and Crossings

Between us and you a great chasm has been fixed.[1]

CATCHING A GROWTH WAVE appears to be the prime reason to innovate. As a motivation this limits where we choose to innovate, why, and for whom.

Like surfers try to catch the perfect wave, entrepreneurs search for waves with steep curves of ascending growth. Seeking the exhilaration from the powerful surge underneath, the wave's lift demands alert readiness and balance to extend the ride. This experience is not unlike what my daughter surely felt when at three years old she would implore me to keep tossing her up in the air only to catch her: "Again, again, again," she begged. Of course, I would indulge her as long as my aging and out-of-shape body could stand it.

The wave is that adoption curve so many entrepreneurial-minded seek. Popularized by Everett Rogers in the early 1960s, Rogers divided his bell-shaped curve into phases through which innovations pass from novelty to normality. Rogers named each phase by the type of adopter: "innovators," then "early adopters," then "early and late majorities." The majorities represent the steepest, fattest and most sought-after parts of the curve. But nearly thirty years after Rogers's first description, Geoffrey

1. Luke 19.26

Moore observed a break in the wave. The continuity Rogers proposed actually hid a chasm between the early adopters and the early majority.[2]

Turns out, the adoption curve is really not all that continuous. Moore's chasm creates a frustrating challenge for innovators. Getting to the steep part of the adoption curve requires a demanding crossing. Moore observed that, at least with technology-intensive innovations, there is a great gulf between early adopters and the early majority, a chasm that many never cross. The illusion of continuity tempts innovators. Surprised by the chasm, they are swallowed up in the midst of the sea, not unlike Pharaoh's chariots, wondering what happened to all that growth they anticipated. The success innovators experience *before* the chasm easily seduces them into imagining that even larger success, bigger markets and more rapid growth are just a matter of time.

The market on the other side of the chasm is actually comprised of risk-averse pragmatists, unlike the more visionary and risk-tolerant early adopters. There is a big difference between the early-but-few visionaries and the later-but-many pragmatists. The former set the trends and the latter follow them, and there is a chasm between the two.[3] Such a chasm cannot be crossed without a focused marketing effort, single-mindedly targeted to a "beachhead," from where an invasion of the larger market can be launched. Moore's theory is still ravenously consumed by hordes of technology marketers.

Less famously James Utterback offered another wave theory of how innovations progress and find adoption.[4] Utterback's two-wave theory suggests what surfers know: waves come in pairs or sets. First there is a wave of product innovation. When cresting, it's followed by a second wave of process innovation. Once product effectiveness is demonstrated then process efficiency becomes what makes the difference. When the adopting marketplace declares what it likes, the "dominant design" sets in. At this point innovators must turn their attention to what makes for efficient production conforming to the "dominant design." Utterback's gap between the two waves may not be as dramatic as Moore's chasm, but a crossing from one wave to the next is still required.

2. Moore, *Crossing the Chasm*, 24.

3. The irony of tracking trends to spot innovation opportunities is that once trends have become apparent, the window of opportunity for innovating may have already closed. Anticipating the convergence or intersection of trends, however, can help in the identification of entrepreneurial opportunities.

4. Utterback, *Mastering the Dynamics of Innovation*, xvii.

Growth curves figure prominently in many other theories of innovation, like Richard Foster's early S-curve theory[5] and Clayton Christensen's popular disruptive technology theory.[6] Despite the persuasiveness of these theories, all track quantitative curves of units offered or products sold, or the number of attempts tried, the number of competitors engaged and of course the holiest of holy grails, growth of the market. Few of them attend to the *value* of the innovation.[7]

Diffusion theory is only part of the innovation story, more interesting to marketers perhaps than innovators themselves. In the classic theory, Rogers calls innovators the first to use the innovation. The designation can be confusing and has even led some to conflate the diffusion of innovations with innovating itself.

Rather than leaving the subject to economic analysis alone, a theological inquiry will look at growth curves, chasms and their crossings a bit differently. Such inquiry just might relieve innovators from the tyranny of growth as the only reason to innovate. The following aims to do just that.

The year was 1986. My boss, Bill Wilson, had just returned from a meeting with his boss, Le Roy Peterson. Peterson was at that time the executive vice president of engineering at Kimberly-Clark Corporation. The meeting between the two was intended, we hoped, to clarify our group's charter. "Exploratory Projects" was the name Peterson had given our staff group. This name afforded us plenty of freedom, which of course, we wanted to keep. But the name left us lacking clarity of purpose and direction, something we also wanted to have.

We had all prepared Bill for this meeting with Peterson. Just a few months before, Richard Foster had published his S-curve theory. Foster suggested innovating companies need to know not only what curve to get on, but also when to get off it. An innovator can be too early and can hang around for too long after the growth has peaked. We all thought it made a lot of sense.

Foster's theory exemplified what our group's purpose should be. At least that's what we thought. *We* should be the group in Kimberly-Clark to identify the curves. These curves would provide targets for the corporation's innovation ambitions. We had armed Bill with all sorts of examples

---

5. Foster, *Innovation*, 89–111.

6. Christensen and Raynor, *Innovator's Solution*, 32–39.

7. Except as can be inferred by the quantitative growth or incline of the curve.

from Kimberly-Clark's own innovating experience with innovations like Kleenex®, Kotex®, Huggies®, and even the one at that time, Depends®.

Bill returned from his meeting with Peterson and the expression on his face wasn't giving us any clues as to how the meeting went. However, we didn't have to wait long to find out. In typical fashion, Bill called us all into the conference room and revealed to us Peterson's reaction.

His response threw us another curve. Anticipating our surprise, Bill reassured us that he had walked a quiet-but-attentive Peterson through all the key points of Foster's theory. Peterson was patient and attentive, and then gave the following response:

"This S-curve is all well and good, Bill. And it even makes a lot of sense. However, what I want to know is what's over here? What's going on there?" Bill, repeating where Peterson had pointed, put his finger on the blank space to the left of the S-curve, *off* the curve.

At first none of us understood what Peterson was talking about. We had no idea what he intended by pointing to the empty space on the chart to the left of the curve. Then Bill said to us, with the confidence of someone who had complete clarity regarding what Peterson meant: "That's where we need to look for the next innovation."

Peterson had convinced Bill that while growth curves are inherently attractive, there may be other reasons to innovate, other places to look for opportunity than those that elicit the largely imaginary and highly specu-lative prognostications of growth. The seed had been planted, a seed that there may be something other than growth worth paying attention to regarding where to innovate and why. About this "something other" an innovation theology has much to offer.

Growth curves are inherently limited and limiting, whether shaped like a bell or an S. These curves measure volume not value; more not bet-ter. Curves track growth, whether steep or flat. Growth curves are avail-able only to hindsight and typically measure transactions, units sold and numbers of adopters. Such curves record popularity rather than value or quality. To be fair, value is often inferred when a curve of growth appears. But inferences are indirect at best.

Despite these limitations, however, the standard measure of success for innovating today is growth. The steeper the growth curve the more suc-cessful the innovation. These growth curves are not limited to commercial realms. Philanthropic foundations seek large-scale impacts, predicated on growth. In fact, the measure of success for an innovation—social or commercial—is whether growth is the consequence and to what degree. Return on investment is too often innovation's only metric.

But is this the only reason to innovate? Must exponential growth be the only answer to the questions of where to innovate, why and for whom?

Basic adoption theory has stood the test of time ever since Rogers first proposed it. Because it is descriptive of the delays and dynamics affecting how innovations find acceptance and spread, adoption theory offers prescriptive utility and predictive value to investors, marketers and innovators alike. However, adoption theory, along with the analysis of most economists, is predicated on the assumption that growth is always possible and always good. Theology might offer a different perspective and alternate reasons to innovate.

THE PROBLEM WITH GROWTH CURVES

First there is a problem with what comes to mind when we think of growth. It is typically extensive, quantitative or volumetric. We call it simply "more." When growth-as-more is pushed to the extreme it becomes excessive, which is aesthetically ugly, distasteful, even gross. When excessive, growth becomes exploitation, what Scripture so often calls iniquity. None other than Adam Smith might have suggested as much when he observed, "In the proportion or disproportion which the affection seems to bear to the cause . . . consists the proprietary or impropriety, the decency or ungracefulness, of the consequent action."[8]

So much for extreme or excessive growth; what of less excessive growth, perhaps at a more modest rate, one that does not immediately evoke an aesthetic revulsion? Even more modest rates growth, however, are viewed as having an extensive rather than intensive character. Extensive growth spreads out, broad and wide. Intensive growth, on the other hand, deepens, penetrates, and develops.

While theology's primary source (Scripture) employs both connotations for growth, theology is likely more interested in intensive than extensive growth. Isaiah speaks of this intensive understanding of growth when he expects the surviving remnant of the house of Judah "shall take root downward and bear fruit upward."[9] Such intensive growth is not only confined to agricultural domains. The Apostle Paul points to this when

8. Smith, *Theory of Moral Sentiments*, 24.

9. Isa 37:30–31.

he reflected on his own efforts, reminding the Corinthians, "I planted, Apollos watered, but God gave the growth."[10] Innovation theology will likely carry this bias for intensive more than extensive growth. It will also likely view growth as anything but a panacea.

Take a look at what Jesus said to one who came to him for a bit of arbitrage. He asked Jesus to tell his brother to divide their inheritance between them. Jesus replied,

> "Take care! Be on your guard against all kinds of greed; for one's life does not consist in the abundance of possessions." Then he told them a parable: "The land of a rich man produced abundantly. And he thought to himself, 'What should I do, for I have no place to store my crops?' Then he said, 'I will do this: I will pull down my barns and build larger ones, and there I will store all my grain and my goods. And I will say to my soul, Soul, you have ample goods laid up for many years; relax, eat, drink, be merry.' But God said to him, 'You fool! This very night your life is being demanded of you. And the things you have prepared, whose will they be?' So it is with those who store up treasures for themselves but are not rich towards God."[11]

To be fair this parable speaks to the *results* of growth, not of growth *per se*, though it does put us on the alert. Elsewhere Jesus speaks directly to the nature of growth itself.

> The kingdom of God is as if someone would scatter seed on the ground, and would sleep and rise night and day, and the seed would sprout and grow, *he does not know how*. The earth produces of itself, first the stalk, then the head, then the full grain in the head. But when the grain is ripe, at once he goes in with his sickle, because the harvest has come.[12]

For Jesus growth is always a gift given, not an achievement earned. And despite all our microbiological and genetic understanding, we still do not fully know how. This growth is beyond the competence, capability or capacity of humankind. This was likely established from the get-go, when "out of the ground the Lord God made to grow every tree that is

---

10. 1 Cor 3:6.

11. Luke 12:13–21.

12. Mark 4:26–29.

pleasant to the sight and good for food" including the tree of life and the tree of the knowledge of good and evil.[13] And according to Ezekiel,

> All the trees of the field shall know that I am the Lord.
> I bring low the high tree, I make high the low tree;
> I dry up the green tree and make the dry tree flourish.[14]

God even reminds a recalcitrant Jonah, "You pity the plant, for which you did not labor, nor did you make it grow."[15] Planting, tilling, keeping, and harvesting are our responsibilities, not growth.

Had Jesus been a part of an industrial or digital age rather than an agricultural one, would his parables have taken on a different shape? Perhaps. We may never know. But whatever the more modern equivalent, I suspect that the growth that comes from the literal or figurative seeds we plant will remain God's to give and not ours to achieve.

The problem with growth is not growth's problem. It is our misattribution of credit for who is responsible for the growth. Believing growth is our doing or the result of our efforts alone is something an innovation theology might be slow to accept, if it allows it at all. Despite this, I suspect that the credit for growth will continue to be largely attributed to entrepreneurs, venture capitalists, philanthropists and those who take credit for innovators' work, or for God's work.

Besides, growth may or may not reflect alignment with God's purposes. We are perhaps all too quick to assume that growth is a sign of God's grace, reflective of God's blessings and validation. Extensive growth is based on more; bigger is better. Never mind that in so many areas we do not really need any more. Greatness is not bigness. Quality and character of content, not volume, is what constitutes greatness. In fact, sufficiency and sustainability are becoming the new criteria for innovation instead of growth.

The metrics of the company of God do not likely reside in volumes so much as in the lasting value, character and content of living with and for others. Either we are calculating a financial return on investment or we are clarifying what is the right thing to do. When calculating the ROI replaces doing the right thing, we allow economic, if not purely financial

---

13. Gen 2:9.

14. Ezek 17:24.

15. Jonah 4:10.

considerations, to preempt considerations of innovating for the common good, and the good of the commons.

Surely, it is our job to till and keep the land; our job to plant the seeds, attend to the kind of soil in which to plant them, and even to cultivate the conditions we believe conducive to sustainable growth. But this kind of growth is not the achievement of human effort. It is the result of the grace of God. Theology's perspective on growth takes it to be more of a grace given than an accomplishment achieved. Jesus used only timeless parables of organic growth in which the growth was not an achievement of mankind. It was a gift of God.

THE URGENT PROBLEM

Any theological critique of the place growth occupies in motivating innovation efforts would be remiss if the work of Herman Daly and John Cobb were not considered. Herman Daly, an economist, and John Cobb, a theologian, collaborated in the 1980s and produced a seminal work entitled *For the Common Good.* That a credentialed economist teamed up with an equally credentialed theologian to reexamine what the majority of neoclassical economists refuse to look at, even still today, is itself worth noting. But their provisional conclusions are even more noteworthy still.

At the risk of oversimplifying their description of the urgent problem, Daly and Cobb make two basic points: first, that the global economy is a subset of the global ecology, and second, that the current growth rate of the global economy (never mind the desired growth rate), far exceeds both the source and absorptive capacities of the global ecology. Put in more theological language, God's creation and God's creatures (including human beings) are headed for a collision, the effects of which we are beginning to see in what Paul Gilding refers to prophetically as the "great disruption."[16] In their last chapter, Daly and Cobb propose a theological basis to guide prescriptive solutions, away from the conventional wisdom of economics, largely because with economists

> no real argument needs to be given for devoting oneself ultimately to the promotion of productivity and growth. No recitation of the horrors that this commitment has inflicted upon human beings, not to speak of the other creatures, no explanation that the physical conditions that made growth possible in

16. Gilding, *Great Disruption.*

the past are rapidly disappearing, no clarification of how human welfare can be met in other ways—none of this has yet sufficed to shake the conviction so deeply rooted in the discipline that growth is both the supreme end and the supreme means for achieving the end. Precisely by limiting the horizons of inquiry one can attain to this state of mind. The rest, economists often think, is "theology," and hence not worthy of their time.[17]

Instead, Daly and Cobb turn directly to that theological orientation for the foundation of prescriptive solutions, even economic ones, based on four points, saying in essence that theology

- provides a check against the idolatry of growth;
- takes a point of view that necessarily transcends one's own individual interests;
- emphasizes believing which engenders commitment, something we are obviously going to need in any solution; and
- provides a necessary orientation and understanding of the future (i.e., hope as distinct from the "dismal science" of economics alone.)[18]

Hence the urgent need to focus on innovations for the common good where the motivation for innovating becomes about sufficiency rather than more, about sustainability rather than size, about substance rather than convenience, about shared rather than individual benefit.

Citing the biblical prophetic tradition, Daly and Cobb observe that

in the Bible the immediacy of God frees people *from* absolute worldly loyalties in order to bring about justice and righteousness *within* the world. The unity of love of God and love of neighbor are affirmed unequivocally. Indeed, the way to serve God truly is to serve the neighbor. What one does to the neighbor, especially the lowly neighbor, one does to God.[19]

Though Daly and Cobb focus their examination on the fallacies of growth at the macro level of global economics and ecology, their theological inquiry has implications for more local levels of business and nonprofits and the lust for growth that often manifests there.

17. Daly and Cobb, *For the Common Good*, 402.

18. Ibid., 401–4, with apologies to Daly and Cobb for any errors from oversimplification on my part.

19. Ibid., 392.

Measurable to be sure, extensive growth is an outcome, not a purpose. Extensive growth attracts attention, but it is a poor substitute for one's sole intention. The purpose of a business[20] is to create (by means of an innovation) and serve a customer.[21] Growth is a possible outcome of serving many customers who become, *de facto*, aggregated into a market. A market is not a customer but an aggregation of many customers with similar needs. Each customer, however, and the value sought by that customer remain, to a greater and lesser extent, defined by their respective and individual contexts. When growth becomes the purpose, then the business takes its eyes off the customer and attends to the market. This is the point at which the interests of the business begin to supersede the interests of the customer. When this happens, the purpose of the business has begun to drift. When this growth becomes the sole purpose of a business it becomes an idol, at least in the context of the business's entrepreneurial vocation to create and serve a customer.

When growth-as-more is pushed to the extreme it becomes excessive, exploitative, iniquitous and abhorrent. But when growth-as-better is pushed to extremes we call it excellence; those who exude excellence, we call virtuosos. Growth is simply too limited and gross a reason and measure for innovating.

If not growth, then what? What could motivate investors, innovators and entrepreneurs to risk crossings (innovations)? One obvious place to start is to "reduce the importance of consumption as a driver of growth and replace it with an enhanced role for investment."[22] The British economist Tim Jackson, teaching at the University of Surrey (UK), also suggests that

> clearly the target of investment would also need to change. The traditional function of investment, framed around increasing labor productivity, is likely to diminish in importance. Innovation will still be vital, but it will need to be targeted more carefully towards sustainability goals. Specifically, investments will need to focus on resource productivity, renewable energy, clean technology, green business, climate adaptation and ecosystem enhancement.[23]

---

20. And by extension, the purpose of any organization.

21. Drucker, *Management*, 61.

22. Jackson, *Prosperity Without Growth*, 138.

23. Ibid.

Innovating in the company of God just might direct our attention to what God is already doing for the common good and especially to those in whom God consistently expresses a particular interest: the vulnerable and dispossessed (e.g., widows, orphans, immigrants and the poor). Or to express it less theologically, Jackson writes:

> The sense of common endeavor is one of the casualties of consumer society. We need to revitalize the notion of public goods; to renew our sense of public space, of pubic institutions, of common purpose; to invest money and time in shared goals, assets and infrastructures.[24]

In short, theological inquiry will surely suggests that we need to innovate for the common good.

CHASMS WORTH CROSSING

Moore's chasms are really more about marketing than innovating. These chasms reflect unmet expectations of growth rates. Such chasms are considerably less substantive than the chasms between chronic problems and sustainable solutions; between the way things should be and the way things are; between the common good and an individual's self-interest; between the ideal and the real, the possible and the actual. More substantive chasms are likely ones that are crossed in the company of God.

Theological inquiry might point to these other chasms and crossings. These are not chasms between different trajectories of growth, nor crossings focused merely on those who are waiting on the other side. Rather, they are chasms between self-interests and God's interests, and crossings that *carry* others from the bondage of self-centered fear to the freedom of trusting in One for whom all things are possible.

The only explicit reference to a chasm in Scripture is embedded in a parable of Jesus recorded in the Gospel of Luke.[25] It is the story of a nameless rich man and a poor one named Lazarus. Both die but end up in entirely different places. Angels carry Lazarus off to reside in the bosom of Abraham, while the rich man is unceremoniously buried and finds himself tormented in hell. The rich man looks up and sees Lazarus, far off. In anguish the rich one calls out to Father Abraham pleading for mercy. "Send Lazarus to dip the end of his finger in water and cool my

24. Ibid., 193.
25. Luke 16:19–31.

tongue." But Abraham refuses, saying, "Remember that you in your life-time received your good things, and Lazarus in like manner evil things, but now he is comforted here, and you are in agony."

And then, as if stepping aside to observe the moral reality that pre-ceded the fate of these two souls, Abraham says, "Besides all this, between you and us a great chasm has been fixed, so that those who might want to pass from here to you cannot do so, and no one can cross from there to us."

Now this is a real chasm—an impassable, unbridgeable divide. There is no connection, no communication, no passage possible across this chasm, either one way or the other. This chasm has been fixed, or so it seems.

But the parable doesn't stop there. It goes on through three rounds of failed bargaining by the rich man.[26] In the first round Abraham re-minds the rich man that the chasm is fixed and impassable. Since no crossing is possible, the rich man then asks Abraham to send Lazarus to the rich man's father. The rich man assumes his father (presumably also dead) is on Lazarus' side of the chasm. Might his father be in a position to warn his other sons so as to avoid the fate that befell the rich man? But here Abraham demurs, "They have Moses and the prophets; let them hear them." So much for the second round.

Undaunted, the rich one tries a third time pleading, "If someone goes to them from the dead, they will repent." Surely Abraham could have responded with a little compassion. But Abraham says, "If they do not hear Moses and the prophets, neither will they be convinced if some-one should rise from the dead."

This chasm is perhaps the greatest chasm of all: the chasm between the living and the dead. Theology might claim that this chasm *has been* crossed, and indeed, is still being crossed; a crossing that requires faith, obedience and the company of God, to be sure. But a chasm that Abra-ham, at least, regards as similar to the chasm crossed by Moses that gave birth to the "old" covenant, indeed, gave birth to the liberated people of Israel, no longer enslaved to Pharaoh's bondage.

According to the Gospel of Luke, Jesus' parable makes explicit what is common between the new chasm to be crossed and the old chasm Mo-ses crossed with the people of Israel.

The chasm between "dead" and "living" is layered with meaning and promise in the company of God. This chasm points to where innovations

26. Is this bargaining a core competence of the rich, or merely a stage in his griev-ing process?

are truly needed and why, and indeed, for whom. To put it simply, what theology can bring that economics cannot is the call to innovate where there is little if any hope, for people who have little if any hope. This is ultimately where the company of God invites us to create new value for others.

Innovating in the company of God is about crossing chasms between different need states not between different growth rates. Chasms of economic inequalities, social asymmetries, racial prejudices, and environmental exploitations are where innovations (crossings) are needed. We need to redeploy our innovating time, attention and devotion to economic sufficiency instead of unbridled growth, to environmental sustainability instead of ecological extractions, to equitable security instead of human exploitation, and to societal solvency instead of precarious, unstable peace.

If theology has anything significant to say to innovating efforts, has anything to contribute to clarifying where innovations are needed, why and for whom, then theology is likely to ask innovators whether what they are doing (why and for whom) has anything to do with the will and purposes of a living and loving God. Should the answer be less than satisfying then a follow-on question might be whether the innovating effort can be realigned with the company of God? If this follow-on question is answered with the question "What is the will of God?" an answer can always be found in who the other is for whom new value is created: those whom Jesus referred to as the "lost sheep" in contrast to the ninety-nine.[27] These "sheep" are not "consumers," much less a market. They are people, who have lost their way, have unmet needs (vs. wants), needs that may be rather basic, more than "virtual" or digital. Innovating in the company of God is surely directed toward these, the least of these.

All this might challenge the conventional return on investment (ROI) logic. "Just so," Jesus says, "I tell you, there will be more joy in heaven over one sinner who repents than over ninety-nine righteous people who need no repentance."[28] Again, "Just so, I tell you, there is joy in the presence of the angels of God over one sinner who repents."[29] Clearly ROI in the company of God is calculated upon a different basis.

We have an abundance of educated talent, credentialed engineers, experienced computer coders, capable material and life scientists and even skilled architects and designers in the "softer" disciplines. What if

27. Luke 15:3–7.

28. Luke 15:7.

29. Luke 15:10.

even a small percentage of them were directed toward challenges facing the care of creation, the correction and prevention of social injustice and the sustainable reconciliation of economic inequities?

Some are starting to point in this direction. One is Jeff Hammerbacher, former manger of the Facebook Data Team and founder of Cloudera, who is often quoted as saying, "The best minds of my generation are thinking about how to make people click ads. That sucks."[30]

Too many of our brightest minds are directed toward designing additional advertising platforms creating more entertainment "content" or improving convenience instead of the care of others and creation itself. If we were innovating in the company of God, we would be more apt to create new value for others that is common, shared and of redemptive and reconciling purpose. Innovations in the company of God will likely be aimed more at what benefits the common good and speak more to our shared physical, economic and perhaps even emotional security. These innovations may at first appear to be islands of care in oceans of indifference and seas of self-reliance. Too much of our innovating chases ROI. The returns are typically measured by scale (i.e., large and/or wide, at least relative to the money or effort invested). In commercial contexts these returns are monetized by profit or shareholder value.

Our current innovating efforts could use a little theology, don't you think? Jesus didn't appear to be particularly enamored with ROI, shareholder value or profit for that matter, though he didn't disallow it either. He was, however, more interested in the one out of ninety-nine lost sheep, or the one out of ten lost coins.[31]

Don't get me wrong. Deploying theological inquiry to judge whether an innovation or related technology is good or bad is overreaching. Doing so would confuse theology with ethics. Nor is the interest here to declare all innovations and their respective technologies morally neutral. The intent, rather, is to realize and actualize the idea that theology can raise the question of purpose more quickly, holistically and compellingly than any other field of inquiry. Sooner or later theology will ask what is the purpose, will or intent of God and if the innovation effort is even remotely aligned with that purpose. Merely asking this question remains a prophetic but hopeful reminder that in the company of God purpose, meaning, and reconciliation are possible.

30. Mele, *End of Big*, 25.
31. Luke 15:7, 10.

CROSSINGS

Experienced practitioners of innovation have long recognized that innovating involves crossing boundaries. Do a key word search with "crossing boundaries and innovation" and marvel at the number of citations (2.8 million) when I tried it. Cross-functional, cross-disciplinary and diverse perspectives are widely recognized as essential to any credible innovating effort.

Successful innovating happens "at the seams" where traditional boundaries are crossed—conceptual, academic and even geographic and cultural. Innovations cross boundaries between what was previously believed to be impossible, improbable or infeasible. Frans Johansson has gone so far as to describe two general types of boundary-crossings manifest in most innovations.[32] One he calls *directional*, where the boundaries crossed reside within a particular field. The other he calls *intersectional*, where the boundaries crossed reside between different fields. In either case, boundaries are crossed.

How the crossing is made may be as significant as that a crossing is required. How the crossing is made will also depend on the nature of the chasm crossed.

Moore's crossing strategy, appropriate for chasms of different growth rates, is to concentrate time, attention and resources on a single beachhead. Borrowing from the success of the D-day invasion of Normandy, Moore's crossings assume chasms like the English Channel, where the way across is by buoyantly traversing the surface of the waters in more or less a straight line. The crossing trajectory is up and over.

The crossings innovation theology likely has in mind will be significantly different, primarily because the chasms in which the company of God is more interested are different—more likely about what separates us from substantive meaning, sustainable value, sufficient satisfactions and shared commons. Crossings of these chasms require a different route altogether.

Since these chasms are less about gaps in growth rates and more about what separates people from becoming who God intended them to be, the crossings carry people rather than marketing messages. These crossings are not about focused marketing strategies, but about reconciling differences and creating a sustainable bridge for others to cross, and keep crossing. The crossings are not likely to be up and over, but down

32. Johansson, *Medici Effect*, 17–20.

and then up; death before resurrection, a sacrifice of self-interest for the interest of others.[33] A seed must sacrifice itself and die before life and intensive growth can come from it.

This may not be simply an interesting theological principle. It may have practical relevance for innovating. Otto Scharmer, Peter Senge and others have made the case for what they call the "social technology of *presencing*."[34] It reflects this down-and-then-up crossing strategy. It resonates with what leaders and innovators have actually experienced in their innovating efforts. "*Presencing* is a blending of the words 'presence' and 'sensing.' It means to sense, tune in, and act from one's highest future potential—the future that depends on us to bring it into being."[35] Senge observes that

> change efforts usually focus on making changes in "them" or in "the system" or on "implementing" a predetermined "change process," or in fixing some other externalized object—rarely on how "I" and "we" must change in order to allow the larger system to change.[36]

When innovating requires the innovators themselves to change, we are now speaking a language familiar to theology, especially from its prophetic sources. There it is called repentance, a turning away from something old that results in a turning toward something new.

While current thinkers are rediscovering this way of crossing chasms, theology might relook at its own primary crossing in a new light. The ancient crossing I have in mind is the crossing of the Red Sea, the climax of the Exodus story.

Given how often we assume familiarity with the Exodus story, it is worth a pause to look at the actual canonical account. Here's the narrative as it is represented in the book of Exodus:

> The Lord said to Moses, "Why do you cry out to me? Tell the Israelites to go forward. But you lift up your staff, and stretch out your hand over the sea and divide it, that the Israelites may go into the sea on dry ground.

---

33. Paul called this the wisdom of God and observed that the world regards it as "foolishness" (1 Cor 1:21–25; 3:19).

34. Senge et al., *Presence*, 218–21.

35. Scharmer, *Theory U*, 8.

36. Ibid., xiv.

"Then I will harden the hearts of the Egyptians so that they will go in after them; and so I will gain glory for myself over Pharaoh and all his army, his chariots, and his chariot drivers. And the Egyptians shall know that I am the Lord, when I have gained glory for myself over Pharaoh, his chariots, and his chariot drivers."

The angel of God who was going before the Israelite army moved and went behind them; and the pillar of cloud moved from in front of them and took its place behind them. It came between the army of Egypt and the army of Israel. And so the cloud was there with the darkness, and it lit up the night; one did not come near the other all night.

Then Moses stretched out his hand over the sea. The Lord drove the sea back by a strong east wind all night, and turned the sea into dry land; and the waters were divided. The Israelites went into the sea on dry ground, the waters forming a wall for them on their right and on their left. The Egyptians pursued, and went into the sea after them, all of Pharaoh's horses, chariots, and chariot drivers. At the morning watch the Lord in the pillar of fire and cloud looked down upon the Egyptian army, and threw the Egyptian army into panic. He clogged their chariot wheels so that they turned with difficulty. The Egyptians said, "Let us flee from the Israelites, for the Lord is fighting for them against Egypt."

Then the Lord said to Moses, "Stretch out your hand over the sea, so that the water may come back upon the Egyptians, upon their chariots and chariot drivers." So Moses stretched out his hand over the sea, and at dawn the sea returned to its normal depth. As the Egyptians fled before it, the Lord tossed the Egyptians into the sea.

The waters returned and covered the chariots and the chariot drivers, the entire army of Pharaoh that had followed them into the sea; not one of them remained. But the Israelites walked on dry ground through the sea, the waters forming a wall for them on their right and on their left.[37]

There is more than enough related to innovation theology in this crossing story to keep a theological inquiry going for some time.[38] Most

37. Exod 14:15–22.

38. Such as the "hardening of Pharaoh's heart" as an apt expression for the resistance that is a part of most every innovating story, or the protective shelter ("pillar of cloud") that repositions itself hinting at the practice of so many experienced R&D leaders who know their role is to offer "top cover" for any vulnerable innovating effort.

relevant to our interests in crossing chasms, however, are the particulars of this crossing. There at least four that present themselves.

First, the crossing is unambiguously an act of God. This act of God is an unanticipated and miraculous intervention, one that certainly challenges common notions of historicity, empiricism and even believ-ability. But if God is the One for whom all things are possible,[39] then such uncertainties fade into the shadows cast by the light of this story's unambiguous attribution of the One who makes the crossing possible. Clearly, the not-so-hidden assumption operating here is that God is both interested and engaged, not the disinterested or disengaged Watchmaker who has designed and made the clock, wound it up, and set it aside to run its course. "The Lord drove the sea back." "He (the Lord) clogged their chariot wheels." "The Lord tossed the Egyptians into the sea." This was not some off-handed, inadvertent effect of a disinterested divine being.

Second, God did not act alone. While clearly God is the main actor in this crossing, God assigns Moses a specific role and responsibility—to stretch out his hand over the sea, twice in fact, both before and after the crossing. Might we say the crossing is an act of God while the timing is in the hands of Moses? The crossing is a collaborative effort, not only between God and Moses. God also seems quite willing to use all means available to embody this intervention, including a "strong east wind" that blows all night long to drive the waters back and the overwhelming potential of the waters themselves to cover. Even the residual moisture of the ground "clogged their chariot wheels." God appears to prefer in-terventions aided and abetted by the collaboration of others—both other people and other natural elements.

Third, those making the crossing stepped forward. This could be an-other example of God not acting alone. However, calling it out separately reminds us that God is likely to have not only a collaborative bias but a preference for inviting us to participate. While the story doesn't leave the Israelites with much of a choice, the biblical witness consistently gives us an image of God as one who invites us not only to follow but to "go forward" (not backward!), regardless of the uncertainty and seeming im-possibilities that going forward may appear to present. Other examples of this include the binding of Isaac[40] or the prior promise to Sarah that

39. See ch. 2, "Theological Assumptions and Practical Purpose," esp. assumption 4.
40. Gen 22.

even though she was well past her potential for pregnancy, she would bear a son.[41]

There are many examples of this call to step forward, especially when we are not sure. Crossings like this evoked the famous definition of faith found in Hebrews: "the substance of things hoped for, evidence of things unseen," and the rather lengthy list of examples that followed.[42] Even Albert Einstein, who crossed significant scientific chasms, alluded to this step-forward faith in the advice he wrote in a letter to his son Eduard, saying, "Life is like riding a bicycle. To keep your balance you must keep moving."[43] Crossings seem to require us to step forward ourselves, even in the company of God.

Fourth, the crossing is on dry ground. Nearly equal to the miracle of the parting of the seas is the dryness of the ground over which the Israelites crossed. The crossing was made on terra firma, offering the sure footing that only dry ground can offer. They neither treaded water in the chaotic seas of ambiguity, nor were tossed about in the turbulence of uncertainty on the surface. The crossing was made on the ground and it was dry.

Innovation in the company of God may likely show up more on *dry ground* than elsewhere—innovations that are substantive more than superficial or virtual; material more than digital. While so much recent innovating effort has gone into the virtual domain, God may have a greater interest in the material domain. This possible preference, provisionally offered here, should give us all considerable pause as we consider where innovations are needed, why, and for whom. Looking to growth perpetuated by virtual realities or aided and abetted by big data, may not be as keen an interest of the company of God.

Herman Daly suggests as much in his observation that

> we have an inordinate faith in solutions by technical improvement and practically no faith in solutions by moral improvement. Growth seems to absolve us from the duty to control population and to share the earth's resources more equitably among members of the present generation and between the present and future generations.[44]

41. Gen 12; 15; 16.

42. Heb 11:1 KJV.

43. Isaacson, *Einstein*, 367.

44. Daly, *Steady-Sate Economics*, 206–7.

Instead of growth, sustainable development might provide a motivation for clarifying where innovations are needed, why and for whom, at least in the company of God.[45] Innovations so motivated will address sufficiency as much as efficiency and its related technologies. Such innovations may be oriented less to throughput than to stewardship, harvesting rates of renewable resources calibrated not-to-exceed regeneration rates while using nonrenewables at rates not exceeding the creation of renewable substitutes.[46] Technological innovations in these areas will be challenging enough and certainly appear more urgent, important and deserving of our technological capabilities than the quest for more convenience or more digital advertising platforms. This is what it may mean for us today to make crossings "on dry ground"; perhaps, dry *common* ground.

Innovations themselves cross chasms. In the company of God these crossings might cross not "over" but down, into and up from the chasm itself. In the company of God, these crossings (or innovations) are not merely transformations. They are transfigurations, incarnations and resurrections; often wordless, nonverbal and empathetic forms of communicating that demonstrate more than describe meaning and value. And what these innovations communicate, if they are even modestly successful, is that the other for whom they are intended is both heard and beheld, and to some extent understood and served. There innovations may reconcile perhaps even more than they redeem, and they cross over on the dry, solid ground of non-exploitive value, value that is recognized even before it is described.

Many chasms can be crossed horizontally. Some, however, cannot be crossed without the intervention from the vertical dimension, the transcendent reality that makes the crossing possible. Such verticality either preempts or dissolves trade-offs possible only when the horizontal is considered. Like a suspension bridge, some height is required, some "looking up" (as did the rich man lifting up his eyes to see Abraham and Lazarus) not only to the other side of the chasm, but upward, to another altitude altogether.

So what? Why do curves, chasms and crossings matter at all?

A close reading of the economic theology derived from Scriptures yields some useful principles, one solid example of which is the set of

---

45. Daly, *Beyond Growth*, 219.

46. Daly, *Steady-State Economics*, 256.

principles Craig Blomberg sets forth.[47] Blomberg readily acknowledges that any attempt to summarize such a large swathe of scriptural passages that touch on economic matters lends itself to oversimplification. However, Blomberg offers what I believe is a prudent and restrained characterization of economics in both Testaments.

Blomberg suggests the law (in the Old Testament) was primarily interested in "restrictions" placed on the use and accumulation of property, "precisely so that people would remember that God owns it all and wants all people to be able to enjoy some of it." As to the prophets, economic injustice, born of the misuse and over-accumulation of property, was a major theme. New Testament economics reaffirms the perspective of the Old on such matters with one exception, according to Blomberg: "Never was material wealth promised as a guaranteed reward for either spiritual obedience or simple hard work."[48]

From both Testaments Blomberg offers five central economic themes paraphrased as follows:

- Material possessions are a gift from God meant to be enjoyed;
- Material possessions are a primary means by which humans turn away from God;
- A symptom of a transformed life will necessarily manifest in acts of stewardship;
- Extremes of wealth and poverty are contrary to the will of God; and
- The material and spiritual are inextricably intertwined.[49]

CONCLUSION

The measure of success for most innovating efforts today is growth. The steeper the growth curve the more successful the innovation. Conventional economics looks to evidence of quantitative growth as the measure of success for both innovation in general and a specific innovation in particular. If an innovation is able to "cross the chasm" between early adopters and the early majority, the entrepreneur has achieved the goal—exponential growth.

47. Blomberg, *Neither Poverty Nor Riches*, 241.

48. Ibid., 242.

49. Ibid., 243–46.

In the company of God, however, success is likely defined differently. Value is not just extrinsic or only instrumental. It is also intrinsic, covenantal. In the company of God people are not only consumers but also children of God. In the company of God growth is something that goes deeper, not just broader, something that is transfiguring, not just expanding. In the company of God relationships are more important than acquisitions, life is more important than transactions, covenants are more important than contracts. While economists may be satisfied with growth as the prerequisite for a healthy economy, engineers satisfied with improvements as essential for progress, psychologists with happiness as the goal, political scientists with a just and ordered society; those with a theological sense may not be satisfied at all, unless the creation and creatures, including humankind, be more closely aligned with the will of God.

Without the benefit of theological inquiry somewhere early in choosing where to innovate, why and for whom, we will likely be left with growth as the sole measure of success. Innovating with at least some theological inquiry, however, just might give us sustainability as an alternate measure. In fact, innovating with some theological consideration just might reframe success as a part of a longer-term succession rather than an unsustainable episode of exponential growth, flattening as it inevitably does when the S-curve peaks.

A biblical theology of innovating might look for a different kind of evidence as the measure of success, not based on quantitative growth but qualitative development. This means that regardless of the ensuing slope of the growth curve, there is something more important than quantitative metrics with which to gauge the success of an innovation or innovator; a significant improvement in the quality of life for the innovation's beneficiary, whether an individual or a community, or a world.

Theology has some experience with curves, chasm and their crossings, though they are not confined to growth and adoption. Theology's curves have to do with deep and dark descents followed by steep ascents—curves "with wings like eagles"[50]—conversion curves of repentant reversals. Its chasms stretch wide and far, and include broken covenants, exilic separations, unbelievable demands and pride-swollen exceptionalism—chasms keeping God from mankind and mankind from God. Its crossings move from death to life, from exploitation to liberation, from man to God and God to man—crossings thought improbable if not

50. Isa 40:31.

impossible, until the One for whom all things are possible made, with and for us, one crossing after another.

In the end, however, what theology can bring to innovating is limited. It certainly cannot bring technological content to innovating. However it can bring inspired, renewed heart, mind and hands to innovators, so long as we are sincerely working in the company of God, aligned with the One who can do for us what we cannot do for ourselves, One for whom all things are possible.

CONVERSATION STARTERS

1. If innovation theology can be located at the intersection between "hard" science (discovery), engineering (invention), value (economics, sociology and psychology) and God (theology), then what approaches might provide counterbalance to the "invisible hand" of the market to motivate innovations for the common good or where the needs of society are greatest?

2. The great majority of technological innovations fail, not for reasons of technical feasibility so much as market acceptance. Might starting early with a theological inquiry, complementing the market and technology development efforts, not only deepen the commitment of innovators, but also focus innovators' attention on where innovations are needed, why and for whom? Might theology contribute to a better alignment with market acceptance?

3. What besides growth will invite innovating, when there is no obvious ROI?

2

Theological Assumptions and Practical Purpose

You set the earth on its foundations.[1]

WHAT DOES INNOVATION HAVE to do with God? What does God have to do with innovation?

"Not much" seems to be the conventional answer. After all, innovating is a human, socioeconomic or cultural phenomenon. It represents nothing more than the intersecting dynamics of technology applications and market diffusions—simply a socioeconomic dynamic.

Such an answer has practical implications for both organizations and individuals. For organizations it leaves decisions on where to innovate and why captive to financial considerations and outcome calculations. It adds kindling to the smoldering notion that economy is more important than community.[2] In more personal contexts the exclusion of any divine interest in innovation leaves individuals with only a calculator to make trade-offs when confronted with tough choices. Why bother to invent solutions that transcend trade-offs if nothing transcendent is at

---

1. Ps 104:5.

2. Marglin, *Dismal Science*, 1. Marglin convincingly argues that community forms a necessary societal "infrastructure" for any economy. Economic development that ignores more fundamental community values and structures undermines the very foundation the economy assumes.

stake? Why be concerned with the deeper, more intrinsic values when the extrinsic ones are "just good enough"?

If God is neither interested nor engaged in innovating then we have limited what interests God. Presuming we know the scope of God's interests is not only arrogant. Such a presumption places us above God—a theologically untenable position. When we answer "not much," we make an assumption about God, an assumption about innovation, and reveal the limits of our own theological imaginations. If innovation[3] has nothing to do with God then we assume there are boundaries on God's interests and relegate innovation to be "out of bounds" for God.

On the other hand, if "something" is our answer, it implies an innovation theology of some kind, however implicit. If God *is* interested and actually *does* have something to do with innovating, then questions like where and why God is interested, and what difference God's interests make, come to the surface. Discerning the nature, character and location of this divine interest becomes not only relevant but perhaps more urgent.

As you might imagine, a basic premise of this and the other essays is that God *does* have something to do with innovation and innovation something to do with God. This is a claim that is accessible through faith, and possibly through the pragmatic logic reminiscent of Pascal's wager.[4] But whether by faith, logic or wager, "something" seems a more prudent answer, and that God's interest in innovation remains regardless of whether innovators—individuals, organizations or companies—are conscious of it or not. If innovation does interest God then making innovation theology more explicit should be worth doing.

In such an effort, we will need to consider where innovation theology can be located in the context of other types of theology and among other perspectives on innovation, like economics, anthropology, technology and diffusion theory, to name a few. What kind of biblical foundations provide the base for such a theology? What is the purpose or function of such a theology? Will it have its own peculiar methods? All these things and more will need to be considered as we start to construct an innovation theology.

---

3. Defined in the next essay as "a structural response to substantive change aimed at creating new value."

4. The 17th-century French philosopher observed that all humans bet with their lives either that God exists or not, and that it is almost self-evident that it is more prudent, if not rational, to believe in God and live accordingly than the alternative. If, it turns out that God does exist and we choose not to believe it, then we are much worse off.

If an innovation theology can be built, it will likely end up an applied theology—one that derives truths and principles from theology proper and applies those principles to innovating practice. Consequently, this essay explores the basic theological groundwork necessary for pouring the foundation for any innovation theology. Such groundwork will need to consider which critical few assumptions about God are essential for such a theology. It will also need to consider what purpose such a theology might serve. Once the foundation has been laid and the purpose clarified, then we should be better positioned to consider the implications and applications of these assumptions for innovating and whether it makes any difference or not.

ASSUMPTIONS FROM THEOLOGY PROPER

Innovation theology cannot aspire to be pure theology or a "theology proper" as some call it. Pure theology explores the existence, nature and character of God, whether based on revealed or "natural" sources. Innovation theology, on the other hand, will necessarily build upon foundation claims made about God by theology proper. That foundation will then be applied to the acts and efforts of creating new value for others in response to substantive change.

While innovation theology may share the same foundation as other applied theologies, the application space has a different focus and interest. Therefore, innovation theology will be interested in parts of theology proper more directly related to its purposes, methods and interests. For example *attributes* of God are likely more essential to any innovation theology than are arguments for the existence of God. As an applied theology, God's existence is assumed, not argued. As a result, little attention is given to arguments for the existence of God in this and other essays. For that plenty has been written. God's attributes, however, prove to be more influential in shaping what an innovation theology might look like.

The aphorism "everything should be made as simple as possible, but no simpler" guides which of the divine attributes from theology proper to select as most relevant to innovation theology. I might add another criteria—those theological claims most self-evident or least controversial. I confess that by saying "self-evident" I necessarily reveal my own theological bias and tradition.[5] If these essays stimulate divergent views, I consider that a success. Should the brevity or architecture of this set of assumptions be considered an egregious theological error, I can only hope this will incite further thinking and may indicate at least tacit acceptance of the invitation to continue the construction project I believe innovation theology deserves.

There are at least four "self-evident" assumptions that will likely be part of any foundation for innovation theology. These four will influence and shape what innovation theology might become and the pragmatic value it may eventually provide. The four are as follows:

1. God exists.

2. God is still creating.

3. God loves.

4. God is One for whom all things are possible.

Another assumption—that Jesus embodied all these assumptions[6]—could easily be added. Some might argue for a shorter list of assumptions, modifying the way one or more of these assumptions is expressed. Still others might object that other assumptions should be included—for example, an assumption or two about Jesus Christ and his death, resurrection and ascension, or about a Trinitarian God, or about grace, atonement, etc. All of these are interesting variations that may be worth exploring.

The modest scope of my intent in this essay is to invite rather than address these possibilities. I hope theological cases will be made in the future for such inclusions, alternate expressions or combinations. My present objective in listing these four assumptions is not to defend as much as to suggest that these may be a bare minimum of the critical few theological assumptions necessary for constructing an innovation theology.

Simplicity and clarity—the criteria at work here—reinforce each other. Simplicity helps with clarity and both clarity and simplicity serve to quiet much debate on theological assumptions so that attention can

---

5. My own theological background is Protestant in tradition, Presbyterian in denomination and Reformed in theology. Hopefully I am not stuck in these perspectives, but readily acknowledge the resulting bias of this background.

6. The implications of Christology on these assumptions and innovation theology may make a significant difference in the architecture of innovation theology and should be considered for further discussion and investigation.

focus on the application space and the practical value an innovation theology can bring.

Each of these four foundational assumptions deserves some attention in order to make their relevance to innovation theology apparent.

Assumption 1: God Exists

Arguments for the existence of God are many and varied. These arguments have garnered attention and study for thousands of years and have been based on revelation, nature, philosophy, "pure reason," pragmatic probability and phenomenology. The recent resurgence of adamant atheists has re-plowed the field of these arguments, sometimes without a lot of consideration for the breadth, depth and longevity of the "prior art." Innovation theology should not take up these arguments. That is the job of theology proper. However, innovation theology will necessarily build upon the outcomes of one or more of these arguments for the existence of God.

Obviously, any effort to construct an innovation theology would not get very far without the assumption that God exists. Whether one or more of the many arguments for the existence of God will have a material bearing on the nature and character of innovation theology, I leave to better theological minds than mine to discern. Suffice it to say for now that any innovation theology that does not include this most basic assumption, for whatever reason, is dead in the water.

There are certain implications of the claim *God exists* that will have a bearing on innovation theology. For example, if God exists, then it follows logically, at least for some, that God is living, interested and actively engaged. Some of this is implied in the next assumption, which makes the implication of God's existence a bit more explicit than the bald statement that God exists.

Assumption 2: God Is Still Creating

Some have conceived of God as a passive watchmaker.[7] Once God finished creating the world, having "wound it up," so to speak, God took a detached position, letting the mechanisms of creation play out.

This view, while still held by many, is not likely to provide a supportive foundation for any innovation theology. Instead, an innovation

---

7. Paley, *Natural Theology*, ch. 1.

theology will likely assume a God who acts and intervenes in both the history of mankind and in the natural processes of creation. This active, even interventionist, view of God is arguably more aligned with the Old Testament witness, and certainly a central assumption behind the intervention of God in and through the pre-and post-resurrected Jesus. The Apostle Paul's bold statement that "the whole of creation has been groaning in labor pains until now"[8] suggests a Creator God who is committed and not finished. A passive, "watchmaker" kind of God is likely not going to be a working assumption of any innovation theology.

While it is theologically appropriate to acknowledge that in creation God established a natural order to things, it does not necessarily follow that once established, God stopped working, or stopped creating. As the psalmist sings it,

> Yours is the day, yours also the night;
> You established the luminaries and the sun.
> You have fixed all the bounds of the earth;
> You made summer and winters.[9]

This verse of the song, however, is preceded by,

> Yet God my King is from old
> working salvation in the earth.[10]

Might not "working salvation" be synonymous with the ongoing creative engagement of God, albeit after the fall? "Do not remember the former things, or consider the things of old," says Isaiah.[11] "I am about to do a new thing; now it springs forth, do you not perceive it?" There is certainly some evidence, theological, scriptural and even phenomenological, to suggest that God is not finished yet.

When and where there is no change, movement or creating there is no life or living. Changing, moving and creating may actually be less the exception and more the norm, though we often default to the opposite. These three are inseparable it seems, though we more often look at them separately. Change, movement and creating are all part and parcel of life and living.

8. Rom 8:22.

9. Ps 74:16–17.

10. Ps 74:12; 40:5; 71:15.

11. Isa 43:18–19.

Take a look at the first two verses of Genesis. Even *before* the first day of creation, the first verse of Scripture describes God as One who is creating. This is as much as we know about God, at least as far as Scripture tells us, thus far in the canon. Everything else we imagine about God we are importing.

"In the beginning God created . . ." is the more familiar translation. However, just as acceptable is another: "In the beginning when God began to create . . ." This translation suggests God may have started creating in the beginning but may not have ever retired from it, except for a day off at the end of each "week." Indeed, if we jump ahead to the seventh day of creation—the day that God rested "from all the work that he had done in creation"[12]—we might get the impression that God was done creating. But the text doesn't quite say that. It says, rather, "God finished *the work he had done.*" This does not imply that God had no more work to do. In fact, taking a day off to rest might imply the next morning God returns back to work, creating. That God is still creating is a reasonable assumption.

Look even more closely at these first two verses in Genesis. Verse 2 says that the "earth was without form and void, and darkness covered the face of the deep, while a wind from God swept over the face of the waters." Even before there is light (God's first act of creating) there is movement. The Spirit of God (*ruah* in Hebrew means "breath" or "wind") is moving. It moves across the waters, which themselves move in reaction to the unseen stimulus. Highly susceptible to stimulus, water is rarely, if ever, still. When it is we call it "dead."

Movements vary. In the subsequent days of creation various creating movements are mentioned, including *separating* the waters above from the waters below (day 2), *gathering* the waters under the sky, and vegetation *yielding* seed and fruit (day 3), *lighting* the earth and *marking* the days, seasons and years (day 4), *bringing forth* every living creature that moves and creeps (day 5 and 6).

Thus far the only "image of God" we have at this point is of a creator: creating, living, breathing, moving. All these partial images don't stand independently from each other. Like threads in a fabric of reality that is woven together, integrated, moving, breathing and living are contiguous, successive and of one continuous flow. Even in the second creation account in Genesis[13] *before* plants or herbs or rain, God forms man from

---

12. Gen 2:2.

13. Gen 2:2–4b.

CHANGE, INNOVATION AND THEOLOGY

the dust of the ground and breathes into this form, specifically into the nostrils of this form, the breath of life. As a result, "the man became a living being."[14] There is a similar explicit equation of life, living, breathing (and the Spirit of God) and movement in Ezekiel's vision of the valley of the dry bones.[15]

Movement implies change, as does the coordinated acts of mind and hand we call creating. Creating, changing and moving is more the norm than most of us think.[16] Even what we most often regard as "given," like the "foundations of the earth and heavens," God can change like an article of clothing.[17] God's presence may be constant, but God's creating is constantly changing, generating, and generous. Genesis, the first book of Scripture, is well named. It is hard to avoid the generative generosity of a creating God.

Assumption 3: God Is Love[18]

This assumption could be regarded as implicit in the second assumption. However, I include it here as its own assumption for two reasons.

The first is to be explicit about the disposition of God toward God's creation, including both the earth, what lives and moves on the earth, and mankind. Love, of course, can and should be viewed as more than a disposition of God. It could be in some mysterious way an (or the) essential attribute of God's entire being. Hence, "God is love." Whether this is a disposition or an attribute of God or the essential being of God is better left to theology proper. So much has been written about this characteristic of God that we can generally accept the widespread consensus in regards to these three words "God is love" arranged as they are.

The second reason for including this assumption may have more to do with innovation than God. Innovators, particularly successful ones, are often seduced by the admiration of others and their own success. Succumbing to this temptation leads to boasting in their own wisdom,

---

14. Gen 2:7.

15. Ezek 37.

16. Carr, *Henri Bergson*, 18. The philosophy of Henri Bergson examines this "fabric" in great detail. Movement is life and life is movement, suggests Henri Bergson. Where there is no movement, there is no life.

17. Ps 102:25–27; Heb 1:10–12.

18. 1 John 4:8.

strength, and often in their resulting wealth. In so doing, these successful role models often end up implying they have a proven and therefore
replicable formula for successful innovation.

However, while their experience and success may be indisputable,
replicability does not necessary follow, logically or in practice. In fact,
"success is often the enemy of innovation."[19] Success can easily erode humility. When we assume "God is love," it may also be useful to remind
ourselves that love is not simply an emotion or a disposition. Love also
has to do with matters of justice and righteousness, even truth and reality. Love and success are two words that do not necessarily comfortably
reside with each other.

Whatever other theological notions people have about God, the
prophet Jeremiah's way of combining steadfast love, justice and righteousness, and leading off with steadfast love—is a combination worth
keeping in mind. It keeps innovators humble, implies an understanding
of love as more than mere feeling, and expresses an inseparable triad of
love, justice and righteousness. This triad avoids a superficial sentimen-
talism of mistaking love as primarily a feeling or disposition. Here's the
way Jeremiah puts it:

> Thus says the Lord, "Do not let the wise boast in their wisdom,
> do not let the mighty boast in their might,
> do not let the wealthy boast in their wealth;
> but let those who boast boast in this,
> that they understand and know me, that I am the Lord;
> I act with steadfast love, justice and righteousness in the earth,
> For in these things I delight," says the Lord.[20]

Assumption 4: God Is One for Whom All Things Are Possible[21]

Of the four, this assumption may be the most directly encouraging for
innovators. As a foundation assumption it is certainly the closest to a

19. Said by David Chernin, former COO of Fox, at a strategy meeting I facilitated
some years ago.

20. Jer 9:23–24.

21. Brueggemann, *Reality, Grief, Hope*, 157. Brueggemann highlights this way of
describing God, citing Soren Kierkegaard. Kierkegaard was not necessarily the author
of this assumption, however, as we can find plenty of direct and indirect evidence of
this assumption in Matt 19:26; Mark 9:23; 10:27; and Luke 18:27.

tautology. For God all things are possible. If there were any limits on God then God would not be God. If we limit God's freedom, competence, capability or capacity by inferring that there is anything that God cannot do, we make a fundamental error in logic, or *theo*-logic. Putting any limits on God is a direct and logical contradiction. We do this more often than we may realize, particularly when we take a detached, objective and reasoned point of view of God.

Such a detached perspective requires a perch from outside the creation, "outside" of God or God's influence, or a more arrogant "looking down upon" God. With any one of these points of view, we end up taking God's perspective—a perspective that we cannot take, by definition. Such a perspective is not only a logical contradiction. It is also practically impossible. That we do it anyway, repeatedly, is one of the great sources of trouble for mankind.

If God is God, then neither you nor I are. Rather, we are a *part of* God's creation and within or under the umbrella of God's perspective and care, a position that by definition we cannot get out from under even if we wanted to or think we can.

This fourth assumption is particularly pertinent to innovation theology, given that innovating has so much to do with converting what is possible into what is real. First-person accounts of innovators and third-person case studies consistently reveal the following pattern of innovating. Innovating starts with a change. The change reveals a problem or opportunity "as given."[22] This is the initial stimulus, inciting innovators to conceive of a few potential solutions and even try them out. Then, inevitably, these solutions encounter rejection and resistance, especially if the solution is new. Somewhere along the way in this process the original problem "as given" morphs into a problem "as understood." Then a more evolved and refined solution is conceived, developed and ultimately introduced. This pattern holds true whether the innovating effort is successful or not, and regardless of the context in which the innovating is done, personal or corporate, social or commercial.

Innovating requires persistence. Many regard persistence as an essential characteristic of entrepreneurs and innovators, for good reason. Innovation, if it is really innovation, will be resisted, if not at first rejected. This was described centuries ago by Nicolo Machiavelli (1469–1527) in *The Prince* in the often-cited quote:

22. Is this "givenness" a grace embodied in purposefulness, task and vocation? Innovation theology might suggest that it is.

48

> There is nothing more difficult to carry out nor more doubtful of success, nor more dangerous to handle than to initiate a new order of things; for the reformer has enemies in all those who profit by the old order, and only lukewarm defenders in all those who would profit by the new order; this lukewarmness arising partly from the incredulity of mankind who does not truly believe in anything new until they actually have experience of it.

Machiavelli's "reformer" is our innovator. Innovating "initiates a new order," whether out of chaos or out of a more familiar context.

As a result, this fourth assumption—"that God is one for whom all things are possible"—is a potent source of persistence and hope for innovators. It provides a powerful countermeasure to the resistance and lukewarmness that innovating always encounters.

Innovating progresses iteratively, whether from concept to commercialization in the economic realm or from insight to transformation in the personal sphere. Multiple iterations of trials and errors—often called learning "loops"—progress through conceptual stages of development to the physical or "realized" incarnations of working prototypes. More often than not these learning loops are buffeted by the headwinds of rejection and resistance. "It'll never work." "It's too expensive." "We've already tried something like that before." "I am not smart enough." Autoimmune reflexes accompany and preoccupy the new wherever it emerges. If there is no rejection, the idea is likely not new. Innovations are often considered impossible at first, based upon the conventional wisdom and accumulated knowledge as well as the entrenched interests of incumbents.

This pattern has been both observed and expressed in many different ways by many different innovators. One was Einstein who put it this way: "If an idea does not at first appear absurd, it is probably not worth pursuing." But the assumption that God is One for whom all things are possible carries a profoundly hopeful implication into any innovating process. Whether innovators are conscious of their own tacit concurrence with this fourth assumption or not, the assumption seems to operate within them enough to work through the resistance and rejections they will surely encounter, both from within themselves and from their peers and sponsors. When this assumption is missing, it can have a debilitating effect on innovating.

When all four assumptions are taken together, innovators have something formidable with which to address the inevitable resistance and rejection that is so much a part of innovating.

There is another assumption that could be added to the four, though it is more anthropological than theological. This is the assumption that God gave humankind the freedom to choose, even to choose not to believe (in) God. It seems self-evident that were we not free to choose whether to believe (in) God and/or recognize the value of being in relationship with God, that we would be in a deterministic, robotic or mechanistic relationship with God. Being in a relationship where there is no such freedom or choice is really not much of a relationship at all. The relevance of this anthropological assumption to innovation shows up in the central role choice plays in innovating, perhaps as central a capability as creativity.

Other basic assumptions both theological and anthropological may eventually end up forming the foundations of innovation theology. At this embryonic stage, however, these four assumptions should provide the bare minimum.

We can now look at how these theological assumptions apply to the practices and principles of innovating, and what practical contribution innovation theology might make.

INNOVATION THEOLOGY'S PURPOSE

Over the past thirty-five years of laboring with the innovating efforts of different companies in different continents, cultures and countries, I have observed *decreasing* interest in innovating especially on the part of incumbent organizations. Ironically *talk* of innovation has increased while investments in innovating have decreased. With all the talk, a shared and common understanding of what constitutes a genuine innovation itself has eroded. I am by no means the only one who has noticed the erosion. Many analysts[23] suggest from an economic point of view that companies in the United States alone are investing in the future at the lowest level in some four decades, despite plentiful reservoirs of cash.

One of the reasons may be a failure of nerve and an impatient desire for quick fixes.[24] I have seen firsthand leaders fail to even ask, much less answer, where and why innovations are needed from their own companies and in their own business ecosystems. Many leaders defer to others to both ask and answer these two most basic questions. Certainly there

23. Rubenfire, "CEO's Partly Sunny Economic Outlook"; Morath, "Secretary Lew Warns"; Christensen and van Bever, "Capitalist's Dilemma."

24. Friedman, *Failure of Nerve*, 2.

are exceptions. However, a significant number of innovation efforts, even ones attracting an abundance of financial capital, are neither structural nor infrastructural. Many are focused on quick fixes and quicker exits with big payoffs, from an app to a cleverly coded user interface.

These "innovations" are hardly structural, barely substantive. The changes to which these "innovations" represent a response are not very substantive themselves. Rather they represent reactions to an uncertain future and reflect aims to skim off the surface rather than create new value rooted below it.

Short-termism chronically prevents leaders from asking where and why innovations should be pursued. Risk/reward ratios, net present value calculations or options-valuation schemes are all employed to calculate whether to innovate. These equations, however, are all far too weak to motivate authentic innovation efforts, even when these calculations do turn positive. The few highly publicized examples of entrepreneurial success with big financial rewards are often based on market capitalization more than profitability, much less the actual value contributed.

It is not much of a secret that most corporate ventures and entrepreneurial start-ups fail. Responding to change aimed at creating new value is difficult. The degree of difficulty presents a near impossible challenge to justify innovating only on calculations and risk/reward ratios. The skepticism of investors whose motivations are more extractive and transactional than generative and relational is typically too great to overcome. Even those new entrepreneurial ideas that don't fail outright, even those that attract an acquirer's attention, or become "liquid" through an IPO, do so *before* demonstrating a profit or positive cash flow. Hindsight does not seem to influence much foresight. Financial markets have a way of distorting signals from economic markets, and even volatile extrinsic values have a way of distorting more stable intrinsic ones.

Entrepreneurs[25] with whom I have had the privilege of working typically *see and believe* in the value they can create and deliver to their customers well before they are able to calculate the returns with any certainty. Some of these entrepreneurs are lining up the opportunities they see first with a point of view in plumb with a higher purpose, not a spreadsheet.

---

25. "Entrepreneur" has also morphed in its meaning. J. B. Say, the French economist, coined the phrase to originally denote one who took considerable risk to create resources and capital from sources and materials that were not generally recognized as carrying that value. See Peter Drucker's discussion how "entrepreneur" is frequently misunderstood can be found in his *Innovation and Entrepreneurship*, 21.

It is not that entrepreneurs shun financial calculations or ignore risk/reward ratios. Quite the opposite. They pay very close attention to the numbers. The bottom line is important. However, what calls them to risk failure and loss is that they *believe* in what they are doing and that it is worth believing in. This is a purpose greater than simply how much they stand to make at the end of the day. Greater purpose and other-oriented value is a central part of the equation in deciding to take the risk in the first place. This is fertile ground for theological exploration, ground wherein theology might plant seeds for answering where and why we should, could, can and need to innovate, and for whom.

PLUMB LINES VERSUS BOTTOM LINES

The prophet Amos had four visions. Of the four, the vision of the plumb line is perhaps the most memorable. Particularly remarkable is what Amos deselects in the description of what he sees. Here's the way Amos conveys it:

> This is what the Lord showed me:
>> the Lord was standing beside a wall built with a plumb line,
> with a plumb line in his hand.
> And the Lord said to me, "Amos, what do you see?"
> And I said, "A plumb line."[26]

If I was Amos and saw the Lord standing beside a wall, I would be hard-pressed to focus on the plumb line. I would likely be more focused on the One who was holding it. However, when Amos replies with the simple "a plumb line," it is hard to miss the implication. Not only the wall, but God is relegated to background. What comes to the foreground is the plumb line.[27]

Change can capture our attention but distract us away from what is most important. The intent of the plumb line is to hold up to us what is central and should not be missed. At the risk of overstatement, seeing

26. Amos 7:7–8.

27. The prophetic plumb line concept will resurface in many of the following essays. At this juncture, it is important to note that there are various pieces of core "code," or "instruction sets" that surface throughout the Old and New Testament (e.g., Jesus' self understanding in Luke 4:18–21 wherein he quotes Isa 61:1–2 is one. Micah 6:8 is another.) Identifying what other plumb lines are particularly potent for innovators may itself be worthy of further development in any future innovation theology.

the purpose of God may be even more important than seeing God. It is a simple yet potent image. The plumb line tightly weaves teleology (the study of purpose) and theology (the study of God) into in a single strand. With the aid of gravity, builders hold the line up to align whatever they are erecting to keep it straight and "on purpose."

The plumb line may have been envisioned first by Amos, but it certainly didn't remain captive of his prophecy. The intent of the plumb line runs throughout the entire prophetic tradition and even through the fulfillment of that tradition in Jesus. As a primary tool of measurement, the plumb line keeps our creative purposes aligned with and to the purposes of God. Plumb lines will likely be a "go to" tool of innovation theology.

Innovation theology cannot offer any magical potion to cure a failure of nerve. Nor are plumb lines substitutes for bottom lines. However, what innovation theology *can* do is encourage the entrepreneurially inclined to seek opportunity that is truly compelling. In fact, the purpose of innovation theology itself may be to challenge and enable the entrepreneurial leader to use a plumb line *before* using a bottom line to discern where innovations are needed and why. The stewardship, sustainability and social and economic benefit of our children's future depends upon it.

CONCLUSION

If on the one hand, innovation has nothing to do with God and God nothing to do with innovating, then we end up with both theological and practical consequences. These consequences are desolate, dry and transactional. Theologically, we risk limiting God—something most theologies would scrupulously want to avoid. Practically we risk creating new but superficial value in our innovating. Value of this kind is no deeper than what can be extracted from transactions. Economists call it "exchange value." It's extrinsic.

When value from transactions replaces new value created for the other we easily misdirect our innovating efforts on wants more than needs. If this goes on for too long, extrinsic value becomes detached from intrinsic value; economic growth gets built on the sands of conspicuous consumption more than the rock of creative contribution. This is not only unsustainable, it leads to what the prophet Micah described as desolation:

> You shall eat, but not be satisfied,
> and there shall be a gnawing hunger within you;

you shall put away, but not save,

and what you save, I will hand over to the sword.

You shall sow, but not reap.[28]

If on the other hand, God does have something to do with innovating and innovating with God, then we end up with different theological and practical consequences. These consequences are consolate, abundant, generative and generous. Theologically, we open ourselves up to the possibility (perhaps probability) that God is still creating in and through the changes confronting us. We also open ourselves up to the possibility that God is inviting us to participate in his creative purposes, to join the company of God, and contribute to its purposes.

Practically, when we assume God does have an interest in innovating, answers to the questions of where to innovate and why become clearer, bolder. We have a divine partner to guide us where to look, and even what to look for. Practically, when we are in the company of God and contributing to his purposes, we discover more compelling meaning, more substantive value and more sustainable confidence. In such company we can move with stronger conviction in discovering where innovations are needed and why, and discover compelling reasons and solutions greater than our own self-interests. This alone should not only improve the probability of success. It will transform the definition of just what success is.

28. Mic 6:14–15.

CONVERSATION STARTERS

1. Where are the plumb lines emerging in today's changes? In today's emerging innovations? What makes it difficult to see the plumb lines?

2. What makes innovations motivated by plumb lines different from those motivated by top or bottom lines (for commercial companies) or even outcomes and impacts (for noncommercial organizations)?

3. If the One for whom all things are possible is still creating, and if we are made in the image of this One, do these assumptions make any difference in how we accept and make sense of change? Any difference in whether and how we innovate in response to change?

4. Since innovation and theology both

   - have much to say about accepting and making sense of change,
   - influence how people respond to change,
   - have much to do with value and value creation,
   - are ways people make sense, and
   - shape culture with positive and negative implications;

   how does one reinforce the other or get in the way of the other?

5. What other assumptions should be included as the basis for an innovation theology, and what difference to innovating will the assumption make? For example, should the crucifixion and resurrection of Jesus be one of those assumptions?

3

Innovating Needs Theology

He woke up and rebuked the wind, and said to the sea, "Peace! Be still!"[1]

STORMS ARE IN THE forecast, some more intense than we have experienced in the past. These storms are not just in the weather. They are economic, political and even personal.

Unseen forces stir these storms into being. Adam Smith's "invisible hand" or Nassim Taleb's "black swan"[2] point to vague origins of disruption that prove impossible to predict. But whatever their origins, when storms emerge from their anonymous beginnings, grow beyond infant states and descend upon us without discrimination, they hit us where we live, locally and personally.

Globalization intensifies competition for raw materials. Commoditization erodes just about every competitive advantage. Democratization undermines every precarious political promise of incumbent administrations. Digitization disrupts stable institutions, with universities looking like the next institution on the cyber chopping block. Wave after wave of change pounds against the retaining walls of society, each wave weakening the political, economic and linguistic borders we were counting on. The effects of each storm are felt personally as well, in the particulars of disappointment, disillusionment, despair, loss, and alienation.

1. Mark 4:39–40.
2. Taleb, *Black Swan*, xxi.

Despite the shelters we have built, private or public, in policy or psychotherapy, storms keep coming. Climates keep changing. The Irish poet W. B. Yeats prophetically described our situation this way:

> Turning and turning in the widening gyre
> The falcon cannot hear the falconer;
> Things fall a part; the centre cannot hold;
> Mere anarchy is loosed upon the world,
> The blood-dimmed tide is loosed and everywhere
> The ceremony of innocence is drowned;
> The best lack all conviction, while the worst
> Are full of passionate intensity.[3]

Volatility, turbulence, and uncertainty all seem to be increasing, perhaps even at an accelerating rate. Whether the rate really is accelerating may be debatable. But both sides of the debate would readily agree, we are living in an anxious time in an insecure world. The anxiety doesn't seem to be subsiding. Some of us are naturally prone to the more dramatic; others, more reserved. And surely our attitude toward change depends in part on how vulnerable we imagine ourselves to be. The mere threat of storms raises anxiety most everywhere, and the anxiety is not just about the storms but about what the future holds after the storms blow through.

Change is always in the forecast, however, whether it's a weather, economic, market or personal forecast. And when change is in the forecast, stormy or not, we awaken to the fact that we will need to respond in some manner and to some degree. Our responses can vary, to be sure. We can insulate ourselves *from* the change, accommodate ourselves *to* the change or we can innovate *with* the change. The degree of anxiety we have about the change will likely influence which response we choose. The more anxious we are, the less likely we will choose to innovate or respond generously to those who do.

I share Edwin Friedman's belief about the "rampant sabotaging of leaders who try to stand tall amid the raging anxiety-storms of our times."[4] Persistent "sabotage" shows up in countless forms of resistance to change and countless rejections of generative responses to it. Resistance and rejection are due not so much to the particulars as to the fact that

---

3. Yeats, "Second Coming."

4. Friedman, *Failure of Nerve*, 2.

the leader took initiative[5]—did something aimed at creating new value for others; in other words, when leaders attempt to innovate. This is one reason why we so often insulate or accommodate rather than innovate.

That theology speaks directly to "anxiety-storms" should not surprise us. Jesus not only stilled the waves and quieted the storm.[6] He was explicit in what he had to say regarding our anxieties in general and those tied to forecasts. "Don't worry about tomorrow."[7] Don't keep striving for what can be consumed. Don't keep worrying, for it is the nations (and companies?) of the world that strive after all these things, and your Father knows you need them. Instead, strive for his kingdom and these things will be given to you as well.[8] We typically understand these words personally. Seldom do we imagine that these words may be equally relevant to us organizationally.

What may be surprising, however, is that theology might also have something quite practical to say about innovating. This is the primary proposal of this essay: that theology has something to contribute to innovation, something needed by leaders and innovators. Put another way, innovation and innovating efforts actually need what theology can offer, a kind of response to change often so overshadowed by anxiety we don't even consider it as an option.

While this may sound like a brash proposal—and it may well be— it is based upon two assumptions: one about innovation and the other about theology. These two assumptions need to be understood before any defense can be made of the proposal.

First, the assumption about innovation which itself includes a dependent assumption about responding rather than reacting to change. We start with this dependent assumption.

5. Ibid., 3.

6. Mark 4:35–41.

7. Matt 6:25–34.

8. Luke 12:29–31.

RESPONSE TO CHANGE

As was said in the introduction, responding to change is different than reacting to change.[9] Responding is a thoughtful, deliberate choosing. Consideration and discernment differentiate a response from a reaction. A reaction has neither. As such, responding to change implies some pause in between the stimulus and response, a pause that is not empty but occupied with clarifying what the options might be, weighing those options, and investigating the nature of the change itself to create additional options. Without the space between the stimulus and response we react rather than respond.

Broadly speaking we have at least three options when responding to change. We can *insulate, accommodate* or *innovate.* The first two are the habitual preferences of incumbents who prefer to maintain their established positions. The latter is the preference of the up-starts, or if you prefer, start-ups. These are the Davids, not the Goliaths—individuals and organizations who know their positions are untenable and are willing to try something new.

Choosing to *insulate* requires an investment in defense. It typically invites us to put something between us and change. Insulation can work for a while though it can easily turn into isolation. Insulation necessarily recruits strategies of self-reliance for as long as there is an accessible supply of resources and energy to sustain it. But self-reliance only goes so far, as the English poet John Donne (d. 1631) put it famously in the first line of his *Meditation XVI*:

> No man is an island,
> Entire of itself,
> Every man is a piece of the continent,
> A part of the main.

Donne's wisdom applies to nations, companies and individuals. In the context of nations, North Korea is an extreme example of the dubious sustainability of insulating. For companies, insulation distorts the feedback a company needs from its environment, whether feedback

---

9. Ackoff, *Differences That Make a Difference*, 108. Ackoff's distinction between a reflex, a reaction and a response is wonderfully expressed in this delightful volume. Ackoff centers the difference in choice. He observes that with a reflex we have no choice, with a reaction we have a choice but we do not make it, and with a response, we have a choice and we make it. We will use "response" in these essays with this definition.

from customers, suppliers or even competitors. Without trustworthy and timely feedback, change erodes profit margins and eventually an ability to attract talent. For individuals, insulation can lead to social or emotional isolation. Neuroscience suggests our natural anatomical wiring is at risk when the duration of isolation is too long, not to mention the health of our spiritual condition. We are social animals. Solitude and celibacy may be appropriate for a time. But as a society we'd run aground if everyone behaved this way. Individualism taken to an extreme leads to defensive insulating responses first and then, eventually, to isolating ones.

Choosing to *accommodate* in response to change requires an investment in tolerance. Accommodation invites us to absorb the change. Accommodation can also work for a while, but it requires sufficient capacity or resilience to absorb and cushion the disruption. Accommodation makes room for differences without really digesting or reconciling them. The digestive challenge is wonderfully illustrated in an experience David Packard recounts about the very early years of Hewlett-Packard. Packard confessed fondness for a truth he often repeated, but first learned from an unnamed retired engineer Wells Fargo sent to do due diligence on the young company. The occasion was the company's need for another round of funding. Because of the many opportunities the company saw in the rising tide of electronic measurement technologies, the engineer told Packard, "David, companies seldom die of starvation. More often they die of indigestion."[10] Indigestion is the risk of accommodation.

Accommodation often leads to diversification. If pursued long enough, diversification eventuates in the divestment of what has been accommodated. It risks eroding focus in mission and purpose. Some call this "strategic drift." In the context of nations, accommodation appears to have its limits, particularly in inverse proportion to the diversity of perspectives the society attempts to hold within it. What we are currently witnessing in Iraq and Syria with Sunnis, Shiites and Kurds is but one example of diverse people finding it difficult to coexist. The European Union might be another example, stable for now. Even the federalism inherent in the structure of the United States is a form of accommodation.

Accommodation can work so long as there are mechanisms of cohesiveness to "digest" the diversity (e.g., a common language). When one company acquires another, the synergies promised[11] end up destroying

10. Packard, *HP Way*, 57.

11. By the deal-makers who feel no responsibility to ensure the "synergies" they promise are realized.

shareholder value more often than they create value. In the context of family systems, accommodation often erodes into unhealthy "codependency" and enabling behaviors, debilitating both the individual and the family. In the context of an individual's response to change, accommodation can only stretch as far as one's conscience or sense of wholeness will allow.

Choosing to *innovate* in response to change requires investments in acceptance, investigation and invention. Unlike insulation and accommodation, innovation invites us to accept and understand the new realities change brings. Innovating requires an adaptive capability grounded in a willingness to learn and modify, unlearn and revise. In fact, innovation can be reasonably understood as a choice-ful act of adaptation to the external environment. It is especially needed when an order that used to make sense no longer does. Reality, or life, has moved and new sense needs to be made. The old order doesn't make sense any more. Sometimes it even appears as non-sense; familiar, yes, but nonsense.

But choosing to innovate—to do something entirely new—does not come easily to those who already have something going they prefer to keep going. The new initiative very early on sets up a "sibling rivalry" for limited resources and attention. This is a rivalry typically won by older siblings.

In addition, innovation will always be less certain, less measurable and less predictable than either insulation or accommodation. Even if the prospect of an innovation promises more sustainable and robust growth, it will always appear more risky, nationally, corporately or individually. In the context of nations, genuine innovation can produce greater productivity, as did the widespread diffusion of higher education, now reaching emerging economies globally. For companies, innovation can lead to growth of both top line revenues and bottom line profitability, often without the costly premiums paid to deal makers for value-destroying "synergies." For individuals responding to change, innovating can lead to lives of greater meaning and purpose than could have been imagined before. Consider the extraordinary example of Viktor Frankl who survived the death camp at Auschwitz and from that horrific experience invented a radically new therapeutic method.[12] Necessity is the mother of invention and often of innovation as well.

If insulation, accommodation and innovation represent three possible responses to change, then what would cause us to choose one over another?

12. Frankl, *Man's Search for Meaning*, 9–10.

When we choose to insulate our choice is ultimately based on our desire to defend or buffer ourselves against some aspect of the change we find disagreeable. The choice may be rationalized as being more practical, cost effective or generally "reasonable." But what "reasonable" means depends upon what is of greater interest at the time.

When we choose to accommodate our choice is ultimately based on preserving as much of our previous position as possible, though we acknowledge some or all of the change that we may or may not like. Like insulation, accommodation may make more practical, cost-effective or prudent sense, and conforms to what is of greater value to the one making the choice. In this case, the choice-maker is interested in preserving his or her position.

If we choose to innovate, however, our choice is ultimately based on a desire to try something new, a desire often pulled by a purpose greater than defending ourselves or preserving our position. For a business this purpose is often found in the one served (the customer) more than the one serving (the company). If this is not a "greater purpose" then it is certainly less self-interested. Some might call this an allo-centric[13] rather than an egocentric purpose. Most simply refer to it as a greater or higher purpose, meaning greater than one's own self-interest, self-defense or self-preservation.

To be sure, choosing to innovate can conceivably include both allo-centric *and* egocentric motivations, particularly as a business must sustain a sufficient profitability if is to continue. But even here, when business continuity becomes more important than delivering value to customers, the business can lose sight of its primary purpose. Providing others with a novel product or service with real value to them works only if in providing that value there is a financial or economic return that exceeds the total costs incurred: i.e., profit. Profits, however, are never the purpose of the business, regardless of the many companies that slip into this mistaken thinking. The purpose is always first and foremost to create and embody a value through which to serve the other.[14]

If choosing to innovate is "driven" by a purpose greater than oneself or greater than the needs of the company, then the relevance of theology should not be all that surprising. Purpose or teleology[15] is at the heart of theology.

13. Other oriented.

14. Drucker, *Management*, 61, 71.

15. Teleology is the study of purpose. See also Ackoff and Emery, *On Purposeful Systems*.

Some might object here, and remind me that teleology is not theology. Technically, this is correct. However, teleology and theology have been warp and weft in the fabric of theological reflection as far back as Plato, Socrates and the roots of all three Abrahamic religions. My point here is not to argue for a teleological perspective on cosmology, often called "creationism" or "intelligent design." Rather, my point is simply that it is difficult if not impossible to separate teleology and theology, as difficult as it was for Jean Calvin to differentiate[16] theology from anthropology, which itself may be another reason to consider innovation and theology alongside each other.

Before wading any further into the main proposal of this essay, I need to lay out the assumptions about innovation and theology, which I can now do having addressed the dependent assumption underlying what it means to respond, rather than react, to change, and what the response options generally are.

INNOVATION DEFINED

Those of us who have been laboring in the field of innovation for several decades have grown tired, even cynical, of the various uses and abuses of the word innovation, particularly of late. Once adopted by the mainstream media the word's meaning was occluded by a vaporous cloud of many connotations. Such is the perennial problem of language. But semantic mutation is particularly pernicious when it comes to words that become desolated by advertising messages. The words lose much of their precision.[17] Such has been the fate of the word "innovation."

As a result, at least for the sake of the following essays, innovation needs to be explicitly defined. A working definition that provides some distinctiveness in denotation while avoiding any obfuscating jargon is to define it as the *structural response to substantive change that aims to create new value*. Mindful that a response is not a reaction, what I intend to do with this definition is raise the bar on what qualifies as an innovation and an innovating effort.

---

16. Calvin, *Institutes of Christian Religion*, 35. Calvin opens his two-volume work: "Nearly all the wisdom we possess, that is to say, true and sound wisdom, consists of two parts: the knowledge of God and of ourselves. But, while joined by many bonds, which one precedes and brings forth the other is not easy to discern."

17. McIntyre, *Caring for Words in the Culture of Lies*, 12.

First, innovating as effort and innovation as the result of that effort are both responses to change rather than reactions or autonomic reflexes to it. Clarifying this intends to avoid the frequent confusion of innovation with change itself. Internal change often becomes confused with external change; stimulus gets confused with response. When such confusion sets it, it is difficult to know whether you are communicating. Categorizing innovation as a response to change, at least for organizations, excludes something called organizational change (or change management) as a synonym for innovation. It is not. As important and necessary as organizational change can be, innovation is something else. Keeping the two separate avoids unnecessary confusion.

Second, by introducing the qualifier of "structural," I am intending to exclude much of what is constantly bubbling at the surface but remains superficial. To illustrate, consider the example of the iPod, often cited as an innovation. Taken by itself the iPod device was not really an innovation when it was introduced. It was another version of an MP3 player—something that had been around for a while. No doubt it was an elegantly designed device. But such elegance alone does not an innovation make. However, when the iPod is considered as one part of a system comprising an iPod, a service (iTunes) enabling music lovers easy access to music, and a new pricing structure that allowed not just albums but singles to be purchased, then the structural elements of the new system can be seen. This iPod/iTunes "ecosystem" *was* an innovation when it was introduced because it changed the then-current structure of music accessibility and delivery.

In the language of systems, when something new alters the structure of the existing system it is likely an innovation. When the degree of newness comes from adding or breaking structure it typically makes for a more seminal invention, no matter what the field. It may be worth noting here that invention and innovation are not synonymous. An invention-less innovation will likely not alter the broader system of which it is a part at a structural level,[18] whereas an innovation with an invention more likely will.

Third, by using "substantive," the depth of change to which innovation is a response is qualified. The intent is to exclude changes that are superficial and transitory, along with responses to them that are superficial and transitory. Many things that appear to be new are called innovations. However, many of these innovations are in name only. They are at best

18. It may alter the business ecosystem, however.

superficial. They reside at the surface layer only. Substantive innovations are typically more multilayered, structural or even infrastructural, causing restructuring at deeper layers of reality no matter what the domain.

There is a significant difference between what might be called "surface innovations" and "substantive" or "structural innovations." To qualify as an innovation—a "structural response to substantive change"—more than one layer is involved. This implies that responses to change that do not extend below the surface layer are likely more often reactive than purposefully responsive.

Fourth is the "aim of creating new value" in this definition. Ever since Adam Smith's *Wealth of Nations*, economists have been fond of distinguishing between "exchange value" and "use value." Commercial innovations will find an exchange value, which, if sufficient, is often a measure of its financial success. When exchange value is insufficient, however, a potential innovation will be regarded as a commercial failure. Exchange value derives in part from the innovation's value in use, determined by the perceptions and realities of the user or customer.

No matter the use value the *innovator* may assign to the innovation, in the final analysis the *user* or customer has the final say. To what extent this underlying use value is associated with an even deeper intrinsic value will be addressed in a subsequent essay. For now, suffice it to say that if there is an even deeper intrinsic value associated with the extrinsic value, then a greater, allo-centric purpose is present. In these instances we have a genuine innovation. Lifesaving therapy innovations from the pharmaceutical and medical technology industries, or sustainable energy solutions may represent areas wherein the intrinsic roots of extrinsic value are easier to discern. In other areas, the difficulty of discerning the intrinsic values under the extrinsic ones shouldn't lead us to conclude that these deeper values are necessarily absent.

"Creating new value"—not merely adding, transferring or rearranging value—sharpens the difference between authentic innovation and its more trivial and superficial pretenders. This is not to equate creativity and innovation, though it does intend to imbue genuine innovation with some degree of originality. What is regarded as original or creative, however, is inescapably derived from the subjective discernment of those who know enough about the domain to recognize something as new.[19]

19. Csikszentmihalyi, *Creativity*, 6.

The community of knowledgeable practitioners is the only source qualified to appropriately apply the designation "new."

With this understanding of innovation, I need to address one more
assumption—what theology is.

THEOLOGY DEFINED

Delineating differences between theology and philosophy, cosmology, the
sociology of religion, etc—distinctions appropriate for a complete definition of theology—are beyond the scope of this essay. However, within the
limits of my ability and this space, I would propose the following simple
definition of theology—what some call reasoned discourse on God and
divine realities. The definition is simply this: that *theology is what and
how we explicitly think and express our experience of, relationship with and
trust in, God.*

Part of my intent in defining theology[20] this way is to return theology to its rightful owners—you and me—not scholars, but laymen and
laywomen, believers, and perhaps even a few agnostics as well. However
we choose to classify ourselves and others, whether as atheist, agnostic
or theist; whether Christian, Muslim, Jew, Buddhist, Hindu, or the more
prevalent "I am spiritual but not religious," theology is in our thinking
and speech, whether we are conscious of it or not. To "do" theology,
therefore, is to examine explicitly what we implicitly experience of our
individual and collective relationship with and trust in God.

Theology shouldn't be confused with religion. Religion is comprised of the shared beliefs, practices and traditions among a community
of people who express and enact their orientation toward the Divine.
Theology is, rather, the explicit expression of implicit belief. As explicit
expressions of the implicit, the purpose of theology is to test the coherence, consistency, relevance and implications of these explicit expressions by means of reason and discourse. With whatever frequency we
subject ourselves to these tests and whatever the test methodologies all of
us express our implicit beliefs regardless of our relative confidence about
those expressions.

---

20. The prominence and role of Scripture as a primary source for theology should
be assumed, unless otherwise stated. This role is addressed in the essay "Innovating
with Company Assets: Scripture and Spirit."

The point is that theology belongs to all of us and is practiced well or poorly by all of us. A hint of support for this premise resides in the repeated Gallup Polls that consistently tell us that over 90 percent believe in God.[21] This definition of theology is intended to be nontechnical but specific enough to enable a reasoned consideration of theology's application into an area that could use it, namely innovation.

CONNECTIONS BETWEEN INNOVATION AND THEOLOGY

Proposing that innovation "needs" theology presumes some connection is possible between them. If innovation is left to the variable whims of its many media-hyped connotations and theology is mistakenly considered the exclusive province of scholars fine-tuning doctrinal propositions, then any connection between the two will likely elude us. However, if innovation denotes a deeper response to substantive change and theology stays close to its primary subject, the connectivity between the two begins to present itself.

There are several aspects to this connection. First, what connects innovation and theology has to do with choice. Choice is a thread woven into the fabric of innovation. Choice is also central to theology as well. How choices are made, and even that we have the ability to choose, reflects a theological claim about free will. Choice deserves to be made more explicit before going any further.

When an individual or company *responds* to change it is reasonable to assume the respondent not only has a choice but also exercises it. Without the ability to choose (key to the ability to respond) change stimulates reactions more than responses. When one has a set of options and the ability to choose, but for some reason a choice is not made, the result is a reaction not a response. Only when one has a set of options, uses the capability to weigh the options, and selects from the set, can it be called a response.

What removes choice from an individual or organization is the absence of options, time or the capability to assess and weigh the options. For an individual, physical addiction is an example of lost choice. An active addict loses her ability to make choices, at least in regards to her

21. More than 90 percent of Americans believe that God exists. This figure has remained relatively constant since Gallup first asked the question in the 1940s. (Frank Newport, "More Than 9 in 10 Americans Continue to Believe in God," June 3, 2011, http://www.gallup.com/poll/147887/americans-continue-believe-god.aspx.)

will power to stop drinking or taking the addicting substance. As a result, the addict's ability to respond departs, leaving the addict to the mercy of her own reactions and reflexes. If and when abstinence is achieved an addict's ability to choose returns, and the recovering addict can become response-able, at least more so than in the past.

Likewise for an organization, internal conditions or external circumstances can degrade the ability of leadership and management to make choices. This can happen when leaders perceive they don't have the time to generate and consider a set of options from which to select. David Packard might call this a lack of digestive capability. Such digestive inability could be a problem of ability, capacity or both. Fear, inadequate vision and a failure of nerve are all likely suspects of this leadership deficiency. Whatever the reason, when otherwise responsible leaders give in to reflex or reaction they sacrifice choice and the ability to exercise it, which is the essence of leadership itself. Having and making choices is central to responding to change. It is an essential ingredient of innovation.

Choice is an essential ingredient of theology as well. God gives us the freedom to choose whether we believe that God exists or not. If we so believe, we are free to choose whether we think God is actively engaged in the affairs of mankind or not. Just these two choices alone—and there are others—are filled with theological implications and consequences for how one chooses to live and how one chooses to view and relate to God. Theology should spend much of its attention and energy in examining the implications, nuances and consequences of these choices.

Just as choice forms the logic of responding to change, the *theo-logic* of responding to change becomes more apparent when we realize that choice is shaped not only by circumstance and the available options, but also by purpose. When responding to change, sooner or later the respondent must revisit their understanding of purpose. Without such a reexamination, the ability to make choices can atrophy or evaporate altogether. Theology and purpose are effectively inseparable, at least in the sense that theology is interested in God's purposes.

A second strand of the connective tissue between innovation and theology might be summarized in Viktor Frankl's often quoted observation that "between stimulus and response there is a space, and in that space is our power to choose our response, and in our response is our growth and freedom."

Innovators have a keen interest in this space and what happens there, as do theologians. The principles of innovation begin to be practiced in this space, as do the claims of theology. Theology will readily contend that God—the primary subject of theology—is not only present but also an active participant in this space. Prayer occurs in this space. Theology will also point to God's presence and participation outside this space, in both the stimulus that comes before and the response that comes after.

Those who believe God to be active and present in this space, and the spaces in front of and behind it, should readily see the theoretical and practical sense of the intersection of innovation and theology. Those who believe God to be a disinterested observer of this space will not likely see this connective tissue at all.

A third characteristic of this connectivity is in the underlying whys and wherefores of change. This is familiar territory for theology. New realities invisibly move below the surface ("the deep") or emanate up from what is unseen. These realities are in theology's backyard, particularly when we consider the unseen and anonymous movement of God's Spirit. If it "sticks to its knitting," theology deals in matters that are unseen, under the surface, and anything but superficial. As a structural response to substantive change, innovation is also interested in what is below the surface at structural, infrastructural and ground layers of change.

A fourth aspect of the connectivity between the two shows up in the practice of each. Centuries ago theology was often referred to as the "queen of the sciences"—a moniker that referred to its inherently interdisciplinary interest.

Historically, separate fields of study comprise the content architecture of the modern university. This architecture evolved from Western European monastic institutions in the High Middle Ages (11th–12th centuries). As separate fields of study evolved, theology was often viewed as the integrator of them all. Theology has a long track record with deeper, broader "cross boundary" inquiries. Just as theology is known for crossing the conceptual boundaries of different domains, experienced innovators recognize boundary crossing as native to innovating practice. Innovation simply refers to this in a more pedestrian manner as "connecting the dots."

In this respect, innovation and theology have similar proclivities for penetrating what is under the surface and widening the field of view to find dots to connect. However, just because there may be some intuitive connection between innovation and theology doesn't necessarily suggest innovation has an inherent practical *need* for theology. This claim deserves closer examination.

INNOVATION NEEDS THEOLOGY

To propose that innovation needs theology does not intend to imply a prepackaged solution theology has to offer to innovation. It intends, rather, to recognize that any response to change aimed at creating new value requires us to make choices within a context. Theology aims to understand God's purposes in a context. Where innovating needs theology is in the search to understand the *intrinsic* value within that context.

The domain of economics has held innovation in captivity for a long time. Economics is a field which many of its own practitioners admit may be much better at understanding the dynamics of supply and demand than the creation of new value. Unlike other economists, however, Joseph Schumpeter turned his attention to the creation of new value. Schumpeter, one of the more influential economists of the twentieth century, popularized the notion that near continuous innovation is more the norm than the exception. Schumpeter viewed capitalism as an evolutionary process wherein advances in society and economic wellbeing happen as a result of a normative "creative destruction."

Thirty-five years after Schumpeter, Peter Drucker reexamined and revived interest in entrepreneurship and innovation. Though an economist also, Drucker's interests were more with the behavior of people than the behavior of goods, services and money.[22] A decade later, Clayton Christensen, also an economist, coined the phrase "disruptive innovation" reminiscent of Schumpeter's theory and reflecting the incumbent interests of his primary audience—leaders in established enterprises. These astute observers, along with many others, have made significant contributions to our understanding of entrepreneurship and innovation. However, even these thought leaders view entrepreneurship and innovation through the lens of economics.

To be fair, the field of economics provides much that has proven useful for managing innovating efforts. However, understanding innovation and entrepreneurship exclusively through the lens of economics is simply too limited. Drucker himself admitted as much.[23] Substantive change and our structural responses to it are too broad and deep to be confined to the domain of economics, corporate management or even one academic discipline alone. An economic lens on innovation may be necessary but is insufficient by itself.

22. Drucker, *Ecological Vision*, 75–76.
23. Drucker, *Innovation and Entrepreneurship*, viii, 13–14.

Innovation practitioners themselves have for years looked to methods and theories from sociology, anthropology, relevant sciences and technologies in their quests to create new value. When it comes to understanding value—what really matters to people and why it matters to them—none of us can leave such understanding up to economists alone. Value, both intrinsic and extrinsic, is at the heart of the innovator's intent. This intent is called to the foreground when any of us respond to change, especially when the change is substantive and the response called for is more than superficial.

The notion of value in general can be sliced and diced in many different ways. However, when it comes down to what is important enough to hold our attention, capture our imagination and extract our money from us, context plays the largest role.

Context—from the Latin *con* and *texere*, meaning "weave together"—is the surrounding set of conditions and circumstances. What shapes and determines what we value is the explicit or implicit purpose discernible in any context. The "text" of meaning is always tied to its context. Text and context are inexorably linked. When we lose, omit or forget an important piece of the context our view into the truth of the situation becomes partial or distorted. Have you ever had someone take what you said out of context?

Context, a seemingly innocuous word, turns out to be the silent partner in what makes value so much a part of the substance of innovation. The perennial challenge for any person or company responding to change, particularly an innovating response, is to turn an idea with potential value into a reality with actual value. In this effort, the starting idea will likely morph, even to the point of looking and being dissimilar to what it looked like in its beginnings. The innovator must avoid ending up with an idea that is feasible but not valuable.

Theology too is keenly interested in this conversion of belief into relevant, purposeful and meaningful practice. Theology is interested in lives that are transformed—from lives of less meaning to lives of more meaning. And when value or God are taken out of the context, theology reminds us, or should, that we are disabled. When value is "out of context," it has no value. It is only "in context" that it carries value. Selling refrigerators to Eskimos reminds us of the importance of context in shaping what is and what is not valuable. The intent of every innovating effort and innovator is to create new value. Here, theology is connected at the hip to innovation, specifically in the deeper notions of value.

We take God out of contexts, partly because God does not fit our concepts and frameworks. We take God out, leaving theology for the theologians, economics for the economists, and innovation for the innovators. This is all neat and tidy for conceptual categorization. However, its correspondence to reality is highly suspect. When God is taken out of contexts by implicitly assuming God is not involved or relevant, we have formed a conceptual boundary to the One who, whether we like it or not, is by definition, not confinable to our conceptual boundaries.

Innovation's need for a theological perspective carries some urgency. The current bias of leaders to accommodate and insulate in response to change appears to be increasing. As I write this,[24] the *Wall Street Journal* posts a report of US Treasury Secretary Lew's remarks saying that companies are sitting on unprecedented piles of cash with a low or no investment mind-set. In this same month, the *Harvard Business Review* published an article by Clayton Christiansen decrying the outdated metrics driving CFOs to behave like cautious controllers, keeping the spigots closed on innovation investments. In the very same issue of *Harvard Business Review* former IBM CEO Sam Palmisano says the problem is not metrics but the maturity of management. Edwin Friedman[25] was less delicate than Palmisano. He called it a failure of nerve more than a lack of maturity.

When it comes to choosing to innovate instead of accommodate or insulate, leaders lack sufficient theological imagination to understand the vocation (i.e., the divine and societal purpose beyond profits and shareholder value) of the organizations of which they are stewards. They may also lack sufficient theological understanding in regards to the notion and responsibilities of a steward. In addition, the contexts leaders consider are often too narrow and parochial. Their choices too often ignore the under layers of intrinsic values from which extrinsic values derive. Consider all the technical and engineering talent, not to mention the massive amounts of private and public equity, being deployed on superficial innovations that are essentially digital platforms for more advertising. Shouldn't we be deploying these creative and financial resources to more substantive, structural and infrastructural solutions that address near crisis issues in energy, environmental healing and injustices displacing millions of people each year, injustices that exacerbate inaccessibility to basic food, water and shelter, not to mention medical care? There is some urgency to innovation's need for theology.

24. June 11, 2014.

25. Friedman, *Failure of Nerve*.

BENEFITS TO THEOLOGY

Likewise, benefits may accrue to theology as it broadens its field of view and considers innovation as an application domain. Ignoring innovation, theology risks being "late to the party" where choices are made and substantive, sustained initiatives set in motion for good or ill.

To be fair, theology has been concerned with culture for some time. But with culture it is difficult to get very much below the surface layer. Deeper, substantive and structural layers are often unaffected. Theology has a chance to influence the character and timing of choices that will affect society (and culture) for some time to come, particularly at more substantive and structural levels, if it applies itself to innovation and entrepreneurship. Culture is more an aggregate of outcomes; innovation more an input. And if theology has a desire to influence them, focus on inputs may be wiser than obsession with outputs.

If innovation becomes an application field for theology, it may prove another source of nourishment to theology's interest in the *works* of God, not just the Word of God. Theology's interest in the works of God—not only past but current and future works—could conceivably be advanced by more explicit links with examinations of innovating efforts and innovation dynamics. These works—still works in process—may be under the surface and unseen but conceivably represent the presence, engagement and activity of God, whether God's presence, engagement and activity are visible or not.

In more common theological language, God's Spirit is alive, moving, free and engaged in all areas of mankind's endeavors and creation's continuing evolution. So, given that the presence and activity of God's Spirit is certainly of interest to theology, wouldn't God's presence and activity include our innovation efforts as well—what many call social, commercial and technological entrepreneurship?

CONCLUSION

Theology has not ignored matters related to substantive change and mankind's responses to it. Both the biblical witness and centuries of scriptural interpretation have closely attended to the prophetic tradition, and this tradition deals directly with change, hope and the future.[26] However, of

26. Change, hope and the future by the way are all areas of great relevance and keen interest to innovators as well.

late, it seems as if theology has kept a safe distance between itself and innovation.

Is there some implicit principle like the separation of church and state that keeps this distance safe? Never mind that theology has often crossed this divide. Prophetic sources have always invited theology to take interest in matters of justice, reconciliation, peace-making and the visible symptoms of change and resistance to it.

Issues of economic injustice in particular play a significant role in innovation, according to Peter Drucker. Though he does not use the word, Drucker points to injustice as one of the more reliable and predictable sources of innovation. Drucker uses the word "incongruity" to name this source, and defines it as the difference between the way things are and the way things should be[27]—a more than adequate definition of injustice. The corpus of theology's prophetic source material repeatedly and consistently calls out injustice, including economic injustice, as contrary to the will and purposes of God. Innovation takes a next step beyond the calling out and calls us *in*—invites us in, if you will—to consider where and how to respond to these "incongruities." Our responses, successful or not, are innovations.

Without engaged interest in structural responses to prophetic proclamation, theology risks a narrow obsession with parochial propositions or after-the-fact commentary on surface by-products of change—what we typically call culture. Neither a passing interest in workplace ethics nor an individualistic orientation to vocation will address the strategies. Neither will theology's cultural commentaries sufficiently address the structures and infrastructures of injustice without also addressing innovations that contribute to them. Effective social action cannot lead to more structural social innovation without both prophetic imagination[28] *and* an imagination for innovation.

Theology's prophetic sources—from Amos through Ezekiel and even to John the Baptist and Jesus himself—penetrate the layers of change to what's underneath. These sources, along with solid theological understanding, can prove to be essential to formulating effective social and commercial innovations more aligned with the purposes of God. But prophetic imagination alone, as necessary as it is, will not be sufficient to

27. Drucker, *Innovation and Entrepreneurship*, 35, 57.

28. Brueggemann, *Prophetic Imagination*, xxiii. "It is the aim of every totalitarian effort to stop the language of newness, and we are now learning that where such language stops we find our humanness diminished."

address injustice. Innovation, both in thought and action, picks up where the prophetic tradition leaves off. A practical theology of innovation *needs* to learn how to speak effectively and hopefully to these response efforts. Doing so promises to realize theology's potential and revitalize its relevance to present and future society.

Storms will continue to be in our forecasts. Climate change threatens to alter the natural boundaries of coastal landscapes. Societal and economic change threatens to reshape the once thought secure boundaries of our private or professional coastlines. Trends start out of sight and mind, but eventually emerge from the shadowy bottoms and distant peripheries to place themselves front and center to meet us locally, personally.

How we individually and collectively respond to change will prove critical to succeeding generations. Where and why we choose to creatively respond in structural and sustainable ways—in other words, where and why we innovate—may be even more important than what the innovations end up being and looking like.

Theology can and should bring light to our choices of where and why we create new value, if not to the choosing itself. Innovating will otherwise remain at best in the shadows, at worst, in the dark, and our shared future along with it.

CONVERSATION STARTERS

1. Are biblical narratives more useful than doctrinal propositions for accepting change, making sense of it and innovating in response to it?

2. If innovating is "creating new value for others," does a biblical theology understand

   - "creating" and "value" in ways that contribute more practical an encouraging guidance and direction than economic or financial understandings alone?

   - the "other" and lead to different answers to where innovations are needed and why?

Accepting Change

4

How Do You Make God Laugh?

Why do the nations conspire,
and the peoples plot in vain? . . .
He who sits in the heavens laughs.[1]

CHANGE COMES IN ALL manner of sizes, shapes, and speeds. It can be massive or diminutive, widespread or local. It shows up in subtle shifts of ambient conditions, or in the pointed detail of particulars. It comes with sharp elbows or soft shoulders, and can feel like an impenetrable wall or a boggy swamp. It can approach slowly with advanced notice, or suddenly without warning. Change comes from seemingly out of nowhere, or from just around the corner; from the bottom up or the top down, or from all sides at once. Sometimes its causes are complex and at other times, a single underlying root.

With such variety it is almost impossible to define change in the abstract. Even within a single context what is called a "change" may be as much a function of the observer's subjective state as it is an objective observation of new realities. What is new to one may be just part of an old pattern to another. Point of view, perceptual distortions and an endless range of variations make it difficult to define where change begins and continuity ends. It is not so surprising then that about the only universal truth that holds about change is that it keeps happening. The ancient

1. Ps 2:1, 4.

philosopher Heraclitus[2] observed "no one ever steps foot into the same river twice." The constant thing about change is that it keeps changing.

As elusive as change is to describe, *accepting* change may be even more elusive. This essay proposes that accepting change often succumbs to the inherent seductions of planning without a theological perspective. However, with a purpose greater than our own and interests other than our own, we are not only better able to accept change, we are more able to create new value in response to it; in other words, more willing and able to innovate.

A light-hearted, aphoristic riddle seems an appropriate place to start for such a difficult subject. It goes like this:

> Question: How do you make God laugh?
> Answer: Tell him your plans.

God's laughter may be more the knowing chuckle of a loving father than the uproarious belly laugh of a sardonic cynic. But regardless of how we might choose to describe God's sense of humor, the riddle reveals more about the persistence of our belief in planning than it does about God.

Planning is one of the more common and pervasive ways in which we deal with change, as individuals or as organizations. Our trust in planning and the methods we devise to predict an unknowable future may be as persistent as change is constant.

Consider for a moment all the intelligence we gather, all the data we mine, and all the technologies we invent for tracking and predicting. We spend an inordinate amount of time and energy anticipating, planning and preparing for changes that we cannot fully or reliability predict. We do this personally, corporately, nationally and internationally. Yet, we still have some difficult *accepting* the change that seems to stimulate all this planning.

THE PROBLEM WITH PLANNING

Planning relies on predictions, whether explicit and formal or implicit and informal. Predictions are at best imprecise, at worst incorrect. Yet we keep predicting and planning. We justify this on what looks like an

---

2. That Heraclitus was sometimes referred to as the "weeping" philosopher may be directly related to his awareness of the constancy of change, requiring of him, presumably, a constant state or process of grieving.

entirely reasonable assumption: if we can't stop change then at least we can anticipate it.

Anticipating change is not accepting it, but anticipating change can seduce us into thinking we are accepting it. "Hope for the best and plan for the worst," we tell ourselves, and then act according to plan. Conventional planning with its reasonable predictions works for the most part, at least for the more routine continuities of our lives. However, when change is substantial and our aim is to do something new, conventional planning can prove counterproductive.

Planning often reflects more of a desire to forestall, resist or mitigate change than to accept it. This is not to say that planning and predicting is not useful or necessary. Quite the opposite is the case. Plans and the projections upon which they are based represent the foundation of prudent management practice, whether in our individual or organizational lives. Planning as far ahead as is possible provides us with at least some time to prepare. And such lead times are especially important for innovating.

Ice hockey star Wayne Gretzky famously suggested that we must "skate to where the puck is headed." This is sound wisdom when time is short and space limited. However, few of us live in well-defined rinks with referees skating alongside, reinforcing rules others may forget. Most of us are saddled with the burden of having to navigate through much longer periods in more open fields with no one there to remind us what the rules are, if there are any, much less when an infraction occurs.

The probability of unanticipated events only increases as our time period lengthens and the scope of our horizon broadens. These longer periods and more porous confines make predicting speculative. This, in turn, makes planning and the plans it produces tentative and tenuous at best. As a result, planning is better viewed as a common form of coping with change more than really accepting it.

Over the years I have designed and facilitated a variety of collaborative planning conversations in different settings and contexts. In each I have noticed two different orientations—one is anticipatory and the other is immersive. The anticipatory relies on projecting the collective imagination into the future. The immersive relies on experience that comes from jumping right in and getting a feel for what is going on now.

Each has its own inherent advantages and disadvantages. Anticipatory approaches look before they leap. In doing so they afford the opportunity to prepare—both for the leap and for the landing. However, these anticipatory approaches often lead to looks that prevent any leap at all. Fear sets in.

Immersive approaches, on the other hand, tend to leap before they look and in so doing create firsthand experiences from which to make further judgments and selections along the way. The risk with this approach however is that the initial leap proves to be a step from which recovery is difficult, if not impossible.

Anticipatory approaches produce plans while immersive ones produce plunges. The former produces predictive information, the latter produces experience-based data. Some balance of the two, if possible, is to be preferred.

The unexamined assumptions we make about time are another problem with planning. Our language and culture affords us only one word and concept for time. The Greeks had two: *chronos* and *kairos*. *Chronos* connotes metered, regular, or predictable time, like hours in a day, days in a week, weeks in a year or even seasons of the year. *Chronology* is the temporal foundation of predicting. *Kairos* on the other hand means an opportune time, time with meaning, or as some say, "God's time." These are times when circumstances line up and intersect to make the moment, episode or period something more than merely another minute, hour, day, week or season. *Kairos* is time with significance.

Most conventional planning assumes *chronos*. Most innovating looks for *kairos*. When organizations attempt to innovate in a predictable and chronological way they end up with thin and superficial innovations. Results of these efforts require extra marketing and promotion just to garner recognition. When we innovate in *kairos* we seek new meaning and new value in changed circumstances and conditions.

The problem with *kairos* of course is that it is only apparent in hindsight. It is not certain in advance to the innovator. Only time (*chronos*) will tell whether now is an opportune time (*kairos*) for responding to change in a way to create new value. Hence, the only alternative to planning when our aim is to create new value is to remain alert to the potential value and opportunity in change.

This is not only a challenge for innovating. It is an age-old problem. Even Jesus and his disciples encountered it and to which Jesus' counsel was essentially "be alert at all times," "keep awake," because "about that day and hour no one knows, not even the angels in heaven."[3] Part of accepting change is acknowledging that we cannot know for sure what comes next or when.

Conventional planning is of little use to us when change demands a response that requires something new. Something else is required of us. It is not the "make it happen" mind-set of those who approach change with a command and control orientation. Nor is it the "let it happen" attitude of those resigned to *laissez faire*. Rather, it is to do our best to plumb the depths of the change, and then plunge in where it is already happening.[4] And our willingness to accept the change—even without knowing fully what comes next—is likely stronger in the company of God. Such willingness is a prerequisite to a plunge that aims to create new value for others.

Those who study emergent systems have already begun to make a serious case for plunging in. Their reasoning acknowledges the limitations of traditional planning and its appropriateness for but a limited number of contexts. In this vein David Snowden has offered a useful framework. He calls it the *cynefin* framework.[5] *Cynefin* is a Welsh word that roughly translates as "habitat." The framework classifies at least four different change contexts in which we will find ourselves. Snowden calls them *obvious, complicated, complex* and *chaotic.*

Conventional planning might work in the obvious and even complicated contexts where conditions are either known or knowable. In these conditions we can approach change with a series of steps—first sensing what is happening, then categorizing or analyzing it, and then responding based on this analysis. However, not all contexts are that stable.

Other contexts have conditions that are so complex or chaotic the conditions remain emergent and unknowable. Sensing and analysis just won't work. Instead, we must *do* something however modest. The doing of something produces feedback from the environment. And this feedback we can use for the next, more informed try or experiment. Snowden and others call these "probes" rather than plans.

Such probing may not be all that new. Martin Luther, who launched the Protestant Reformation in the sixteenth century creating complex if not chaotic conditions to be sure, seemed to have this immersive approach in mind when he offered his now famous advice to "sin boldly" as

---

3. Matt 24:36–44; Luke 21:7–36.

4. The second assumption—God is still creating—can imply that God is not necessarily waiting for us to engage in creating (see essay on theological assumptions).

5. *Wikipedia*, s.v. "cynefin."

God is even bolder still.[6] Luther believed he and we would be acting in the company of God.

HORSE AND CART

When change is upon us two questions vie for our attention. "What are we going to do?" is typically the most urgent one. It often overshadows the other one, which is "What do we think is going on?" Answering the more urgent question first has the unintended effect of overwhelming any answer to the other question, even to the point where the other question is never asked. Many have learned the hard way, however, that it is better to understand and accept the change before responding to it, at least as much as time will allow. This holds especially when the response calls us to create new value. Clarify what is emerging *before* choosing where and how to respond.

My own introduction to this principle occurred over three decades ago. I had been called to an important meeting. I knew it was an important meeting because all the vice presidents of the operating functions of Kimberly-Clark Corporation's consumer division would be there—manufacturing, marketing, sales, logistics, etc. Steve Wiley, the vice president of strategic planning had designed the meeting and invited me to facilitate the discussions. It was a three-day offsite held at the Four Seasons Hotel in Los Colinas, Texas. I was definitely the youngest, most junior person at this meeting, wet behind the ears. If anything went wrong, I was a handy, expendable scapegoat.

It was the middle of the morning on the second day. One of the more senior of the vice presidents, Jim Bernd, got up during the conversation to get another cup of coffee. After pouring himself a cup, he slowly turned and started to amble back to his chair at the conference table. Before he got to his chair, however, he interrupted the conversation and said, "You know, we do this kind of thing every year or so. We argue with each other, debate all the issues and end up eating too much and drinking too much. Then we come to some sort of agreement with each other that

6. Luther, *Saemmtliche Schriften*, Letter 99, paragraph 13. "God does not save those who are only imaginary sinners. Be a sinner, and let your sins be strong (sin boldly), but let your trust in Christ be stronger, and rejoice in Christ who is the victor over sin, death, and the world. We will commit sins while we are here, for this life is not a place where justice resides. We, however, says Peter (2 Peter 3:13) are looking forward to a new heaven and a new earth where justice will reign."

we all feel good about. But when we leave, and go back to our respective responsibilities, we all end up doing whatever we were planning to do before the meeting. Why do we keep doing this?"

Needless to say the meeting came to an abrupt halt. I did what any facilitator would do. I called a break.

During the break, everyone scurried off to pay phones (remember those?), grateful to have some excuse to avoid the awkwardness of the moment. Bernd, Wiley and I stayed behind and huddled together to try and figure out what to do next. It was clear that continuing as planned was not an option. The emperor—the meeting's agenda—had no clothes.

I listened quietly as these two senior leaders hemmed and hawed, back and forth. I could tell that neither one of them had any idea what to do next. Neither did I, but no one expected me to. Then, one of them said, "We are just not being honest with each other. We are not saying what we really believe."

The word "believe" caught my ear. I interrupted the two and said, without realizing the full import of what I was saying at the time, "Then let's just invite these guys to say what they really believe." When I said that the two of them turned and looked at me quizzically. It was Wiley who asked, "We can do that?" And I said, not really knowing, "Sure. I'll just ask them." And that is what we did. And it worked. For some reason, unknown to me at the time, the meeting and conversation transformed itself in front of our eyes.

A brief moment of honesty had occurred, a modest moment of truth, if you will. Perhaps it was because the one who spoke so candidly was toward the end of his career and willing to take a risk to point out that the "emperor had no clothes." Or perhaps, unlike others, Bernd had been through more cycles of this kind of planning than had others in the room. He just couldn't bear repeating the same unproductive pattern one more time. Perhaps there was something or someone else at work in this moment. Whatever the reason, what followed was clearly a more authentic and honest conversation, without a pre-envisioned or predetermined outcome. It proved cathartic to the leaders in the room, and transformative to the meeting and its results.

Prior to that moment we had had the cart before the horse. We were just following a process. In that brief moment the unperceived and unspoken was perceived and spoken. All it took was someone to tell the truth. People stopped posing in front of each other and started listening to each other. Each became genuinely more interested in listening and understanding the other than in being heard and understood themselves. They actually began to hear each other.

The moment was a brief crucible. It broke the prescribed process of the meeting. Otherwise powerful political rivals in the room expressed what they really believed. They heard differences in what each believed would happen and why. When differences revealed themselves the tragic narrative that had remained stuck in entrenched positions started to loosen up. All the various maneuverings of self-interests, hidden and not-so-hidden agendas, began to subside. The horse got back in front of the cart, partly because of Bernd's honesty, and partly because we started to address a different, prior question first—"What do we think is changing, whether we like it or not?" Coming to some common point of view on this prior question enabled us to ask and answer the "urgent" question ("What are we going to do?") more thoughtfully, clearly and coherently than before. But we could only do that *after* we had asked and answered the prior question—what do we think is going on? Moments like this turn out to be essential not only for accepting change but for creating new value as well.

At least three things happen when change is truly accepted: someone tells the truth, an old narrative gives way to a new one, and a catharsis occurs. We cannot hope to accept change or create new value in response to it without these three things—telling the truth, seeing a comedic future where before there was only a tragic one, and giving in to the catharsis that can transform us in the process.

We need to look closely at each of these, and a theological perspective proves to be a potent help in understanding all three.

TELLING THE TRUTH

Someone stepped forward and told the truth in this moment with the Kimberly-Clark executives. It was not just a "truth as I see it" kind of truth. It was a truth that everyone there immediately recognized and could no longer deny.

When someone—it only takes one—tells the truth like this it comes as a statement of the obvious. "Obvious" literally means "in the way." It may not really *be* obvious before it is expressed. It becomes obvious only after it is told, not before. But when it is, it becomes a truth that sets us free,[7] a liberation of sorts, not just for an individual, but for everyone else who is involved.

Who ends up being the one to tell the truth may not matter as much as the truth that is told.

However, the teller stands under the truth also and is just as subject to the truth as anyone else. In this particular instance, it turned out to be the oldest, most senior member of the group. Perspective and wisdom often comes with age and experience. But what matters more than perspective and wisdom is the truth's telling by one who is also implicated in the truth told. As such, it is a confessional kind of truth telling. Contrition is experienced and expressed. "A broken and contrite heart, O God, Thou will not despise."[8]

When a truth like this is told or confessed, it exposes a gap, the gap is between what is real and what is planned. This is especially the case with predictions. When truth is told and heard, it has a way of revealing the distinct possibility that our view of reality—our truth—may not be the whole truth. Such truth can remind each of us that "now we see as in a mirror, dimly . . . now I (only) know in part."[9] Remembering this is humbling. It is also liberating. It produces a freedom for choosing to respond rather than react to change. This is genuine acceptance of change—when we are left with a choice and a willingness and readiness to exercise that choice.

Moments of truth create their own awkwardness, however. We don't really know what to say. We feel both a desire to break the deafening silence *and* a reluctance to say anything for fear it will sound superficial or be taken the wrong way. Before the awkwardness fades, the silence permits the truth to linger a bit longer. It is a truth that cannot be fully or finally understood so much as experienced.[10] Just for as long as the fading lingers there is a chance to accept the change named in the truth told. When told we catch a glimpse of the new realities and implied value that can be created in response.

7. John 8:32.

8. Ps 51:17.

9. 1 Cor 13:12.

10. Buechner, *Telling the Truth*, 21.

There is something about the telling of the truth, the describing of it, the calling it out, that silences everyone. This includes the more skeptical, cynical and "Pilate" within or among us. Pilate asked Jesus, "What is truth?" And the silence that replied was deafening.

If Pilate's question was not rhetorical that silence must have been uncomfortable for Pilate as well. In fact it was so uncomfortable that he went back to those anxious for the reassurance of a plan, custom or protocol. And despite Pilate's admission that he finds "no case against him," Pilate chose the most expedient thing to keep the peace. Like so many leaders caught between a rock and a hard place, Pilate ignores the truth that even he sees, and follows the plan.[11] Many would say Pilate was just doing his job.

The experience of truth is fragile and temporary. Other competing truths, half-truths and illusions creep in. Doubt, skepticism and cynicism numb our taste for the truth, leaving us with indifference, even contempt. The educated ask, "Where's the data?" The sophisticated ask "So what?" Like Pilate, the urbane cynically ask, "What is truth?" revealing less about the truth and more about their own disdain for anything not immediately aligned with what is expedient and pragmatic. Self-interest and postulates of plausibility weigh too prominently to permit much interest in truth.

Such moments of truth are of keen interest to theology, however, not only due to their revelatory affects but also because of their transformative potential. These moments are often turning points. Something new happens.

Moments of truth are of equal interest to innovation, for much the same reason as they are to theology—their revelatory effects and transformative potential. In these moments innovators get to see and experience firsthand what is "in the way"—the obvious new realities change is bringing. A call and a need to create new value are embedded in these moments. Without these moments we give in to the anxious urgency to answer the "what are we going to do?" question. And in the process, we end up blind and deaf to what is right in front of us, and it is our plans that blind and deafen us.

Though obvious in hindsight, the new realities change brings can be difficult to accept when we are in the thick of things. The opportunity to create new value can be just as difficult to see as well. How many of us have asked, "Why didn't I think of that before?" and still failed to realize

11. John 18:33–40.

our plans and predictions were blinding us from the new? It is often the former things, the things of old, that prevent us from perceiving the new things that spring forth.[12] These former things are part of what we project into the future, the predictions upon which our plans are based. Moments of truth break through these former things and enable us to sense and accept the new.

We often give more attention to our plans than to the predictions upon which those plans are based. Sometimes all we can see is the plan. However, when we look beyond the plan and into the plausibility of the predictions those plans build on, what we find is an underlying narrative. All too often, without consciously choosing it, that narrative defaults to a tragic and deterministic one. This is a story line with an inevitability that reinforces the plausibility of the story.

Predictions are simply parts of stories we make up about the future. Sometimes we are conscious and deliberate about making up these stories. Sometimes we do so without realizing it. But whether conscious or not, the story lines we create serve our need for plausibility. We need to believe that there is a credible path from here to there, for how we get from current conditions to what is predicted, particularly if the future predicted differs from the present we experience. This is the same regardless of whether what is predicted is good news or bad. The narratives we imagine "fill in" the gap between our current reality and the future reality we envision.

The underlying narrative arc can easily become hidden by both plan and predictions. The hiding is seldom intentional, if even conscious. What we believe will happen and how it will emerge often remains in the private confines of our own minds, unexamined from a lack of genuine dialogue with others. Even in highly collaborative planning, more airtime is often spent debating the plan than the predictions. And even when the predictions do become the subject of debate, seldom does anyone look at the underlying narrative structure.

When left unexpressed and unexamined, predictions and their accompanying narratives are not only difficult to work with, they disable the implementation of the very plans built upon them. This is particularly the case when there is some disbelief about one or more of the predictions. This disbelief can end up sabotaging the entire plan. When expressed, however, predictions (and the plan itself) can't help but be improved,

---

12. Isa 43:18–19a.

where improvement is not so much in the precision of the predictions as in the strength of conviction.

When diverse perspectives are expressed, shared and refined, it sharpens our perceptions of what the new realities are, what they mean and why they may be relevant. When expressed, these predictions can then be tested, refined and honed. It may not eliminate the uncertainty the future holds. But with a narrative that is explicitly shared, readiness and willingness to carry out the plan can't help but increase.

This is what happened in that moment with the Kimberly-Clark executives. Private predictions and implicit assumptions about the business found expression. They weren't perfect or precise expressions, just shared. Each participant awoke to what others were telling themselves about the future and how the business worked. What they heard were different stories about the same future, different assumptions about how the same business worked. The plan was no longer the subject of their debate. Rather, it was their beliefs about the future, and what causes what, that was of greater interest. This led to a healthy, authentic dialogue that fostered much more open-mindedness, deeper listening, and eventually a plan in which all of them believed.

The lesson here is that while our narratives about the future may be fictions, we often unwittingly treat them like fact. When we make and follow a plan we put our trust in a story we have created about the future. Making that story explicit is essential. This is more about story *creation* than story telling, though in the telling we can try out whether we believe it or not.

Plans express intentions. Intentions reflect assumptions about the future—always a fiction we intend to turn into fact. Therefore, it is not only prudent to consider the type of narrative that goes with our predictions. It is essential.

FROM TRAGIC TO COMEDIC

Narratives of the future, like all stories, have beginnings, middles and ends. In fact, the shape of the arc formed by the beginning, middle and end can indicate what type of narrative it is—whether tragic or comedic.

Tragic, deterministic arcs tend to move up and then down before resolving in a downward trajectory concluding in some form of demise or death. Those looking for a repeatable formula, and especially those who believe they have found one, are at risk of telling themselves deterministic and tragic narratives about the future.

Comedic, improvisational arcs tend to move first down and then up, before opening up to something unexpected. The story ends in lift—an updraft more than a downdraft. The ending is life giving, not life ending. The narrative resolution of a comedic arc may not be as neat and tidy as what occurs in a tragedy. But the energy and attitude tend to be more attractive and attracting.

Innovation favors the comedic and improvisational more than the tragic and deterministic, as does theology. The gospel is bad news before it is good news. The movement of its narrative arc is down and then up. It doesn't end in demise and death but in resurrection and life. That theology and innovation share the same bias for the comedic should nurture a continued relevance for what theology might have to contribute to innovating.

Famously Nicodemus asks in response to Jesus' claim that one must be born anew, "How can anyone be born after having grown old? Can one enter a second time into the mother's womb?"[13] Nicodemus asked the question each of us asks when we sense our relevance is slipping away, whether as individuals or organizations. On the road to Emmaus Cleopas didn't recognize the resurrected Jesus. Stuck in a tragic narrative, Cleopas asks him incredulously, "Are you the only stranger in Jerusalem who does not know the things that have taken place there in these days?" Where have you been? And ironically, it turns out Cleopas is the one who is clueless.[14] Don't remember the former things, Isaiah says, nor even consider the things of old. "I am about to do a new thing; now it springs forth, do you not perceive it?"[15]

Nicodemus and Cleopas ask questions that come out of a tragic, deterministic narrative. Their tragic questions are answered from a comedic reality, however. Isaiah's question, on the other hand, comes out of a comedic, improvisational and open narrative. Was it Voltaire who described God as a comedian playing to an audience that refuses to laugh? Tragedy begins with a rise and ends with a fall. Comedy begins with a fall and ends with a rise.

13. John 3:4.

14. Luke 24:18.

15. Isa 43:18–19.

The good news, for both theology and for innovation is that the truth comes not from a tragic narrative but from a comedic one. When moments of truth happen the truth has a way of relocating us "narratively." It tells us where we are, both in space and in time. We are not merely in chronological time (*chronos*) but in a time with meaning (*kairos*). And our task is to discover, uncover or co-create that meaning. And the value of the meaning and its hope is derived from the narrative. It is not necessarily where we want to be, or where we think we should be. Rather, it locates us where we actually are, in accepting the change.

Contrast this with conventional planning[16] which favors more closed, tragic and deterministic narratives. Perhaps it is simply tragedy's penchant for closure or resolution. Or perhaps it is our desire to shun fantasies that are simply unrealistic. Fairy tales are entertaining but unbelievable.

Whatever the cause, when predictions reflect a tragic narrative, innovation is disabled. Open-ended futures make planning more difficult. Resolutions are harder to reach. Plans are less conclusive, uncertainty more apparent. But when the comedic energizes our outlook, it invites innovation.

Ambiguity and uncertainty are ultimately resolved in tragic narratives, more so than they are in reality. In comedic narratives ambiguity and uncertainty are the stuff of which surprise and improvisation are made. To traditional planning, ambiguity and uncertainty look like viruses. To innovation they look like fertile ground.

This is not merely the preference of the pessimist's view that the glass is half empty or the optimist's view that the same glass is half full. It is not simply a matter of attitude, disposition and outlook. Rather, it has to do with a deeper, albeit often unconscious, commitment to the shape of the arc underlying the "account of the hope that is within us."[17]

When desire for precision takes precedence in our predictions—more than reality will reasonably allow—the consequence is a choice for a tragic, deterministic and closed narrative in our future. The more precise we imagine our plan needs to be, the more exacting our forecasts, the shorter the time frame and narrower the field of view.

This may work in operational planning contexts or when as individuals we plan more routine matters in more stable, controllable environments. It leaves conditions barren and desolate for innovating.

16. Planning of the type wherein innovation plays a minor role, if any at all.
17. 1 Pet 3:15.

Plans can also distort the predictions upon which those plans are based. When the expression of our plan's intention takes precedence over an honest acceptance of change's new realities, plans begin to shape predictions, rather than the predictions shaping the plans. We succumb to self-fulfilling prophecies. The cart gets in front of the horse. Our interests and desires influence the predictions we make.

In circumstances wherein our planning is more pressing and urgent, the tragic more than comedic can slip in. And when change is significant, these shorter time frames and narrower views can debilitate. Even in contingency planning, when we have predicted unfavorable conditions, plans are likely to reflect our own interests and desires. There is nothing inherently wrong with this. In fact it is important to clarify what our intentions and desires are, as we are able. However, if we are aiming to create new value, the emphasis cannot be on *our* plans so much as the change-born need of others.

This is one reason that incumbent organizations find it so difficult to innovate. They become wedded to their plans and the implicit narratives upon which those plans are based. Often these are closed, deterministic and tragic narratives of the future. It's depressing—psychologically and economically. This same dynamic can hold for us as individuals. The more invested we are in the rituals, routines and desires to perpetuate our current realty, the more likely we are to miss the new realities change brings. We unconsciously default to an assumed future with a tragic narrative.

This brings us to another essential dynamic that happens in these moments of truth, wherein the plan often gets in the way of the truth, a truth that is absolutely necessary to perceive if we are to create new value for others.

A moment of truth is impossible to plan. It's more of gift received than an outcome achieved. Something happens to, with and among the participants. This "something" is what makes the moment significant. *Kairos* emerges out of *chronos*. The moment comes "out of" regular time and is recognized as special—a moment with meaning, primarily because a catharsis occurs.

TRUSTING CATHARSIS

Catharsis is a purging, purifying, cleansing and liberating experience.[18] Aristotle was the first to draw our attention to what a catharsis can do. He spoke about catharsis as the effect theatrical tragedy has upon an audience. According to Aristotle, tragedy leads to a purging of pity and fear (*Poetics*). While it is not entirely clear whether Aristotle implied that the benefits of catharsis come only to theatrical audiences, it is clear that Aristotle saw in catharsis a way for us to regain a balance of emotion and perspective in our minds and hearts.[19] Both ancient spiritual practice and modern psychology (including Freud and others) picked up on the relieving and healing effect of catharsis and incorporated it in various treatment strategies. While Aristotle may have at first described catharsis as the effects of tragedy, subsequent thinkers[20] have extended it to comedic effects as well.

Catharsis is an uncomfortable but healing experience. What was repressed is finally expressed. Once expressed some relief is received. Then the hard work of transformation begins. Catharsis often happens within the context of a crucible—a heated experience through which a corrupting element is purged and the carrier is cleansed, typically not without some difficulty.

Crucible and catharsis are often confused. A crucible is a container that can withstand very high temperatures. Crucibles are used to hold contents—metal, glass or pigments—intended for purification. Catharsis is the cleaning and transforming process the contents go through in the container. Whatever the form of the container—crucible, cross, loss—catharsis is what happens to the contents inside. The container or crucible is not changed. The contents are.

Crucibles and catharses come in many different shapes and forms. The intensities of the heat and resulting purgation range from dramatic and emotional relief to mild and cognitive insight. But whatever the shape, form and intensity, catharsis leaves one changed for the better, not so much by personal achievement as by persistent sacrifice—the giving up of emotional attachments or intellectual preconceptions that no longer serve and are likely in the way.

---

18. *Shorter Oxford Annotated Dictionary*, s.v. "catharsis."
19. Powell, "Catharsis in Psychology and Beyond."
20. Scheff, *Catharsis in Healing, Ritual and Drama.*

Cathartic moments punctuate our individual and collective narratives of growing up, a growing up that never really ends. In my case, I was fortunate to have a mother who would anticipate my passage through these moments by giving me a little tough love, saying to me often, "It's character building." This simple phrase continues to prove true even long after she died.

Whether dramatic or incremental, catharsis results in a more emotionally balanced state from which a clearer perception and willing acceptance of change is possible. From a theological view, catharsis can transform an otherwise tragic narrative into a comedic one. The effects of catharsis are purifying and freeing at the same time. It relieves, heals and resolves. In so doing catharsis produces a clean and clear access to what is real, pure and true.

In purging one of pity, as Aristotle observed, catharsis leaves a capacity for understanding instead. It can turn pity and fear into understanding and hope, two capabilities that are coincidentally essential for creating new value. Here again, the interests of theology and innovation naturally converge.

Catharsis cultivates empathy. "Empathetic identification with the end user" is both an expression and principle well known and widely practiced by innovators. Understanding the need in context is one of the first things an innovator must do in creating new value.

Believing that one can fully "identify" with the other, however, has always seemed a bit presumptuous to me. Walking a mile in the shoes of another may help me to understand the other's experience, including how they feel and what they see from their point of view. But assuming that I can completely identify as the other not only takes something away from them. It also risks overestimating my own capability and underestimating the ever-present corruption of my own biases and points of view. But "empathetic identification" from an empathizer who has not experienced catharsis is likely to produce pity more than understanding.

Empathy may be an acquired skill, but without catharsis the intention and contributions of the empathetic can prove ineffective. Empathy can be a "power tool in the hands of the weak to sabotage the strong."[21] It can absolve the other of responsibility for getting into and out of the circumstances in which they find themselves, not resolving anything. Edwin Friedman makes the point this way:

21. Friedman, *Failure of Nerve*, 24.

> Empathy may be a luxury afforded only to those who do not
> have to make tough decisions. For "tough decisions" are deci-
> sions the consequence of which will be painful. The focus on
> "need fulfillment" . . . leaves out the possibility that what another
> may really "need" is *not* to have their needs fulfilled, in order to
> become more responsible.[22]

Many attempt to practice empathy and end up with more "over-standing" than understanding. This is partly because empathy is easier to describe than it is to authentically practice, and partly because, as Aristotle seemed to know, pity and sympathy are often substituted for understanding. This is a classic example of the good being the enemy of the best. Without experiencing catharsis an innovator may practice empathy[23] but produce very little by way of creating new value. Engaging without becoming enmeshed, and caring without taking freedom and choice *from* the other, requires an understanding born from one's own cathartic experience.

Creating new value requires accepting and understanding change in more than merely a superficial way. It requires not only changing our points of view. It requires allowing and trusting a change within ourselves as well. This is the theological notion of repentance (*metanoia*—changing our way of thinking and acting). Einstein pointed to the same truth when he recognized that "the significant problems we face cannot be solved at the same level of thinking we were at when we created them."

Accepting change is not simply a cognitive reframing of our perceptions. It changes us inside as well. We can remain detached and objective for only a little while. None of us is immune to the penetrating effects of change. We cannot resist, deny and delay change forever. Those of us who have tried are likely to have learned how unworkable these strategies turn out to be in the long run, sometimes in the short run also.

Accepting change is not simply the job of recognizing the new realities outside of us. It is also an inside job, a change of our values and orientation. We may be able to change our point of view without experiencing a change within, but we are more likely to understand the other more deeply only after we have ourselves changed.

Innovation theology might come to suggest that the comedic often comes out of the tragic, that resurrection is only possible to those who

22. Ibid., 137.

23. All sorts of ethnographic techniques are currently in use to discover unmet needs among corporate innovators attempting new product development.

have experienced death—a purgation of their own self-interests so that they might live to and for the interests of the Other and others. In fact, it could be that with a theological point of view, a catharsis might actually transform a tragic narrative into a comedic one. Innovations themselves may be what result from cathartic transformations of organizations and individuals.

THE PROBLEM OF SELF-INTEREST

One of the few agreements among those who study innovation is that entrepreneurs seem to do it better than intrapreneurs. Start-ups innovate better and faster than ventures initiated by established companies. The evidence is overwhelming. Yes, there are occasional successes for intrapreneurs. But for the most part, innovations tend to originate where there is no internal (sibling) rivalry for resources. An incumbent organization's own self-interest gets in the way of giving full attention and complete understanding to the interests of others—even prospective customers. But while most agree, there is little consensus as to the cause.

You might think that with all the resources, knowledge and R&D of large, established companies, these organizations would show a better track record of innovating. Some attribute this dismal track record to pride that builds up before the fall.[24] Others believe it's due to the dilemma incumbent organizations cannot escape—"stick to your knitting" on the one hand, or "do something new" on the other.[25] Most view the problem from an economic point of view. A few view the problem as a lack of leadership. But none take a theological perspective—a perspective that has a decidedly different take on self-interest than does classical economics.[26]

This dilemma is not unfamiliar to theology. A theological perspective will assume self-interest as a significant part of the *problem*. Theology can draw upon a rich set of narratives related to self-interest and sibling rivalries, not only with theological perspectives but practical wisdom. For transcending self-interest there is always Paul's explicit counsel, patterned

24. Collins, *How the Mighty Fall*, 2.

25. Christensen, *Innovator's Dilemma*, xiii.

26. Smith, *Wealth of Nations*, 485. Adam Smith's notion that individual pursuit of one's own self-interest will still be "led by an invisible hand to promote an end which was no part of his [the individual's] intention," has served as a foundational belief in economics for some time.

after the example of Jesus: "Do nothing from selfish ambition or conceit, but in humility regard others as better than yourselves. Let each of you look not to your own interests, but to the interests of others."[27] And for dealing with sibling rivalry we have to look no further than the stories of Cain and Abel,[28] Joseph and his brothers[29] or the parable of the prodigal son and elder brother.[30]

These are all narratives of hope, more comedic than tragic, more surprising and improvisational than deterministic and predictable. When we continue to think of innovation only from an economic perspective the prospects are dismal. Economics, on its own admission, is the dismal science.[31] It tends toward a tragic, closed and deterministic narrative. Theology deals in hope and intrinsic values; economics in extrinsic ones.

Innovation is most often conceived of in terms of profit making, close to matters of investment and return. However, if innovation is the creation of new value, it must first be valuable to the one the innovation intends to serve. Value to the provider or innovator depends upon value to the end user or customer. This first value, theologically speaking, is an expression of love of neighbor and perhaps even love of God. In this sense the interest of the other is first and foremost, an interest other than one's own self-interest. As a result, should we be thinking of innovation as essentially a *moral* activity before it is an economic, technological or creative one? By moral I mean here simply the ability to consider interests other than one's own.[32]

From a theological point of view innovation itself might be viewed in an entirely different light—one that is keenly concerned with the love of God and the love of neighbor. In fact, is innovation even possible without some degree of altruism, some degree of putting one's own interests aside and giving oneself over to the interests of another? At first glance this sounds like a stretch, and may be. However, when one considers the animating power and freedom of God to do a new thing—the Doer being by definition the One for whom all things are possible—innovators may not want to dismiss this too quickly.

27. Phil 2:3–4.

28. Gen 4.

29. Gen 38–47.

30. Luke 15:11–32.

31. Thomas Carlyle in the 1849 tract called *Occasional Discourse on the Negro Question* was apparently the first to refer to economics as the "dismal science."

32. Niebuhr, *Moral Man and Immoral Society*, xi.

If the essence of innovating is creating new value, then value is key. If value is understood as extrinsic or exchange value then innovation will remain confined to an economic phenomenon. But if value is understood as intrinsic, if whatever the value is and however it is embodied, is truly valuable to the one—the beloved for whom it is intended and formed—then is it not possible that innovations are embodiments of love of neighbor? Regardless of the commercial transactions associated with the buying and selling of this value, a transaction that can and does erode the love for which it was created—is it still not, at least in intent and design, an expression of love?

This may hold true for individuals but may not for organizations. Reinhold Niebuhr made a powerful case for this in his classic *Moral Man and Immoral Society*. Niebuhr observed that

> individuals are capable of preferring the advantages of others to their own . . . a rational faculty that prompts them to a sense of justice . . . but these achievements are more difficult, if not impossible, for human societies and social groups. . . . In every human group there is less reason to guide and to check impulse, less capacity for self-transcendence, less ability to comprehend the needs of others and therefore more unrestrained egoism than the individuals, who compose the group, reveal in their personal relationships.[33]

Niebuhr's skepticism regarding the capability of any organization to behave morally strikes many as unduly cynical and pessimistic. But if Niebuhr is even partially correct, it may go a long way toward explaining the mystery of why existing organizations have more difficulty creating new value than do new ones.

Even if we disagree with Niebuhr's skepticism, theology clearly has an interest in the love of God and the love of neighbor—two distinct but inseparable realities according to most theologies rooted in the biblical saga. Cain's question ("Am I my brother's keeper?"), the parable of the Good Samaritan, Jesus' summation of the whole law, and much of the biblical library is concerned with these two realities—two realities that arguably form a foundation for any theology.

So, what of self-interest? Jesus' citation of the second great commandment—"love your neighbor as yourself"[34]—assumes that we love

33. Ibid., xi, xii.
34. Luke 10:27; Matt 22:39; Mark 12:31.

ourselves before we can love our neighbor. When this assumption does not hold, as under conditions of shame, it becomes practically difficult to love our neighbor or anyone else for that matter. Love, here, of course, is not limited to just a feeling. It is a creative act which when done selflessly, creates value for the other.

French philosopher Auguste Comte was the first to coin the term "altruism." It represents the opposite of egoism or self-centeredness. The human motives underlying altruism are still being debated, at least within the frames of psychology.[35] One side holds firm to the position that humans have an inherent, selfless capability, while the other side counters that what appears to be a selfless act really benefits the giver and is therefore motivated out of self-interest. Whether neuroscience will bring any resolution to the debate may not be known for some time. However, theology has likely never found much to debate. The close coupling of the love of God and love of neighbor leaves little room for isolated or individualistic self-interest.

Direct experience confirms this. When we give without thought of a return and even anonymously, it feels good. The good feeling may be one of relief, a reprieve of sorts, with an otherwise lingering preoccupation with ourselves. Or the good feeling may be due to an inherent alignment with the love of God and of neighbor. At the very least, when we are fully engrossed in doing something for someone else, without expectation of any return, we are relieved of the distractions from any self-interest, if but temporarily. Creating new value for another seems to require this. Self-interest makes it difficult for established organizations—concerned with protecting and defending what they have going—to take the risks to create something new and valuable for others.

However we view altruism, whether a form of self-interest in a clever disguise or the God-given capability of individuals, theology certainly makes it clear that this love of neighbor is inseparable from the love of God and the sought reality for anyone in the company of God. The question is what we do with whatever lingering self-interest is there. This is not simply a problem that confronts the religious. It confronts organizations trying to innovate and individuals trying to accept change. But here, theology has something to offer as well. It is the radical message of *kenosis*.

---

35. See the works of C. Daniel Batson at Princeton Theological Seminary.

THE "SOLUTION" OF KENOSIS

Kenosis is a Greek word that denotes "emptying" and a theological principle that takes a radical position regarding self-interest. *Kenosis* is used in one of the earliest creedal affirmations of the first churches. Found in Paul's Letter to the Philippians, its beauty and potency is as striking as its truth is timeless and profound:

> Do nothing from selfish ambition or conceit,
>
> but in humility regard others as better than yourselves.
>
> Let each of you look not to your own interests,
>
> but to the interests of others.
>
> Let the same mind be in you that was in Christ Jesus,
>
> who, though he was in the form of God,
>
> did not regard equality with God
>
> as something to be exploited,
>
> but emptied (*kenosis*) himself,
>
> taking the form of a slave,
>
> being born in human likeness.
>
> And being found in human form,
>
> he humbled himself
>
> and became obedient to the point of death—
>
> even death on a cross.[36]

This truth has survived generations of experience shaped by many crucibles animating many cathartic moments. It continues to do so. Going into those crucibles are tragic, deterministic narratives. Coming out of them are hopeful, open, improvisational and even comedic ones. Forget the former things, the old ideas. God is about to do something new. Even now it springs forth. Don't you see it?

The value of every innovation resides in the interest of the other—the one for whom the innovation is intended. What the other finds valuable, what is useful to them becomes explicit at the moment of birth for any commercial enterprise. It is the moment when it attracts and retains its first paying customer. The payment is a sign and seal confirming value has been recognized if not realized.

The extrinsic or exchange value—the price the company charges the customer—is derivative of value the customer assigns to the product or

36. Phil 2:3–8.

service. Whatever ends up being the price-value relationship, however, it was an interest in the other that started the whole ball rolling in the first place. This interest in the other is intrinsic before it takes on an extrinsic quantification. The interest of the other is not only the heart of innovation. It is the heart of a business as well and the company that provides it. Love of neighbor.

Self-sacrifice, including the sacrifice of self-interests, is essential if something new and valuable is created for another. And when such new value is created, it transforms what is otherwise a tragic, deterministic narrative into a comedic, improvisational one.

It is easy to lose sight of this basic interest in the other, especially when businesses grow. Success, ironically, born out of a basic interest in creating value for another, without which there would be no business to begin with, ends up creating a lot of self-interest as well. And as self-interest grows it can often overshadow the interest in the other. Walt Kelley (d. 1973) must have had something of this in mind in his creation of the comic strip character *Pogo*. One of the more famous of Kelly's cartoons had Pogo speaking from the Okefenokee Swamp: "We have met the enemy and he is us."

Planning can get in the way of creating new value for the other because innovating requires the ability to put aside one's own self-interests in order to focus on the interests of others. Plans have a way of carrying forward the self-interests of either the one doing the planning or the organization for which the planning is being done.

CONCLUSION

On those occasions when I have told the aphoristic riddle about how we can make God laugh, I invariably receive one of two reactions: a knowing smile or an awkward chuckle.

The knowing smile suggests a quiet recognition of the truth. The truth, of course, is humbling. "Thy will, not mine, be done." Reminiscent of the Lord's Prayer, either the one he taught us, or the one he prayed himself in the Garden of Gethsemane.

We are never quite sure in either one of these prayers whether the prayer is an explicit petition for the way things will be or an implicit confession that our desire may not line up exactly with God's. It could be that both meanings are intended. The knowing smile and quiet recognition is of the gap between our plans and God's purpose. Therefore, we should always proceed humbly.

The other reaction is a polite but awkward laugh. This reaction typically comes from someone who is heavily invested in the plan, whether his career or the progress of the organization's plan. For him the truth of the riddle is a little unsettling. Even the slightest consideration given to the possibility that a Greater Power may have other plans is disquieting to the planner, to say the least, particularly a thoughtful and thorough one, who is assuming he or she has figured it out.

However, responding to change in a way to create new value is more likely to come from those who have learned how to accept change than from those who have not. Those who are more likely to innovate in response to change are those who are ready to trade in a tragic narrative for a comedic one, who also accept the fact that the external changes before us will require a catharsis within us. In the long run, it may be easier to empty ourselves of our predictions, plans and expectations, at least if we seek to close the gap between our own goals and those of the company of God.

CONVERSATION STARTERS

1. If our plans cause God to laugh, is there any reason for planning?

2. In which current economic and societal tragedies—global or local—do we see emergent signs of the cathartic laughter of God? Does recognizing the comedic in such laughter lead to hope?

3. Is self-interest unavoidable? Can the biblical challenge to love—God, self, others, and even enemies—be a catalyst for innovators, or simply a crucible?

5

Change Wounds; Grieving Heals

By his wounds we are healed.[1]

THE ROLE IMAGINATION PLAYS in innovating is as widely recognized as it is poorly understood.

Discovering, inventing and solving require imagination. Imagination is also essential for accepting change. However, not all imaginations are equal or work the same. Neither are imaginations merely cognitive, or a matter of the intellect. Imaginations are endowed with emotion, can be wounded by the losses that change inflicts, and yet, can grieve and heal.

This essay looks at four different types of imaginations involved in accepting and responding to change, and proposes that theologically informed imaginations may be more practical than we might think, particularly when a response to change is aimed at creating new value.

An underlying premise of what follows is that grieving the loss of what was frees us to respond to what is, and when we are thus freed, we are enabled to create new value—i.e., to innovate. Much innovating fails despite the application of creative imaginations, individual and collective. Even brilliant and knowledgeable imaginations can be wounded. But responding to change with healed imaginations can lead to more substantive innovations.

From hundreds of collaborative problem-solving efforts in various industry and organizational settings I have repeatedly observed anxious

---

1. Isa 53:5.

imaginations grappling with problems before the anxiety subsides. This is far from optimal. Anxiety can distort and even cripple imagination.

The late Edwin Friedman tells of a nurse who came across a biological fact in a medical journal that caught her attention. Friedman's recollection reads this way:

> When a wound occurs there are two kinds of tissue that must heal, the *connective* tissue below the surface, and the *protective* tissue of the skin. If the protective tissue heals too quickly, healing of the connective tissue will not be sound, causing other problems to surface later, or worse, never to surface at all.[2]

Anxiety might focus and motivate the mind on change and its implications, but anxious concern also amplifies dis-ease. It tempts imaginations to get to a solution quickly—a fix more than a solution, really. For example, when organizations and individuals realize they don't have something in mind, or what is "in mind" is not possible, a rush ensues to whatever anxious and defensive imaginations may conceive. What gets conceived is often mislabeled "innovation," partly as a way of justifying it. Giving in to this temptation leads to quick fixes.

We are chronically impatient problem solvers, quick to get to a solution. Many false starts, abandoned efforts, and loads of failure litter innovating landscapes. In our rush to solve we leave losses un-grieved. This pattern of behavior may be the root cause of the difficulties individuals and organizations have in their respective attempts to respond to change.

Examples might include the threatening effects of climate change or the looming shortage of water. For organizational landscapes it may be the inequities of income. On personal landscapes it could be divorce, death of a parent or even worse, loss of a child. There are countless other examples as well. Losses like these penetrate through protective tissue and slice into the connective tissue underneath.

When change is significant, it cuts through both the protective and connective tissue of our lives. Penetrating changes of this sort require structural and substantive responses which themselves heal both protective and connective tissue. Superficial responses run the risk of denying, delaying and distorting responses required for healing at a deeper, more sustainable level.

Responses to what is below the surface may arguably deserve more of our attention than those on the surface, but we should be cautious here.

2. Friedman, *Generation to Generation*, 45.

Healing is necessary in both protective and connective tissue layers. This is what caught the eye of Friedman's nurse. One layer affects another. What appears superficial can have surprising effects on the more substantive.

The role and contribution imagination plays is significant and worth looking at more closely, because how we imagine change and our response to it is one of the few things than we can affect—an effect to which theology makes a significant contribution.

Mental images of change form early, even subconsciously. What we imagine and how we imagine it is shaped by our unconscious prevailing mind-set.[3] It is like the proverbial fish out of water. When out, it becomes aware of the water it was in. Similarly for us, it is difficult for us to be aware of our own mind-sets, unless and until we are taken out of them, as when we visit another culture and catch a glimpse of what is peculiar about our own.

Our imaginations can reflexively form images of change too quickly. Reasons for the quickness can be explained from a psychological, neurological and theological perspective. A psychological perspective might compare and contrast fixed mind-sets with growth mind-sets.[4] A neurological perspective on imagination might suggest that imagination does not happen only in the brain, but in a more distributed fashion.[5] A theological perspective will take a different view.

One such perspective comes from what Old Testament scholar Walter Brueggemann calls the "dominant" and "prophetic" imaginations.[6] Brueggemann finds these two types of imaginations saturating the Hebrew Scriptures. I suspect they influence the New Testament Scriptures as well. Thanks to his brilliant exegesis, Brueggemann's prophetic and dominant imaginations serve as the primary architecture for this essay, the point of which is that four different types of imagination are required of us when responding to change: *dominant, prophetic, emancipated* and *innovating* imaginations.[7] When we *react* to change we are employing only one of these imaginations—the dominant. When we *respond* to

3. Meadows, *Thinking in Systems*, 162–65.

4. Dweck, *Mindset*, 2–14.

5. Wilson, *Hand*, 39.

6. Brueggemann, *Prophetic Imagination*, xix.

7. These four represent an expansion on Brueggemann's two—prophetic and dominant, though even Brueggemann seems to allow for the third—the emancipated imagination. Should my improvisations corrupt Brueggemann's forceful and persuasive biblical scholarship, the mistakes are mine, not his.

change, however, we employ the prophetic, the emancipated and the innovating imaginations.

A brief definition of each imagination is necessary here.

- The *dominant imagination* views change defensively as a threat more than an opportunity. Self-interest[8] is at the heart of the dominant imagination. This imagination tends toward conservation and preservation more than innovation.

- The *prophetic imagination* critiques the dominant imagination and views change as evidence supporting its criticisms. Deeper purpose and intrinsic value (e.g., love, justice) is at the heart of the prophetic imagination. This imagination is focused on what is real and true in what is changing.

- With the window opened by the prophetic imagination, the *emancipated imagination* is freed to envision what might be possible. Interest in others and in closing the gap between what is and what should be (i.e., justice, righteousness) is at the heart of the emancipated imagination.

- A liberated imagination can lead to the *innovating imagination*. The innovating imagination is interested in what is possible now. At the heart of the innovating imagination is what can be embodied or realized in the present—new value that narrows the gap between what is and what should be.

Innovating imaginations are unlikely to get beyond the superficial without the prior work of the prophetic and emancipated imaginations. Imagining what is possible now without the prophetic breaking through the dominant and without expanding the field of what is possible, leaves us too often with superficial innovations.

The current tools of neuroscience, including brain-imagining technology, are woefully insufficient to give us evidence with which to measure or describe how the imagination actually works, much less why.[9] However, neuroscience has confirmed that thinking and feeling are inseparable. Imagination always works with and through the amygdala where emotions are processed. This is but a reminder that a healed imagi-

8. Whether "self" is an individual or an organization.

9. Conversations with marine biologist and neuroscientist Dr. Stuart Thompson (Stanford University) and Dr. Stuart Brown, MD (National Institute for Play—play science).

nation is not simply a function of neuronal circuitry, but is also a matter of emotional balance and spiritual purposefulness. A whole and healed imagination is more than just what's in your head or how you "process information." Healed imaginations, theology might suggest, are those free to imagine what the One for whom all things are possible might be capable of choosing in the creation of new value.[10]

We look at each of the four imaginations below as each reacts or responds to change. In so doing I believe we can see why grieving is so necessary as a precondition to a healed, innovating imagination. Let's take a look at the dominant imagination first, and specifically how this imagination encounters change.

CHANGE AND THE DOMINANT IMAGINATION

The lens through which you and I see change is shaded by the degree of our investment in the *status quo*. On the one hand, change comes as a threat, disturbance or disruption if we are satisfied with the way things are. Substantive change threatens to break the flow that we work so diligently to continue. This is the incumbent's natural point of view.

For those who are not satisfied with the way things are, change can bring welcome relief. Such change is perceived and received as better than none at all. This is the natural perspective of non-incumbents for whom living under dominance is oppressive. However, even non-incumbents may prefer to stay with what is oppressive but familiar. With Pharaoh in hot pursuit, the Israelites looked back and complained to Moses, "It would have been better for us to serve the Egyptians than to die in the wilderness."[11] Dominant imagination can be preferred even by those dominated by it.

Where a dominant imagination engages with change it is quick to evaluate and slow to investigate. Such reflexes may serve us well for detecting immediate threats—perhaps a legacy of our evolutionary biology. But such quickness is prone to error[12]—a chronic problem for this imagination's way of dealing with change.

Security and stability are the primary concerns of the dominant mind-set. Extrinsic values are of greater interest than intrinsic ones.

10. Taylor, *My Stroke of Insight* (TED Talk).

11. Exod 14:12.

12. Kahneman, *Thinking, Fast and Slow*, 19–30.

Intrinsic value is dismissed as academic, impractical and not real world. Of course, this is from the point of view of an imagination that associates "real" with what resides in the superficial layer.

This is not to imply that the dominant imagination is devoid of a theological perspective. The dominant imagination could arguably be considered the most religious of all four imaginations. However, what typifies its theological mind-set is an anxious relationship with God, at the center of which is an unsecured, transactional contract. Investments in ritual embody "sacrifices" intended to resecure God's favor, or at least secure a better balance in the transactional contract, which of course, is never completely satisfying, either to the practitioner or, likely, to God.

Competition and rivalry infect the dominant imagination. This is the case whether the dominant imagination operates in biological, economic or ethical domains. In the biological domain nature is a place where only the fittest survive. When the concern is economic the external marketplace is where competition is good and monopolies are bad and within organizations (internal marketplaces) the competition for limited resources is left to internal rivalries to eliminate anyone who cannot produce a better return on investment. When the domain is ethics, utilitarianism tends to hold sway. Cain's question "Am I my brother's keeper?" comes off as a rhetorical question when heard with a dominant imagination.

Across these domains (and even in the maintenance of the boundaries between them) the dominant imagination favors dichotomous pairs like either/or, victor/victim, prodigal/elder. It ignores change that often shows up in the seams between domains, which is where innovation typically takes root.

Even the subject of innovation itself is vulnerable to a dominant mind-set. Popularized by Clayton Christensen, the current theory of innovation is captured in an unwittingly redundant phrase "disruptive innovation."[13] Christensen bases his theory on Joseph Schumpeter's observation that capitalism has an incessant dynamic of "creative destruction." Christensen's target audience represents established corporations thinking they may want to disrupt themselves before a competitor does. The means of disruption is innovation. Never mind that established organizations are loath to disrupt themselves.

13. Christensen, *Innovator's Dilemma*, xiii, xviii–xxiii.

In this theory innovation presents an inherent dilemma for the established enterprise. On the one hand, keep the current business going to satisfy shareholders and customers but run the risk of being eventually disrupted by some upstart with a "just good enough" solution. Or, on the other hand, disrupt your own business by innovating and beating the upstart to the new solution. In the process, however, one ignores the obligations to shareholders who may prefer a stable stream of revenue.

What Christensen expressed so well reflects the dilemma inherent in the dominant imagination itself, particularly when it convinces itself that it wants something new. It tries to jump over the prophetic imagination and go right to an innovating imagination because it can't quite bring itself to grieve the loss experienced in the new realities change brings. Had the Schumpeterian[14] "creative destruction" been expressed with a greater theological precision—"destructive creation"—it might have shown leaders a way through their dilemma. Might they have seen what others[15] had seen earlier, that innovation is a basic, unavoidable and creative endeavor? It is the dominant imagination that evaluates this as something "destructive."

"Creative destruction" is not confined to organizations. It shows up in the realities of personal lives as well. Personal and spiritual despair at the destruction created can be experienced deeply. Displaced and disaffected workers, along with stagnating wages and increasing income disparities are but a few of the economic symptoms of creative destruction. There are emotional, familial and spiritual consequences as well. Perhaps destruction's path to despair is another reason why economics is nicknamed the "dismal science."

When the dominant imagination encounters change it first narrows its field of view. "Let's get specific." "Can you give me a for instance?" Narrowing has the advantage of quick traction for problem-solving on the hard pavement of specifics. However, narrowing comes with specialization and blindness to the broader context, which may be a good thing for operating efficiencies. But specialization and contextual blindness prove fatal for innovating. Value is derived from context and innovating is about creating new value. For the dominant imagination this is an

---

14. Schumpeter, *Capitalism, Socialism and Democracy*, 139. Joseph Schumpeter (d. 1951), a Harvard economic historian, used both "creative destruction" and "destructive creation" to describe capitalism's "incessant" dynamic of industrial mutation the means of which is technological innovation.

15. Drucker, *Management*, 61.

acceptable risk to take because of its inherent inclination to restore order and preserve the *status quo*. Its interests are primarily in stability and continuity with the past. Its stewardship is about efficiency and optimization. Reactions to change should be fast and lean.

The dominant imagination seeks compliance first. Surface layers are designed to conform as well as protect. When change brings loss, the dominant imaginations will "carry losses forward" to use an accounting phrase. This means to spread or amortize the costs out for the future to worry about. Spreading is a surface act and amortizing serves to numb the feeling and deaden the impact. This makes sense to the dominant imagination. It is more interested in conservation and preservation than innovation and will be more interested in protective tissue improvements than those which run deeper.

Though change may wound the dominant imagination, this imagination will do everything it can to contain the loss and keep change limited to the surface. In contrast, the prophetic imagination seeks to expose the loss. The prophetic does this to enable healing of connective tissue so that emancipated and innovating imaginations might find their voices and bear fruit.

CHANGE AND THE PROPHETIC IMAGINATION

Where the dominant imagination reacts to change with anxiety, the prophetic responds with lament. Mourning the losses that arrive with change is nearly impossible for the dominant imagination.

Bereavement does not come easily for the prophetic imagination either. Grieving is not pleasant, never welcome, rarely sought. Losses *im*press and lament *ex*press what the prophetic imagination has felt and seen. Lament arises not from the love of the way things are, but from the love of God—of the prophet for God, of God for the prophet and for the people to whom the prophet speaks. In such love there is a hope that may not lessen the impression of loss, but makes its expression possible.[16] Such expression is not possible to the dominant imagination rooted as it is in control more than love.

Lament is not this imagination's only response to change. Critique is the other. Just as the prophetic has an inherent willingness to grieve, it also has a penchant for truth, particularly truths that penetrate through

16. This reflects the theological notion of prevenient grace.

protective tissue in which the dominant imagination is so invested. Unlike the dominant's preference to avoid, deny and perpetuate—even perpetuate knowingly what change reveals as illusory—the prophetic imagination uses realities "on the ground" to pierce the delusions of the dominant imagination. Demonstrable, indisputable and undeniable realities—unpleasant, unjust realties—are the prophetic imagination's currencies.

This may be one reason the prophetic imagination turns out to be so inconveniently realistic. It is especially keen on firsthand and unmediated experience—truth felt directly in what is manifesting now, realities that mind and heart prefer to soften. Prophetic imagination is critical, not for the sake of being contrarian or iconoclastic. Its criticism is animated by the desire to acknowledge and express that which the incumbent imagination prefers to cover over. This insistence on direct experience has been described[17] as the first task of innovation—to diagnose the realities of change.

In order to acknowledge and express reality, as unpleasant as it may be, it must first be felt. This may be simple, but it is not easy for the prophet or the innovator to do. The dominant imagination has a host of ways to numb or "narcoticize" the losses change brings, from pixilated distractions on wirelessly connected devices to pharmacological anesthetics.

We lose touch with what loss is without the prophetic imagination. We talk more often about pain rather than loss when we really mean loss. We can't quite bring ourselves to say it. What we call "emotional pain" or "psychological pain" takes up residence in an increasingly expensive second home in our self-assessments. This is troubling. It denigrates the physical trauma of those whose bodies are racked with real, physical pain.

Few of us would ever consider ignoring physical pain and attend to "emotional pain" first, yet the dominant imagination seems to have found "painkillers" to avoid grieving. No one yet has invented a "loss killer."

Suffice it to say that physical pain evokes a more immediate reflexive reaction, whereas emotional and spiritual loss evoke a more considered response. When anesthetics for physical pain are used for emotional, relational and spiritual loss we not only lose our ability to grieve, we become numb to the realities of change.

17. Drucker, *Innovation and Entrepreneurship*, 35. This is also an explicit principle and practice of Toyota's Development System (Morgan and Liker, *Toyota Product Development System*, 32) which in Japanese is referred to as *genchi genbutsu*, meaning roughly "go to the source."

Loss for the dominant imagination is at worst a temporary interruption, at best a deduction to "carry forward." The dominant imagination would rather remain detached. "After all, it's not personal, it's just
business." With the prophetic imagination however, loss is personal,
deeply felt because the prophet is not immune from the critique or its
implications.

Injustice is often revealed and manifested in the change itself. The
prophetic imagination views change as a part of the realignment of reality with God's purposes, a footprint or evidence that God is at work in the
world, whether we are a part of that work or not. This is the essence of
the prophetic plumb line the prophet Amos saw in his imagination.[18] The
plumb line is held up by the prophetic imagination not to realign reality,
but to realign us. Theologically the prophetic imagination takes its cues
as much from changes on the horizontal landscape of our lives as it does
from the constancy of divine purposes on the vertical or transcendent
plane. The criticism of the prophetic imagination is rooted in the justice
of God.

The prophetic imagination starts with relatedness and reframes the
domain—whatever the domain happens to be. In the domain of biology
life is called "creation" rather than "nature," an ecosystem where everything is created, related, has value, even intrinsic value, more than the
sphere where survival goes to the fittest. In the economic domain, the
prophetic imagination sees external marketplaces as places where products are "goods," services express care if not love, and organizations are
places for creative collaboration and cooperation; where relationships
are included in the list of "resources" to be stewarded; where returns are
reinvested more than taken. In the ethical domain, Cain's question ("Am
I my brother's keeper?") is no longer rhetorical and always answered with
an unambiguous "yes."

Across these domains and even in the maintenance of the boundaries between them, prophetic imagination favors not dichotomous pairs
but the both/and. The prophetic attends to what and who is caught in
between, in the gaps the dominant imagination will deny.

When the prophetic imagination responds to change its first move
is to deepen its field of view. "Let's get to the root." "What are the underlying issues?" In this move the prophetic demonstrates its primary interest

18. Amos 7:7–9.

in connective tissue. It is relatively disinterested in the superficial, except as it may signal what is wounded underneath.

The prophetic is not simply *on* the leading edge. It *is* the edge. What sharpens the edge is the undeniable, *prima facie*, the self-evident. Ruptures in connective tissue are more important than breaches in firewalls of protective tissue. Relatedness is what is at stake for the prophetic. The prophetic cannot imagine "carrying losses forward." It is more inclined to take them, take them all, and take them now. What this imagination seeks is not order and stability restored, but hearts broken and contrite. These are matters of connection more than protection.

Mourning is a primary process of the prophetic where realities of change impress and express both loss and truth. Its voice is lament in verse and song, not the calculations of cost/benefit or risk/reward ratios. The prophetic imagination is not about a quick and shallow reaction but a deep and penetrating response. The prophetic imagination is more interested in how change affects relationships, more interested in getting real with what *is*, and less interested in preserving and conserving what *was*.

While Schumpeterian economists refer to innovation as "creative destruction," the prophetic imagination will describe innovation as "destructive creation"—a purgation of loss to begin with that ends in purity and wholeness.

Such a deep wound in America's connective tissues is something Walter Brueggemann lays open.[19] He sees the destruction of the 9/11 terrorist attacks as analogous to the destruction of the Jerusalem in 587 BCE, an example of how change speaks its prophetic critique to American exceptionalism. His prescription is also strikingly relevant to what is required of innovators:

- *accept* the realities of change by exposing the illusion of ideology,

- *grieve* the loss(es) that can no longer be denied, and

- *discover* hope amid the despair.

"Exceptionalism" infects established organizations and manifests in entitlement mind-sets harbored by individuals. These perennial "prophetic tasks" apply not only to organizations in need of reclaiming their relevance. They pertain to one's personal life as well in reclaiming a renewed sense of meaning and purpose. Such reclamation efforts for

19. Brueggemann, *Reality Grief Hope*, 1.

organizations especially begin with an urgent question: where are innovations needed and why?

CHANGE AND THE EMANCIPATED IMAGINATION

Grieving may not ever be over, but an imagination freed from the insidious shackles of the dominant is one that can see possibilities neither the dominant nor the prophetic can. Thanks to the work of the prophetic, this emancipated imagination no longer has to wrestle with the denial of loss or its containment in protective tissue. Its interest and focus are elsewhere, in the possibilities of healing. The emancipated imagination is all about new tissue formation. The emancipated imagination knows that the wound must remain open. The wound needs fresh air to breathe and enable the healing to begin. This is where the emancipated imagination begins.

Even after change has been accepted, imagination can still be captive. Change-born resentments, self-interest and self-reliance frequently remain, restraining and warping imagination even after the prophetic has exposed and critiqued the dominant. Each of these three captors can hold even the most creative imagination in exile. Thus, it is worth dwelling briefly on each one.

Resentments are likely the most pernicious. They are hardened clumps of petrified anger, condensed by time and preservation. Change can leave legacies of indignation, bitterness and regret, and these legacies captivate and cripple imagination.

The one who harbors resentment is of course the one who is hurt the most. Held by either incumbents or victims, resentments always seem to poison the holder more than the target. Often targets are not even aware of the resentment held by the other. Unresolved injustice or irreconcilable conflicts—typical offspring of substantive change—nurse resentments, justified or not. Expectations so often disrupted by change are simply resentments under construction.

Love, in the form of forgiveness received, breaks the bonds of resentment. Forgiveness is the cessation of resentment. It frees both the forgiven and the forgiver at the same time. Like a pair of scissors that cuts the threads of resentment, forgiveness frees more than forgets.

Self-interest also restrains an otherwise emancipated imagination. "What's in it for me?" or "What's the return on our investment?" The questions themselves put self-interest in front of interest in others and prevent the conceptualization and generation of ideas that embody love without a return.

To some extent, even a customer's interest and the interest of company serving that customer will be somewhat at odds, to be sure. Such interests are never fully aligned. Some might argue this inherent conflict of interest is an inescapable, irresolvable dilemma of capitalism.

But the value at the heart of every innovation first benefits the other. Priority given to self-interest will prove counterproductive, especially in the early stages of innovating. Companies that put their own interests ahead of the interests of their customers will find it nearly impossible to innovate. Another will come along and take those customers and lead them where the incumbent does not want them to go.

Albert Einstein—one of history's more emancipated imaginations—recognized this constraint of self-interest on the imagination when he said that "nothing truly valuable arises from ambition or from a mere sense of duty; it stems rather from love and devotion towards men and towards objective things."[20]

Selfless love breaks the bond self-interest holds on our imaginations. Selfless, sacrificial love is the antidote to self-interest. The Apostle Paul said it clearly and simply: "Let each of you look not to your own interests but to the interests of others."[21] St. Francis repeated it in his prayer, asking for the desire to console more than be consoled, to understand more than be understood, and to love more than be loved.

The illusion of *self-reliance*—often thought of as a virtue—is another fetter that keeps imagination in bondage. "Free thinking" is regarded as desired in our otherwise homogenous culture. "Out-of-the-box" thinking is encouraged and techniques to promote it are taught in business schools across the globe. But knowledge of what went into constructing and constricting the box to begin with is a necessary precondition to know whether one is truly thinking outside of it or not. Just as art is the product of an individual creative imagination, innovation is the result of imaginations informed and enabled by others collaborating in the service of the creation of new value.

Many of us might like to think of ourselves as independent or original thinkers. However, even if there is a modicum of truth to the

20. Einstein to F. S. Wada, in Dukas and Hoffman, *Albert Einstein, the Human Side: New Glimpses from His Archives* 46.

21. Phil 2:4.

independence of our thought and the originality of our ideas, imagination depends upon the discoveries, knowledge and experiences of a great "cloud of witnesses." Others have not only paved the way before us, they surround us with a diversity of perspective that as individuals we cannot readily attain on our own. The company and community of others—some near to our awareness and some very remote—nourish and shape our imaginations with metaphors, analogies and directly relevant experience. Imagination, even an emancipated one, is communal more than individual.

Einstein located the emancipated imagination "where the world ceases to be the scene of our personal hopes and wishes, where we face it as free beings, admiring, asking and observing. There we enter the realm of art and science."[22] A truly emancipated imagination is not simply what is left over from the prophetic.

Einstein went on to say that if we choose to portray what we see and experience in the language of logic, we are then engaged in science and technology. If, on the other hand, we choose to communicate in ways not accessible to the conscious mind, then we are engaged in art. But whether art or science and technology, "common to both is the loving devotion to that which transcends personal concerns and volition"; in other words, a purpose greater than ourselves. This is not only an emancipated imagination, but a theologically informed one as well.

In the final analysis what binds and blinds an otherwise emancipated imagination is self-centered fear. Perfect love casts out this self-centered fear[23] and liberates the imagination so healing can begin. Theology actually has much to say about this truly emancipated imagination.

The emancipating of an imagination may be a gradual process. It takes time and a safe, protected space—a place to breathe. Awakenings of emancipated imaginations don't typically happen all at once.

The window of possibility may not open very wide at first. All that is needed, however, is an opening, no matter what the size. And this opening has already been provided by the prophetic imagination. It has cracked the window open, even if only a little. And with just a little opening, the fresh air from the outside—the breeze[24] of the possible—comes

22. Dukas and Hoffmann, *Albert Einstein*, 37.

23. 1 John 4:18.

24. The Old Testament Hebrew word for wind—*ruah*—is also the same word for the breath or Spirit of God.

rushing in. And if this breeze is believed to be from the One for whom all things are possible, then the possibilities will start to enter and multiply.

Like an awakening, even the ones that happen daily in the familiar time and space of our own bedrooms, there is at first a stirring from the sleep we are leaving. This is accompanied by an increasing awareness of our first thoughts. Then an awareness of our senses and finally an opening of our eyes to where we are and what is happening around us. Similarly the emancipation of imagination is a kind of an awakening—a "coming to." In coming to, the emancipated imagination puts on its own pair of glasses calibrated to the possibilities that can be imagined in whatever the response might be.

Believing is the way the emancipated imagination perceives both change and possible responses. By "believing" I do not mean what the dominant imagination regards as propositional "belief."[25] Rather, by "believing" I mean trusting *in* some one, some thing or some power greater than one's self.

Trusting is at the heart of an emancipated imagination. It's more about problem exploring than solving, more about mystery appreciating than myth explaining: "the assurance of things hoped for, the conviction of things unseen."[26] This is what Jesus invited followers to emulate, his own example of believing.

The emancipated imagination embraces change with the arms of appreciation and wonder. It picks up where the prophetic imagination leaves off. The emancipated is free, thanks to the prophetic, to now imagine both the mystery and deeper, intrinsic meaning of the change that is happening. It is also free to imagine the broader range and depth of possibilities that a response might take.

While the unpleasant realities of loss may not have vanished, the emancipated imagination opens itself to deeper mystery and possibility. The emancipated imagination is not wishful thinking, if grounded in prophetic realities. The loss is already accepted, even appreciated. A window of opportunity has opened. Mystery becomes more attractive than mastery. An emancipated imagination may even come to look at the loss grieved as a potential asset, an appreciating one to be used in the construction of something new. As Dee Hock, the founder of Visa International, said in looking back on the challenges he had to work through:

25. Cox, *Future of Faith*, ch. 5. For too long believing has been understood as "believing that," such as a belief *that* something is true, or *that* this really happened.

26. Heb 11:1.

> When it becomes necessary to develop a new perception of things, a new internal model of reality, the problem is never to get new ideas in, the problem is to get the old ideas out. Every mind is filled with old furniture. It's familiar. It's comfortable. We hate to throw it out. The old maxim so often applied to the physical world, "Nature abhors a vacuum," is much more applicable to the mental world. Clear any room in your mind of old perspectives, and new perceptions will rush in. Yet, there is nothing we fear more.[27]

The emancipated imagination is playful, provisional and vulnerable. It is free not only *from* dominant thinking and the tyranny of self-interest, but free *for* imagining "what ifs." It is free for speculation and for the conception and expression of new hypotheses, fresh combinations and novel solutions. It is provisional in the sense that the mystery appreciated is more likely to reveal what a glance can never produce.

But the emancipated imagination is also fragile. It is easily broken by anxious tension characteristic of protective tissue. Who of us hasn't experience the instant deflation of another's negative comment? New ideas are rejected less often because of their inherent deficiencies than due to hostile, nervous atmospheres within which they first express themselves.

The initial move of an emancipated imagination is to broaden its field of view. This requires crossing domain boundaries. These are boundaries the dominant imagination would rather maintain and enforce. It is never just a psychological, sociological or economic matter for the emancipated imagination. Domain boundaries are revealed to be porous and penetrable. In fact, innovation relies on these boundary crossings, and always has.[28] Domains themselves are legacies of dominant imagination.

The emancipated imagination is not without risk. One is the habit of imposing the practical on the possible. We make assumptions, really presumptions, all the time about what we consider possible or not. A partially emancipated imagination is likely to do the same. A fully emancipated imagination—one that is truly in the company of God (the One for whom all things are possible), approaches the kind of faith that Jesus said could move mountains, the amount of faith contained in a mustard seed.[29]

Slips back into the dominant imagination present another risk. Thinking out loud together in the company of others helps, but even the

27. Hock, *Birth of the Chaordic Age*, 135.

28. Johansson, *Medici Effect*, 35–87.

29. Matt 17:20.

company of others is constrained by the inherent limitations of who is doing the collaborative thinking. Individual and collective imagination will always be limited by experience and expertise no matter how diverse and relevant. Negative attitudes, self-centered interests and insufficient trust along with an unclear purpose can also erode the benefits of diverse minds.

However, a truly emancipated imagination will emerge when diverse minds gather for a single, higher purpose. Accompanied with believing hearts and in the active presence of the One for whom all things are possible, this kind of imagination cannot be very far from the kingdom of God on earth—the company of God. Such an emancipated imagination is as close as we are likely to come to a healed[30] imagination.

But innovating is not simply about generating new ideas. It is about giving physical form to conceptual substance, or in theological language, "making the word flesh." Such acts of creation and incarnation not only require the company of God. They require something even beyond an emancipated imagination. They require an innovating one.

CHANGE AND THE INNOVATING IMAGINATION

While the emancipated imagination *conceives* of possibilities in response to change, the innovating imagination seeks to *actualize and realize* those possibilities. This turns out to be a significant difference. While both imagine the possible, the innovating imagination is tasked with not only conceiving but realizing what is possible *now*.

Contrary to popular opinion, innovating is not idea generation. It is about embodying or prototyping—trying it out. Patent attorneys refer to this as "reductions to practice" or "preferred embodiments." Innovating imagination converts the conceived into the real, true and valuable, not just in its physical form but also in the form of its implementation and delivery.[31] Embodiment must happen not only in the product, service or program itself, but in the way in which it is introduced and integrated in the lives of the ones the innovation is intended to serve. This is true for any innovation, whether a commercial product, a nonprofit's service, an educational program or a therapeutic technique.

30. A "healed" rather than a "healthy" imagination may be a better articulation, given theology's understanding of reality as "fallen" or that we are living "in between" times or, if you prefer, the more Pauline view that all of creation still groans as it awaits the final redemption (Rom 8:22).

31. Moore, *Dealing with Darwin*, 61. Also Cheverton, *Maverick Way*, 241–59.

Innovating imaginations attempt to convert the possible into the workable without sacrificing value or newness. In a way, the innovating imagination is an emancipated imagination directed and applied to making it real now. It is not limited to models or prototypes but deployed repeatedly in multiple iterations of conceiving, fine-tuning, interpreting, re-hypothesizing, experimenting and learning. Prototypes and trials are mediums of the innovating imagination. It is where the embodying occurs.

The sweep of Scripture chronicles God's repeated and persistent attempts to incarnate God's love for creation. Many of these attempts and embodiments were brand new things. Some of these demonstrations proved miraculous. Some were more mundane, plausible events. But whether mundane or miraculous, all of them together tell a consistent story of a persistent, patient and engaged God who has not given up. A God who keeps creating is a God who keeps incarnating, constantly making word flesh. Innovation theology should have much to contribute here especially.

Inventions find form and substance in solutions that solve problems and provide value. Varieties of nontechnical, human and organizational conflicts often arise in the process of finding form and substance, however. People have "stakes to claim" and "axes to grind" and "nests to feather." Inventions disrupt all these stakes, axes and nests such that resolutions to conflicts caused by the new solutions themselves are necessary.[32] Innovating is not just about *solving* problems. It's also about *resolving* conflicts.

Some conflicts simply result from asymmetric interests in the marketplace, idiosyncratic preferences or operating legacies. In the early days of personal computers, for example, the less elegant MS DOS operating system from Microsoft found much wider acceptance than the more elegant Apple Macintosh, largely because MS DOS was distributed more widely with IBM's trusted name and its larger more established sales and distribution system.

The late Russell Ackoff, a dean of design and systems thinking, encouraged us to use our innovating imaginations not simply for solving.[33] Certainly *solutions* are to be sought through the application of scientific methods. There are also *resolutions*—new covenants between the parties to a dispute that prove to be innovations in relationships. There are also *dissolutions* wherein problems simply disappear due to a new design, one

32. Vincent, *Prisoners of Hope*, ch. 7.

33. Ackoff, *Differences That Make a Difference*, 1–3. I have made some theological interpolations to Ackoff's original observations on resolutions, dissolutions and absolutions.

that reframes and reconfigures the presenting problem. The problem simply goes away.

New designs and architectures that dissolve chronic problems take a whole systems view, reimagining with a broader field of view, as for example, endoscopic procedures that preempt the need to crack a chest for cardiac surgery, or digital cameras dissolving the need for film. There are also *absolutions* that represent still another alternative that might represent "low hanging fruit" for innovation theology.

The tissues that protect us, more than the tissues that connect us, prevents us from using our innovating imaginations. Jesus himself seems to have pointed this out in his parable of the unshrunk cloth and old wineskins.

> No one sews a piece of unshrunk cloth on an old garment; if he does, the patch tears away from it, the new from the old, and a worse tear is made. And no one puts new wine into old wine-skins; if he does, the wine will burst the skins, and the wine is lost, and so are the skins; but new wine is for fresh skins.[34]

The innovating imagination starts and ends with a focus on both the wine *and* the skins, both the protective and connective tissue need repair if not replacement. The new value God is creating, with or without us, is both intrinsic and extrinsic. The innovating imagination has to do with both content and form in what is possible now.

When it is deployed in the company of God, the innovating imagination becomes less of a fight or a struggle. Sometimes all we have to do is "be still."[35] With the innovating imagination Cain's question is no longer a question. It has become an affirmation: I *am* my brother's (and sister's) keeper, always. There are no longer prodigal sons, or elder brothers, just siblings who have no rivalry because all enjoy and appreciate their Father's attention.

Relief, recovery and restoration are all important aims. But these aims are not innovation. Innovation aims to create new value. This is another equally important purpose of the company of God, but not the same as restoration or return. "Remember not the former things," Isaiah declared, "nor consider the things of old. Behold, I am doing a new thing; now it springs forth, do you not perceive it?"[36]

34. Mark 2:21–22.
35. Exod 14:14; Isa 30:15; Ps 46:10.
36. Isa 43:18–19.

That God is more than willing and capable of doing new things is often forgotten when we are confronted with change and the need to respond. The source of this amnesia is likely the dominant imagination. But not only is God willing and able to do new things, Isaiah seems to suggest God is already engaged in doing those new things. God is not waiting around for us to agree. And it's not just Isaiah. Paul seems attuned to God's engagement in innovation when he says in one of his classic asides, "seeing that you have put off the old nature with its practices and have put on the new nature, which is being *renewed in knowledge after the image of its creator.*"[37] Not only is God interested and engaged in newness, Paul implies that God's very nature appears to manifest an interest in a renewing.

Peter also assumed that God has an agenda of creating something new—nothing short of new heavens and a new earth."[38] And not just Peter, but also the author of Revelation was interested in God's innovating in the vision that concludes the book of Revelation: "Then I saw a new heaven and a new earth . . . he will wipe away every tear from their eyes, and death shall be no more, neither shall there be mourning nor crying nor pain any more, for the former things have passed away."[39]

Innovations that reorder and disrupt are sought, not because they reorder and disrupt, but because these innovations create value in connective tissue. These innovations are not superficial. They go to the roots—some call them "radical" innovations. They resonate with what is intrinsic and virtuous not mediated or "virtual."

A constant temptation for the innovating imagination is to sacrifice what is possible on the altar of what is probable. Invention becomes a burnt offering on the altar of convention, or what is most excelling on the altar of what is more expedient. The dominant imagination will reasserted itself when such sacrifice is made. When this happens we forget or degrade much of what the prophetic and the emancipated imaginations have brought.

The temptation is strong. Why not dispense with all this talk of grieving loss and embracing the critique of the prophetic? Who really needs to widen the field of view and consider what might be possible with an emancipated imagination? What we really need is a feasible solution.

---

37. Col 3:9–10.

38. 2 Pet 3:13.

39. Rev 21:1, 4–5.

Let's get practical and go right to it. The need is urgent. Who can argue with this logic?

LOSS AS ADVANTAGE

Change affects the deserving and the undeserved. Losses always accompany change, whether anticipated or incurred. I have learned this firsthand as a lab rat in the many and varied experiments of my own life. Even welcome change brings necessary losses.

Our attitudes toward loss are difficult to separate from our orientation to change. Research in decision-making strongly suggests that most of us would rather avoid loss than risk gains.[40] This preference for loss avoidance makes it more difficult for us to accept change, and so we prefer conservation or preservation rather than innovation.

A conservation mind-set estimates what remains in the reservoir, compares this with the current rate of drain, and forecasts when the reservoir—money, time, knowledge, etc.—will be used up. The basis of the comparison is a projected gap (anticipated loss), and its purpose is to save resources, or prolong the life expectancy of the reservoir. A conservation mind-set pays attention to the volume of the resource supply and the rate at which it is being used.

A preservation mind-set looks at loss differently. Preservationists are more interested in the purity, quality and character of the content than the level of its volume. The preservationist seeks to protect the purity of what's in the reservoir even more than save its quantity. The preservationist sees the content as worth preserving in its original state. Loss for the preservation mind-set is a loss of essence or purity or character—loss through contamination or corruption.

An innovation mind-set looks at loss still differently. For this mind-set, losses are a symptom of change more than a gap in supply or a corruption of purity. While still losses, the innovation mind-set sees in the loss a telltale to what may be a better, as yet unseen and still uncertain future. As this mind-set has a purpose of creating new value, losses will necessarily be viewed in this light.

Some might think this view of loss lacks compassion. And to some degree this criticism is warranted. However, it does have the advantage

40. Daniel Kahneman and Amos Tversky developed prospect theory—a seminal theory in behavioral economics—for which they were award the Nobel Prize in 2002.

of viewing losses of any kind not as something to prevent, delay or guard against. Loss actually becomes a part of the new set of conditions, even a potential asset.

This is a completely different orientation to loss. Conservation and preservation view losses as essentially negative, things to resist, slow down, and protect against entirely. An innovation mind-set tends to view losses as an inevitable part of change. This attitude toward loss demands emotional intelligence,[41] one that views loss as not only inevitable and constant, but a signal to pay attention to, if not an invitation to accept.

This is not to imply innovation should be preferred over conservation or preservation. All three represent viable responses. Rather, it is simply to acknowledge that loss is an inescapable consequence of change, and as a result, our attitudes and strategies for dealing with loss are worth examining.

CONCLUSION

Though we know in our minds that change is constant, we fear in our hearts the loss so often associated with it. This internal tug of war between what the mind knows and the heart desires can easily distort perceptions of the new realities change brings.

Before the new realities of change can be accepted the loss of the old reality must be accepted. Accepting and understanding these realities are necessary before any serious response can hope to create new value. The truth is that grieving is necessary before the new realities change brings can be fully and cleanly accepted.

We need to grieve the passing of what once was before we are free to respond to what is. Innovation theology can and should help us to do this. It is more able than economics or even cultural anthropology—organizational or individual—to do this, because theology goes further and deeper in its understanding of loss than other "ologies."

Any innovation theology worth its salt should first speak clearly about the necessity of grieving our losses. Then and only then can it speak

41. Bill Wilson started Kimberly-Clark's early disposable diaper business on a research budget. Wilson demonstrated high emotional intelligence when Jack Kimberly told him directly to stop work on diapers because of all the losses. Bill kept working—with his team—on diapers. Bill's persistence proved to be arguably the most productive act of insubordination in Kimberly-Clark's history. Diapers remain the company's number one profit maker. Cheverton, *Maverick Way*.

prophetically about seeing, accepting and appreciating more confidently the new realities brought by change. Innovation theology sees the necessity of grieving as a precondition to accepting and appreciating the new realities change brings with it. The prophetic imagination is what breaks through the dominant so that emancipated imagination might bear fruit in the innovating.

Change can get our attention. The dominant imagination often captures it. But love can free imaginations otherwise held captive by the dominant. Not a sappy love, but a prophetic love, a love that critiques and laments, is a love that longs for something new, valuable, true and good; something that is trustworthy and lasting; something that promotes healing. It is a kind of love that seeks to participate in the new thing that God is already doing.

CONVERSATION STARTERS

1. How much of our imagination about the future is dominated by what we think possible (and impossible)? What percent of our thinking is genuinely open to a God for whom all things are possible?

2. Where do we hear or see the prophetic imagination today? Are there signs of a related emancipated imagination nearby and does such imagination point to where innovations are needed and why?

3. What realities of change have we yet to fully grieve in accepting the "new normal"? And in what context? Were we to fully lament their loss what might that allow us to imagine?

6

Change as Invitation

Deep calls to deep . . .[1]

IS CHANGE AN INTERRUPTION or an invitation?

Many view change as an interruption. As a variation from the norm, change brings with it something different. It interrupts the flow of things, never mind that the flow itself might be change. It's perceived as a divergence from what has been and what was expected. Of course, the same can be said about innovation. It brings something different, is a variation from the norm, and diverges from what was expected.

Both change and innovation can *appear* to be interruptions, even disruptions. As such, both change and innovation often can and do take negative connotations. However, change can be viewed in a more positive light as well. When present circumstances may be less than desirable change can bring welcome relief. But even if change brings no obvious relief, it can be seen as an invitation, if we so choose.

Innovation theology may be biased toward the possibility that change represents an invitation. If we assume that God is still at work, still creating,[2] then the changes we experience could just as well reflect this ongoing work as not. It could represent a divine invitation. Reframing change in this way is not merely an interesting thought experiment. It carries practical benefits and makes theological sense.

---

1. Ps 42:7.

2. See previous essay, "Theological Assumptions and Practical Purpose."

This essay explores both the theological and practical implications of viewing change as an invitation. What follows proposes that change is just as likely to carry an invitation from God, as it is an interruption. In fact, change could be both. Just this possibility should give us pause. To state the proposal concisely: *change may deliver a divine invitation to freely, fully and creatively participate with the company of God in creating new value for others.*

Several ideas are embedded in this proposal and for the sake of clarity, should be made explicit up front.

First, by *change* I simply mean significant external movement and differences emerging in the natural, physical, societal and cultural environments in which we live, as individuals and as organizations. I am not so much referring to internal or psychic change as I am external changes to which sooner or later we will be required to respond (or react).

Second, by *divine invitation* I mean to imply vocation.[3] A more conventional expression might say that God "calls" us to respond. Saying that in change God *invites* us to respond fits a bit more snugly with the character of change. The relevant word in Scripture (*kaleto* in Greek) is and can be translated either as "call" or "invite," depending on the scriptural context in which the word is used.

Freely has to do with God's desire for us to choose whether we accept the invitation or not. The choice is ours. This has a direct bearing on innovating effectiveness. A voluntary attitude turns out to be essential to innovating, which is one reason employees have difficulty innovating. Likewise, *fully* has to do with whether we are lukewarm or all in, which is another characteristic typically regarded as essential to innovating and of likely interest to God.

Co-creative participation intends to imply what you might think—a collaborative activity between God and people. In other words, we get to participate in God's creating if we so choose by accepting the invitation.

And finally, *the company of God*—an expression I intend as a vernacular surrogate for the kingdom of God on earth—reflects the collaborative community of others, all of whom are stakeholders in the purposes of this company, regardless of the degree of their awareness of the company's presence and purpose.

3. Vocation, from the Latin root *vocare*, means voice. It is often translated "call" or "calling." Both imply a someone rather than a something—one who has a voice, one who calls to others, a caller. Unfortunately, vocation is often fused with career only.

As an interruption change is negative, an inconvenience at best, an invasion at worst. Responses to interruptions tend to be begrudging—something we *have* to do, not something we *get* to do. They typically take the form of reluctant compliance. "We have no other real choice." Though we may be able to delay our response, sooner or later we know we will have to attend to it. Such a response garners the least amount of effort. We really would rather get back to whatever it was we were doing.

As an invitation however, change can *call* us to reconsider the trajectory of our present course. Surely when we are invested in keeping things the way they are we can miss the invitation entirely. But when we can no longer ignore or deny the change, reassessing where we are and where we are headed becomes the only appropriate, rational and prudent thing to do. In this view, change itself can extend an invitation to us to rethink and reconsider.

Bring a theological perspective to change, and it will naturally cause us to ask where, or more accurately, from whom the change is coming. Inconvenient or irritating interruptions may just possibly be divine interruptions. Receiving an invitation from a living, still creating, loving One, for whom all things are possible, may cause us to respond differently.

When God may be the source of change—a host inviting us—we can more easily see our selves as potential volunteers who participate in God's ongoing creating, rather than as victims of the change, or even victors over it. Put another way, if God is the host who sends out invitations embodied in the changes we encounter then we may be on God's guest list. This implies the host would like us there, participating, contributing, co-creating with God in this ongoing work.

Unfortunately the default mode for many is to view change primarily as an interruption. In this mode, our readiness to innovate will lag. Reasons for this come from our investments in extending and defending the *status quo*—as individuals and organizations. Investments in our self-images may be another reason. These self-images reflect who we think we are in the context of our more familiar current realities—identities drawn from our work, our roles in families, organizations, churches, etc.

But when we turn from change-as-interruption to change-as-invitation, our response can easily move from one of begrudging obligation ("I *have* to do this") to voluntary willingness ("I *get* to do this"). Perhaps even more importantly, our attitude shifts from receiving the new realities of change as bad news to receiving these new realities as good news, particularly when we consider from whom the invitation is coming. In short, when we view change as invitation, we are more likely to at least take a closer look at the opportunity to create new value for others.

ESSENTIALS OF INVITATIONS

Most of us assume we know what invitations are and even the socially acceptable protocols that go with them. In fact, invitations are so familiar we seldom consider what is assumed.

The dictionary defines "invitation" as an act of asking and encouraging someone to come, attend and take part in some experience beneficial to both the invited and the host.[4] An invitation does not compel so much as it attracts.

Invitations carry a few basic elements: a host, guests, the event to which the guests are invited, and a purpose or intent of the host. Take a closer look at each and the dynamics that go along with them.

Hosts create the guest list and typically do the inviting. Invitations come from some*one* rather than from some*thing*. Invitations reflect the intention and purpose of the one from whom it originated. When we receive an invitation our first question is typically "who is this from?" With an interruption, however, our question is more likely to be "Now what?"

The question of who is doing the inviting is often quickly followed by a second: "Why was *I* invited?" It is the very nature of an invitation wherein guests are named only by the host. Recipients become invited guests only as and when the host invites them.

Another element of an invitation is the event itself—a future time and place—typically named in the invitation itself. Location and timing of the occasion to which one is invited are tightly coupled with the reason for the event. An invitation can point to what brings occasion and reason together.

What the host envisions for the event is tightly intertwined with who the host wants to show up. An invitation not only implies that there will be guests. It implies an intention on the part of the host that cannot be fulfilled without the attendance of some or all of those on the guest list.

None of these elements are considered part of an interruption. When we are interrupted we are not likely to ask "why?" or "why me?" except rhetorically. An interruption has no host, guest list or guests, and quite possibly no intention, explicit or otherwise. Rather, what interruptions

---

4. *New Shorter Oxford English Dictionary*, s.v. "invitation."

look for is attention. Interruptions are disinterested in hosting much of anything. Nor are they willing to wait. If there is any motivation, purpose or reason behind an interruption, it will often remain obscure. Interruptions can remain devoid of discoverable intent, and discoverable intent is essential, not only for making sense of change, but also for discerning where innovations are needed and why. Without a substantive where and why, innovations languish in superficial novelty without sustainable or substantive value.

All this is fertile ground for innovation theology to explore further. My limited purpose here is simply to make explicit how invitations differ from interruptions. Host. Guests. Time, place, and purpose. These are essential to invitations and largely missing in interruptions.

Behind an invitation is a host envisioning a future event that gathers others. The host's vision remains partial and incomplete without the presence and participation of the invited. That host, guests, vision and its realization all come together at a specified future time and place is so much more purposeful and encouraging than an interruption. Viewing change with this invitational frame carries more potential to accept and embrace change and even respond in ways that create new value.

With invitations the dynamics are set in motion before the event occurs. Roles, intention and occasion come into play when an invitation is sent, and even more when received. When change is viewed as an invitation, understanding this invitational dynamic can help us understand how to respond.

Lead time alone gives us a practical reason to view change as an invitation. Looking at change *before* it happens not only enables anticipation. It cultivates the ability to respond instead of react. Interruptions come with little if any warning. They evoke reactions more than responses. Considered response is always preferable to reflexive reaction. During lead time both host and invited have time to prepare.[5]

Think of the basic dynamics of any invitation-response sequence as comprised of three stages. The first happens *before* acceptance, the second *after*, and the third is *showing up*.

Before acceptance an invitation must be sent. When change is the envelope of an invitation, we may not always recognized it as such. Invitations embedded in change probably come to us in more implicit and

5. Systems thinking might call this lead time a delay and classify it as a structural element. Biblical theology might look at delay as a grace and sign of God's long-suffering patience.

subtle ways than do formal invitations. Some come to us quietly, subtly, with early and weak signals. More often than not the weakness of the signal is a function of the volume of noise going on in our preoccupied minds and lives. But even if we are alert and paying attention, the invitations in change are often expressed nonverbally in wordless movements and actions wherein we detect a difference however subtle.

The good news is that most are fairly adept at reading wordless signals. Consider signals sent in the context of conversations. Often-cited studies[6] estimate that 55 percent of what is actually "heard" comes from body language, 38 percent comes from the tone of voice while a mere 7 percent of what is received is carried by the spoken words. The research confirms what most of us already know: actions speak louder than words. This holds for the invitations expressed in change as well.

Sometimes the signals are received, recognized and considered, and sometimes they are missed or dismissed. The scriptural record bears this out as well. Large chunks of historic narrative recount God repeatedly inviting the nation of Israel to do justice, love kindness and walk humbly with God.[7] Sometimes God invites directly, verbally, through prophets. At other times God invites without words: from unwitting nations engaged in military conflicts[8] to surprising turns of events, as when the entire city of Nineveh repents for Jonah,[9] or even the more commonplace, as when Ruth refuses to leave her mother-in-law Naomi, despite the desolate prospects for both.[10] Verbally and nonverbally, in story after story of change, God repeatedly invites the nation of Israel to change its way of thinking and acting.

That God sends out invitations embodied in change—with and without words—shouldn't really surprise us.[11] What actually is more surprising is how often we seem to ignore the probability that God is still inviting us today. Do we really need God to spell it out for us, or is it that God's nonverbal signals are so subtle we entirely miss the invitation?

The second stage begins when an invitation is accepted. *After acceptance* is analogous to what physicists call a state change. With invitations,

6. See the work of Albert Mehrabian on nonverbal communication.

7. Mic 6:8.

8. Biblical scholars often cite Isaiah's reference (Isa 45:1) to how God used the Persian King Cyrus as but an agent for God's own purposes.

9. Jonah 3:10.

10. Ruth 1:8–18.

11. Ps 19:1–4.

the state that changes is the social contract of the relationship. The relationship between the host and the invited is altered by acceptance. The invited make a commitment to the host to show up. The host, having already made a commitment, now, with acceptance from the invited, turns that commitment into an expectation. What was a *desire* of the host now becomes an expectation. Such a shift may carry implications for the resilience of an innovator's commitment, particularly in regards to the resistance innovators will encounter. In fact, when God's desire becomes God's expectation it can strengthen commitment and resolve.

Invitational dynamics have one more stage. When everything is ready and the event (or change) begins, those who accept the invitation turn commitment into presence, intention into action. They *show up*. This is also the moment when the host shows up as well. Mutual presence, of the One who is still creating and of the invited, comes together. The invitation is accepted *and* fulfilled. Shared presence and purpose with each other begins. This is when and where the company of God is "at hand."

GOD INVITING

When change and our response to it is viewed through a theological lens—as a divine invitation rather than an inconvenient interruption—we begin to understand change and our response in a new light. We can see our response more clearly as a commitment (to the host) to show up, freely, willingly and fully to participate in what the host has prepared for us. If God is still creating then what the host is preparing for us in change is a chance to contribute. Viewed as an invitation, change carries at least the possibility, if not the probability, that the host not only wants *us* to show up, but will be there as well.

The freedom of the invited to accept or decline is implicit. An invitation is not a requirement or a command. Accepting or declining the invitation has its own consequences and costs, to be sure. However, when a genuine invitation is accepted it is reasonable for the host to assume that the invited show up *wanting* to be there. The invited willingly participate without obligation or coercion. The desires of the host and the desires of the ones who accept come together. This is a potent union, particularly for creating new value.

Most veteran innovators recognize that a free and voluntary mind-set is essential for innovating. In contrast, an employee mind-set often proves insufficient. Without voluntary acceptance of change, many end up viewing themselves as victims of change, compelled or coerced by circumstances. Willing acceptance, however, enables us to be fully present for responding.

When the response aims to create new value, nothing less than our full attention and presence will do. When strings are attached, obligation easily creeps in. Compliance comes to shape the presence and posture of the invited. Participants compelled, coerced or under some external compulsion to show up, end up less prepared, less present, less giving and less committed to the occasion and to the host. For those who are not there under their own volition, the occasion is an inconvenience, an intrusion and ultimately, an interruption.

Sometimes acceptance implies that the invited will prepare.[12] At other times the only preparation possible is to show up. But whether prepared or not, an invitation implies that the host will prepare something ahead of time. This is not far from the common belief that God has plans for us.

AN INVITATION'S DEEPER PURPOSE

Underneath the protocols of invitations is something even more important, especially for innovating: a relationship. Behind every genuine invitation is a desire to establish, build and deepen a relationship. This may be the most important reason for reframing change as an invitation from God.

When value is created it is impossible to conceive the innovation much less create it without a relationship with the other for whom the value is intended. When it comes to innovating, nothing happens except out of relationships—relationships between people, between people and what they are learning, and between people and their ideas. This may be the deeper, underlying reason for the invitation, and it is certainly the foundation for a life with meaning and purpose, whether for a human being or for a commercial business. As Peter Drucker reminds us, the very purpose of a business is to create a customer.[13] This is not only a relationship. It is a relationship based on created value.

---

12. Matthew's version of Jesus' parable (Matt 22:11–14) reveals what might happen if one accepts the invitation and is not prepared, or at least appropriately dressed for the occasion.

13. Drucker, *Management*, 61.

While there are all types of relationships, it is instructive to array various types across a theoretical continuum. One side of the continuum might be called "means" and the other "ends." On the "means" side are relationships that serve some purpose other than the relationship itself. These relationships have a "give and get" or transactional character. Ultimately, relationships on this side of the continuum are more contractual than generous. They may serve the individual interests of the respective parties, but even if the interests are mutual, their respective gains are centered in each individual's own separate interests and serve the purposes of those separate interests. Transactional relationships are more about what one can *get out* of the relationship than *give to* it.

In contrast, on the "ends" side of the continuum are relationships that serve no other purpose than the common and shared interests of the relationship itself. These relationships tend to have a more generative, generous and trusting character. There is a giving and for-giving quality to them.

Innovations are conceived, born and nurtured on the generative side of this continuum. The value created may eventually migrate toward the transactional side. But it is born and nurtured on the generative side *before* moving over toward the transactional side. When start-ups or well-established enterprises try to create new value from the transactional side, efforts tend to be short-lived and rarely substantive. When we are too quick to calculate what we will get out of our efforts, or too anxious to show "outcomes" and quantitative impacts, innovating ends prematurely, partly because the effort has drifted over to the transactional side too soon. When relationships are given time and space to remain on the generative side of the continuum, however, new value can be created and nurtured and allowed to find forms that work for the intended.

A widespread but misguided belief is that entrepreneurs start out with the idea that they'll make it big and do so quickly. In reality, however, "successful entrepreneurs whatever their individual motivations create value by contributing" rather than trading or dealing.[14] Being other-oriented is a practical necessity for creating new value. Obsession with "what am I going to get out of it" cripples innovating efforts from the beginning. Contributing enables the entrepreneur to focus on real and substantial value for the one served. It is an entrepreneurial requirement essential to innovation.

14. Drucker, *Innovation and Entrepreneurship*, 34.

In a personal context, this selfless orientation toward the other is what Viktor Frankl observed in the most extreme conditions from his experiences in a concentration camp. Frankl discovered that those who seek their own happiness are likely *not* to find it. Happiness is a by-product, not a goal. The goal is to find meaning, particularly meaning in a purpose greater than your own self-interest.[15] Personal happiness comes from finding and pursuing that, or being found and pursued by it. Happiness, like profit, is a collateral consequence of pursuing value for someone else.

Whether the context is an entrepreneurial or personal one, investing in what one can *give to* the relationship leads to more value more quickly than concentrating on what one can *get out* of the relationship. The former is a generative act; the latter, a transactional one.

All of these implications are in play when we receive an invitation, whether we are conscious of them or not. Likewise, all of these conditions are present if we consider change as an invitation from God. Viewing change as an invitation instead of an interruption makes us more willing and able to accept, respond and participate in the opportunity to co-create new value in the company of God.

JESUS' ATTENTION TO INVITATIONAL DETAIL

The practical implications of invitations are nowhere more apparent in Scripture than in the fourteen chapter of Luke. Here Luke weaves together three distinct vignettes with Jesus saying something about invitations in each. The detail with which Jesus looks at invitations is striking. One reason for the intensity and granularity of Jesus' interest here is perhaps because these vignettes precede his enumeration of the onerous costs of discipleship. The consequences of accepting and following through on the invitation can be significant if not severe.[16]

Responding to change with an aim to create new value is not for the faint of heart. The consequences of acceptance are significant and demanding. For those who take up the challenges of discipleship or for those who take up the challenges of innovating, the sacrifices required

15. Frankl, *Man's Search for Meaning*, 145.

16. Luke 14:25–33, where accepting and following through on the invitation to follow Jesus means (1) hating those closest to you and even your own life, (2) carrying the cross, and (3) giving up all of your possessions.

and the consequences experienced are dear. Many are invited. Few follow through. In the company of God, however, God can and will do for us what we cannot do for ourselves.

Take a look at what Jesus said to the invited guests. Jesus first deals with those who have already accepted the invitation and shown up.[17] Jesus says, "When you are invited [and show up,] sit down at the lowest place, so that when your host comes, he may say to you, 'Friend, move up higher.'"

This is the third "state" we named in the dynamic of invitations. It reads more like an instruction set from Jesus on where to sit. Many might dismiss this as a trivial concern or an antiquated example of deferential social protocol. But for innovating it turns out to be as significant and substantive as it evidently was for Jesus.

What does this have to do with anything besides showing a humble deference to the host? Does it have anything to do with responding to change or creating new value?

Innovating proves difficult for those in preferred seating. Incumbents are typically those who occupy and hold these seats. Success experienced by incumbents, however, proves to be the enemy of innovation. It works against creating new value for others. An incumbent perspective tends to "over-stand" rather than understand. To truly understand the new realities change brings, one must view these new realities from the ground up.

The trajectory of over-standing goes up and over. The trajectory for understanding goes down and under. True understanding is born out of humility and looking at the context from below. The truth of this has been expressed in various ways. For example, MIT social psychologist Edgar Schein calls this trajectory the unlearning that necessarily precedes the deep learning of something new.[18] More recently C. Otto Scharmer points to the "U" as the shape of the path anyone must traverse if authentic understanding is to be realized.[19] Only through humility can we start to appreciate and understand. Scharmer convincingly suggests that before one can make any sense of change or even hope to create new value in response to it, one must go deeper, even to the point of letting go much of what one thought was true. This resonates with what I believe Jesus intended when he said, "Truly I tell you, unless you change and become like children, you

17. Luke 14:7–11.
18. Schein, "Anxiety of Learning."
19. Scharmer, *Theory U*, 27–47.

will never enter the kingdom of heaven."[20] It is not unlike the way he concludes this parable in Luke: "For all who exalt themselves will be humbled, and those who humble themselves will be exalted."[21]

Habitual bias for preferred seating distorts perception and blocks understanding. It is natural to want to extend our incumbency. But this will turn the invitation of change back into an interruption. Change will appear either an inconvenient interruption or a threatening disruption. Incumbents are by definition those who have the luxury of not having to learn.[22] As for the Pharisees with whom Jesus was sharing the meal when he told this parable, preferred seating was difficult to give up. But it is precisely this kind of seating that prevents us from accepting change, responding to it, and effectively co-creating new value with the company of God.

HOSTS

Between the first and the third parable[23] Jesus turns his attention to the role of the host.[24] This could be a special word to leaders. In contexts of innovating these hosts are often called "sponsors"—executives with the power, authority and resources to provide safe haven for otherwise vulnerable early stage efforts aimed at creating new value.

In Luke's retelling of it, Jesus speaks directly to his host, a leader of the Pharisees.[25] Jesus offers what appears to be advice about who should be on the host's guest list. A closer reading reveals the concern is not just about *who*. It is really about *why*. Jesus is interested in the host's motivation. The concern is about conflicts of interest, even the appearance of a conflict. "Do not invite your friends or your brothers or your relatives or your rich neighbors, in case they may invite you in return and you would be repaid." Rather, invite those who *cannot* repay, Jesus tells his host, because "you will be repaid at the resurrection of the righteous."

---

20. Matt 18:3.

21. Luke 14:11.

22. Attributed to the late Czech social and political scientist Karl W. Deutsch.

23. The second parable on invitations in Luke 14:15–24 is not referred to explicitly as a parable and may indeed be an extension of the first parable. However, in v. 16 Jesus seem to be starting the second parable (see Bovon, *Luke 2*, 364).

24. Luke 14:12–14.

25. Luke 14:1.

The implication is as striking as it is challenging. Giving more than receiving, creating value more than extracting it, is the primary motivation for innovating. For commercial organizations there is certainly a practical requirement to make a profit from the innovating effort. For individuals we would want to experience some satisfaction for our efforts and sacrifices. However, when profit becomes confused with purpose, innovating becomes harder to justify. When personal satisfaction becomes our interest, we can miss seeing and understanding what is of value to the other. Even change loses its invitational character. Transactions become more important than relationships and little if anything happens in creating new value. If new value is to be created, hosts must ask themselves why it should be created and why their organization is the one to attempt it. If intentions are to contribute—to give more than get—then the effort to create new value will likely be more aligned with the company of God.

When someone resolves to create value for another, initially the value being created is rarely clear, much less confirmed. The proposed value must be received and put to use by the one for whom the value is intended. It is essential to get an untested innovation into the hands of the one for whom it is designed. Experience "in use" precedes any trustworthy assignment of value. When the primary intentions are more about the expected return—what the innovator is going to get out of the deal—then a conflict of interest arises. The ensuing effort is suspect from the beginning. It becomes even more difficult to gain any experience for the untested innovation.

Early prototypes must be offered to customers to try out. These early prototypes are themselves invitational more than transactional. At this stage, the value being created has yet to be confirmed. The only way to confirm it is to invite those for whom the value is intended to try it out. If anything is sought "in return" it is the value of the potential relationship with the invitee and perhaps a chance to try again.

Evidence of positive and pure intent is inherent to the creative act, especially when the goal of what is being created is new value for another. Such creative effort does not happen out of transactions. It happens out of relationships—solid, trusting ones with plenty of mutual generosity and respect.

It is a bit surprising how many believe innovations emerge out of the transactional marketplace. They do not. Markets do not innovate, much less respond. Markets react. Markets also recognize and provide transactional access to new value to be sure. But the new value itself is created and nurtured elsewhere. It is this elsewhere that is often ignored even by those who are intent on extracting value from innovating.

Innovations always start with intentions that are more about what one can contribute than about what one can "get." An example can be found in what is still, despite some tough years, an icon of innovation, the Hewlett-Packard Company (HP). It was just this principle—contribution comes first, returns come later—that David Packard and Bill Hewlett turned into a regular practice in the early years of the company. Packard expressed it this way: "The key to HP's prospective involvement in any field is *contribution*. . . . We always asked, 'How can we make a contribution based on our strengths and our knowledge?' Then we'd ask, 'Who needs it?'"[26] The two founders of HP did not ask first what they would get from their effort. Rather, they asked themselves where they might be in a position to contribute value.[27]

The motivation of innovators should be on balance more about making a contribution, more about creating value, than on extracting returns. When leaders confuse profit with purpose, such confusion infects attitudes about change and disables efforts to create new value. This confusion happens often enough, frequently amplified by impatient time horizons and a surprising ignorance of the necessity for the "protected" space that caring and committed relationships require to nurture and raise an innovation.

This is a prime reason why innovation is so difficult for so many otherwise seemingly competent and able individuals and organizations. This is also where a theology of innovation should be able to make a significant contribution. Theology is deeply familiar with matters of greater purpose and relationships that serve no other purpose than the relationship itself. Transactional orientations can erode relationships built on love—both love of God and love of neighbor. This was a chronic problem recognized by the prophets.[28] And this will always be an issue when the question of value is center stage.

Theology is also familiar with the generative and creative dynamic that animates a gift and the giving of it. Lewis Hyde looks at these dynamics in an economic context in his book *The Gift*. Hyde's analysis affords

26. Packard, *HP Way*, 96–97.
27. Ibid., 146.
28. Mic 6:6–8.

a practical foil for an innovation theology to address the intersection of purpose, profits[29] and value creation.

Hyde observes that a gift behaves differently than a commodity. The sale of a commodity turns a profit. Gifts do not *earn* profit so much as they "give increase."[30] The "vector of increase in a gift exchange stays in motion by following the [gift], while in commodity exchange the increase stays behind as profit."[31] The very value we attempt to create when we innovate is diminished by the sheer extraction of a portion of it for profit. Attempts to account for the value *before* it is created or confirmed often shut down innovating efforts before they get off the ground.

Many who attempt to innovate often completely miss this necessary and inconvenient truth. This is especially the case in commercial contexts where pressures are great to calculate imagined returns even before the reality of the value is confirmed. Calculating anticipated returns, and then believing the calculations, often kills attempts to create new value before they start. Prototypes are never put into the hands of those for whom they are intended. Invitations are never sent, hosts step back from being hosts at all. And we are left with transactions instead of relationships.

THE INVITED

Luke's third vignette[32] deals with those invited who have yet to show up.

As the parable tells it, all of the invited declined. Each one ends up making excuses as to why they chose not to accept. Each has more important matters to attend to, including matters of property, projects and personal relationships. These are incumbent matters. Accepting and showing up would be an interruption. Word gets back to the host that all declined and, understandably, the host is angry.

Then something striking happens in Luke's telling of it. A distinct shift in word choice alone sends the signal. Luke suddenly stops using "invite"[33]—a word Luke uses no less than ten times in ten prior verses.[34]

29. Or outcomes from nonprofits.

30. Hyde, *Gift*, 38–39.

31. Ibid.

32. Luke 14:15–24.

33. Luke reserves one more use of invited (called) in his conclusion to the parable in v. 24 and this is to punctuate and contrast the consequences for those who were invited but refused.

34. Luke 14:7–17.

When all have declined, the host stops inviting and starts enrolling, even compelling them to attend. The host has his servant *bring in* the poor, the crippled, the blind and the lame—those who not only cannot repay, but may have a harder time showing up on their own. These need assistance just to get themselves there. Even after these have been brought in, the host's house is still not filled. Here Luke uses the word *compel* to describe what the host will do to fulfill his plans and accomplish his goals.

This is the same word Paul used to describe the divine constraint he felt he was under.[35] It is the same word Aristotle used in his *Metaphysics*, meaning the force of "immanent necessity"—a condition that is essential (in Latin it is *conditio sine qua non*)—without which the event would not happen.[36] In the Old and New Testaments the word means "constraint."[37] In other words, change eventually constrains and compels as and when its original invitation is ignored or declined. Our response to it becomes a necessity and obligation, no longer the free, willing and voluntary response that was desired at first with the invitation.

Luke leaves us with an image of God's ever widening reach, a reach that is not thwarted by the lack of acceptance from those on the original guest list—those who declined. God's will in change "*will* be done," whether the invitation offered is accepted or not. The new is often rejected in its early form, often by the very entrenched and incumbent interests it was intended to serve. But eventually, like spreading ripples on the surface of the water, the invitation shows up in ever widening places, sometimes where least expected. This is a recognizable pattern in both change and innovation.

When change first becomes apparent we are invited to respond. The invitation may expire, but the change does not. It will eventually happen with or without us, regardless whether we accept or decline. Eventually change becomes impossible to resist, regardless of our efforts to ignore, delay or deny.

Invitations have time limits. Change does not. Change keeps moving. It does not wait. God still creates. When the invitation expires, unaccepted, it turns change from an invitation to an obligation, from an opportunity to create new value to a necessity. As a necessity it forces

---

35. 1 Cor 9:16.

36. *TDNT*, s.v. "anake" (1:344).

37. Ibid.

adjustments and coping, which in turn leave us with little inclination or time to respond. We react.

There are consequences to whether we respond to change and how. The consequences affect us more than they do the change itself. Any host would prefer the invited to accept. It's reasonable to assume that God also would prefer us to accept the invitation and show up and participate freely, willingly and under our own volition. However, whether we accept or not, the banquet will be held, the change will happen, with or without us.

Luke concludes the parable with a description that sounds very much like a prescription. It describes the consequences for those who decline. They do not get to taste the dinner. They do not get to participate, make a contribution, or even respond.

This extended parable in Luke seems to leave us with a choice. In our response to change, will we choose to be those who make it happen, those who let it happen or those who are left wondering what just happened?

CONCLUSION

An invitation mind-set toward change can help us to view change as something to accept rather than something to insulate and defend ourselves against. Seen as an invitation, we should be more ready to explore the change, more willing to appreciate the new realities emerging in it, and more prepared to leave behind what is likely not going to work. We should be more able to create the new that is more valuable for others. This invitational attitude toward change will likely be at the heart of any innovation theology.

If there is any merit in reframing substantive change as an invitation from God, not simply an interruption, then it is this invitation to innovate in and with the company of God. This is good news—not necessarily easy or comforting news—but surely good news. For when an organization or individual attempts to respond to change in a meaningful way, it is something one organization or person cannot do alone. Accepting an invitation implies we will be in the company of others. And when that company is the company of God, I know of no other news that could be better.

As we accept the invitation God is extending to us in change, we not only begin to accept the new realities that come along with it. We also accept an inclusion in the company of God, the One for whom all things are possible.

Proposing that God does have something to do with change, and does have an interest in how we choose to respond, makes a theological claim. Such a claim is not simply theoretical or theological. It is also practical.

By discerning and keeping God's interests in mind, both in change and our responses to it, we will be better able to accept change and even make the kind of sense out of change that is required if any new value is going to be created. Reframing change as an invitation rather than an interruption enables us to become creative contributors rather than reluctant reactors.

Innovating in the company of God has as much to do with our acceptance of God's invitation as it does with God's accompaniment with us in the particulars of our response.

This is a company operating at the intersection of the kingdom of heaven and the kingdoms of earth, an intersection with which we should be familiar. It is where we live.

CONVERSATION STARTERS

1. What current changes are most clearly invitations from God? What are the symptoms and signals that suggest God's interest and invitation?

2. Where might God be inviting innovations now and why?

3. Is making a contribution or competition more important in our willingness to innovate? Why? Might theology suggest the former and economics the latter? Can/should these two motivations for innovation be balanced? If so, how?

4. If generosity is so important to (early) innovation, how can it be nurtured and extended, particularly when it is so vulnerable?

Making Sense of Change

7

Making Sense in the Company of God

What are human beings that you are mindful of them?[1]

ACCEPTING CHANGE IS ONE thing. Making sense of it is another. Both are prerequisites for responding to change, both required for innovating, and both engage the head and heart.

We may never fully accept change unless and until we make sense of it. Likewise, we may never really make enough sense of change until we accept it. The line where making sense starts and acceptance ends may not be so easy to draw.

The difficulty in drawing such a line comes in part from familiarity. Making sense is something most of us are doing all the time, whether we are conscious of it or not. More pronounced occasions of change may cause us to be more aware of our own sense-making, if only because we have to work harder at it. But even on these occasions we are unlikely to pay much attention to *how* we make sense of change. Like the sawyer with too much work, it is difficult to take time out to sharpen the saw.

Sharpening the saw of sense-making is what this essay is about. What follows considers *how* we make sense of change and demonstrates how a theological perspective brings practical benefit to these sense-making efforts.

---

1. Ps 8:4.

Because making sense is so second nature to us, it makes sense here to clarify what sense-making is and is not. An example is always helpful, albeit a dramatic one.

In August of 1966, a friend and colleague, Dr. Stuart Brown, was enjoying his new status as an assistant professor of psychiatry at Baylor University. A call came to him from Texas governor John Connolly. The governor was requesting a full investigation into what quickly came to be known as the Texas Tower Massacre.

Charles Whitman had just ascended the tower at the University of Texas in Austin, killing fifteen and wounding thirty-one before being gunned down by an off-duty police officer and a courageous citizen. Even before Whitman climbed the tower he had killed his wife and mother. Seventeen dead. Over thirty wounded. Few of Whitman's victims knew him; few were known by him.

Connolly wanted to make sense of this senseless event. How many others like Whitman were out there? Could anything be done to prevent this in the future? Stuart took charge of the psychiatric evaluation of Whitman, perhaps the most crucial part of the investigation—a formal and well-funded sense-making effort.

When the investigation began, most speculated Whitman was a raving, deranged and paranoid maniac. But a surprisingly different picture emerged from extensive interviews with people who knew Whitman. He turned out to be a "seemingly loving husband and son; an ex-Marine, who had been the youngest Eagle Scout in the history of the Boy Scouts."[2] The normal, achieving, even impressive image in the foreground was shadowed by a background of an over-controlling father who incessantly abused Whitman's mother, along with a barely noticed but surprisingly lifelong pattern, or absence of one: Charles Whitman never played.

Stuart confessed to me that at first he really didn't think much of Whitman's own absence of play. It was a minor note in the report to Connolly. But when other studies of dark and nefarious cases came to Stuart for investigation—a dubious result of the notoriety of this case—he began to notice a recurring pattern. The pattern has now come to be called "play deprivation." What Stuart first saw in Whitman's background showed up in the psychiatric evaluations of others whose crimes were as heinous as the resulting carnage was tragic. Since the confirmation of this pattern,

2. Brown, *Play*, 94.

Stuart has given the better part of his professional career to tracking the evidentiary science behind play.[3]

What makes Stuart's experience such a good example of sense-making is the presence and sequence of several factors.[4]

First, someone noticed something that no one else had noticed. It is at first *noticed* as something that doesn't quite fit—something that stands out in contrast to the flow of things. In this case it was the absence of play.

Second, what was noticed becomes *noted*. The note is published or made available to a broader community, allowing what one person notes to be noticed by others.

Third, there was some *delay* before others actually start to notice what was noted. Even Stuart himself did not pay as much attention at first to what he noted in Whitman's evaluation, at least not until he started noticing a similar pattern in other cases. Such delays arise because experts tend to overestimate "the likelihood that they would surely know about the phenomenon if it actually were taking place."[5]

Which leads to a fourth factor in the sense-making sequence: how *identity and reputation* of the one who is doing the noticing and noting affects how the sense is made.

The sense we make of change is often questioned or rejected by the one who makes the first sense to begin with. Experts learn to keep to themselves the first sense they make. This is due to the near universal experience of encountering events that at first seemed so implausible most of us hesitate to report it for fear we will not be believed. "Because I don't know about it, it must not be going on." The hesitation "not only discourages curiosity . . . but also frequently creates an antagonistic stance" toward the newly noted.[6] This self-imposed silence constrains and delays the sharing and ultimate validation of the sense made. Identity, reputation and even parochial interests appear to get in the way of making a sense that can benefit others.

While Stuart's experience is dramatic, all of us have our own bank of sense-making experiences. Some of those experiences come from making sense of the movements and contrasts that interrupt the continuity and flow of our lives. Some of these movements and contrasts we would

---

3. See the National Institute for Play website (nifplay.org).

4. Weick, *Sensemaking in Organizations*, 2.

5. Ibid.

6. Ibid.

call life changing. Others might be merely bumps on the road or potholes in our way. Some changes are harder to make sense of than others. As we get older we accumulate more sense-making experience and we become more aware of just how much we don't know. At the same time we can become more tolerant of the imprecision of the sense we *can* make, and the perfect sense that we cannot.

Our own interests, identity and biases shape the sense we make for ourselves, even when it makes little or no sense for the other. Likewise, what makes sense to the other may not make complete sense to us. But if we are to create new value for another, we can only succeed when we see both sense and value made, and the other sees it too.

Typically the sense we make of change we make for our selves first. When we do, the sense we make is about orienting or reorienting the way we see and understand the world, in light of what just changed. Making sense of change for others, however, requires us to express and embody the sense we make in what the other finds valuable.

When we make sense without the company of God—without a theological perspective—the sense we make may have a shorter shelf-life and be of less value. It's likely to make any related innovating effort more challenging than it already is. Making sense of change in the company of God, however, can make all the difference in the world, not only for the other, but for ourselves as well.

SENSE-MAKING

Interpreting is not sense-making. Sense-making surely includes interpreting but is not the same.

What is interpreted is typically a static text or spoken word. In contrast, making sense has us confronting dynamic, ambiguous contexts with ill-defined boundaries. Creative poking and prodding are called for. An interpreter's detached and objective view is necessary but insufficient. Probing the environment around us—the living contexts that we want to make sense of—produces feedback and this feedback tells us something fresh, real and trustworthy. It gives us direct experience with which to learn more about how our environment responds.

Interpreting concentrates on discovery and an accurate and complete diagnosis. In contrast, sense-making includes both invention and discovery—inventing the probes and discovering what the context "says" back to us when it is probed. Those who study sense-making suggest that when trying to make sense of change we are typically more interested in effective engagement than accurate assessment, timely response more than thorough analysis, and even creating new value for others more than ensuring objective diagnosis of the situation.

Making sense of change is never confined to cool cognition. Emotions and memories affect and infect the entire sense-making process. This is especially the case when someone or something precious to us is at stake. From sensors that receive the signals to the interpretive cognitive processing mechanisms embedded in our thinking, even to the way we form the meaning we "make," sense-making is an open, complex and dynamic process, vulnerable to all sorts of missed signals, distortions, misinterpretations and misunderstandings.

The perceptual, cognitive, affective and memory mechanisms involved in our individual sense-making comprise a complex tangle of interwoven and iterating sensors, processors, memories and feedback loops. The sense we make is really revealed, discovered, and invented as much as it is made. For an individual, the sense-making system may be more neurological, though it is not without a social dimension. For an organization, the system may be more social, though it is not without cognitive and affective dimensions.

Several factors set sense-making apart from other ways of explaining things, like understanding, interpretation and attribution,[7] partly because sense-making is not done in the abstract. Rather it happens within our identities, our near term projects and the broader narratives of which we are a part.

Identity. Sense-making is constrained by the sense-maker's own sense of self. Who we imagine ourselves to be and where we are—in life, in career, in some imagined pecking order—will influence what we sense and notice to begin with.

I learned this early in my experience facilitating small groups of scientists and engineers called together for problem-solving and invention. Collaborative problem-solving is not just about finding inventive solutions together. It's also about making sense together. While the explicit purpose of each meeting was to solve whatever the stated problem was,

7. Ibid., 17. Weick names seven factors—identity, retrospect, enactment, social, ongoing, extracted cues, and plausibility. I have condensed his list down to three for the sake of brevity and, of course, for the sense I am attempting to make in the three essays of this section.

there were always other "agendas." Part of the job of a facilitator is to make sure these other agendas don't divert energy and focus from the stated purpose which these other agendas have a way of doing.

Anticipating these other agendas is impossible. There are simply too many of them, and too much variety, complexity and transience to make it worth giving any of these agendas any attention at all, except for one. The one exception turns out to be the same for every individual at every meeting, regardless of the individual. It's an agenda that accompanies each of us all the time: to establish, build or maintain self-esteem. It is a very safe bet that this agenda is current and active for every person, always. Should this identity agenda in any way be threatened, it can and will sabotage the stated purpose.

As a result, I learned subtle and efficient ways to attend to these identity agendas for each individual: giving him credit for whatever contribution was made, or writing up her idea in words that she used, or acknowledging each by name. Rarely did I ever encounter individuals whose identity needs exceeded the attention deposits I could give. When identity needs are quiet, there is less noise from within to interfere with a full-bodied attention to the task at hand. But when worried about establishing, maintaining or building our identity, individually or organizationally, the worry is likely to interfere with the clarity of perception and reception of the signals change is sending.

Identity influences the sense we make and how we make it and the very things we sense to begin with. If identity is in crisis or threatened in any way, it will distort the field of our perceiving. A still,[8] secure and quiet identity is unlikely to interfere, deny or even delude the sense-making effort.

Current Projects. Most of us are always in the middle of things, and the things with the middles we are in are our projects. When change muddles these middles we instinctually use our current projects to help us make sense.

When change comes, among the first questions asked is whether the change or any part of it is relevant. "Does it matter?" Does this change threaten a delay or serendipitously advance the cause of any of our projects? Our criterion of relevance has more to do with what's on our plate than with the new realities emerging in the change. If we cannot see and

8. Ps 46:10.

find a way to do something about the change in the context of our current projects, then we are more likely to ignore it than try to make sense of it.

To a large extent our current projects determine what is relevant to us. Our projects—individually and collectively—filter what is signal from what is just noise. These filters are also woven with the threads of our experience and expertise. What we imagine is relevant helps us filter *out* what we can ignore and filter *in* what we can use. Relevancy is partly a function of our current set of projects and partly a function of our previous experience and accumulated knowledge. In short, our current projects, experience and knowledge define what is relevant and calibrate the porosity of our filters.

Most of us have more than one project on our plates, not to mention a variety of different experiences and knowledge bases upon which to draw. This variety and plurality is both good news and bad news. The good news is that we have a rich and robust set of experiences, knowledge and projects we will use to make sense of any change we encounter. The bad news is that there are many possible meanings that can be "made," depending upon the variety of projects on our plate and the experience banks from which we choose to draw.

As a result, ambiguity is the challenge more than uncertainty when we make sense of change. The irony here is how often we think we need more information when we are trying to make sense of change. What we really need is clarity even more than certainty. Uncertainty is a problem that is solved with more and better information. Ambiguity and confusion are problems solved with greater clarity. What is needed when change overwhelms and confuses is not more information. What is needed is clarity about preferences to help the sense-maker determine what matters.[9] Our current projects, along with our past experiences and accumulated knowledge can help address the ambiguity and even the uncertainty challenge. But our projects, experiences and knowledge will always remain a limiter.

Longer-Term Narrative. Our longer-term aspirations are another influence on how we make sense of change.

One of the first things we ask is whether the change is more threat or opportunity. Answers will depend largely on how the change intersects with our longer-term goals and directions, or perhaps more importantly,

---

9. Weick, *Sensemaking*, 27–28.

how it advances or hinders our progress in the narrative flow and direction of our lives. This is the case for both individuals and organizations.

Retrospective and prospective views play into how we make meaning in the present. Having a sense of where we have been and where we are headed gives us a narrative within which to make sense of what just happened, whatever it is, and whether it is relevant or not. The plots and subplots of our individual unfolding narratives help us locate ourselves and understand the present, especially when change appears without sense or warning.

Interestingly enough it is plausibility even more than accuracy (and verifiability) that contributes more to the sense we try to make. Karl Weick puts it this way:

> In an equivocal, postmodern world, infused with the politics of interpretation and conflicting interests, and inhabited by people with multiple shifting identities, an obsession with accuracy seems fruitless, and not of much practical help, either. Of much more help are myths, metaphors, fables, epics and paradigms. Each of these resources contains a good story . . . [and stories] explain [and] energize.[10]

MAKING SENSE IN THE COMPANY OF GOD

Theology deals in stories that explain and energize. In fact, it is the very purpose of theology to make sense of the stories we are living, not just to explain but also to energize, not just to bring understanding, but also hope. Theology contributes to the way we make sense by bringing a transcendent, deeper or greater purpose to all three of these sense-making factors—our identity, our current projects and our longer-term narrative.

Theology can quiet the needs of our identities and reminds us that we are creatures of the Creator's making, beloved children of Our Heavenly Father, and servants of a company and mission that is greater than our own, as the servant songs in Isaiah so potently remind us.[11] In regards to our current projects, theology assumes the potential in each of these projects, no matter how seemingly mundane or secular. Everyday projects can carry what Paul Tillich calls our ultimate concern.[12] And in

10. Ibid., 61.

11. Isa 42:1–9; 49:1–12; 50:4–9; 52:13—53:12.

12. Tillich, *Systematic Theology*, 1:13.

regards to our long-term narrative, theology invites us to see ourselves as participants in an ongoing and larger narrative of the company of God.

Without a theological perspective, making sense will be more difficult, gaining clarity more vulnerable to the quest for more data, and filtering out the noise more challenging. Theology may be essential to sense-making in general, and especially useful in making sense of change.

Like theology, innovating itself is also an act of sense-making, especially in regards to change. Change was central to what management thinker Peter Drucker described as essential to innovators. These entrepreneurial people are

> not content simply to improve on what already exists, or to modify it. They try to create new and different values and new and different satisfactions, to convert a "material" into a "resource," or to combine existing resources in a new and more productive configuration. And it is change that always provides the opportunity for the new and different. *Systematic innovation therefore consists in the purposeful and organized search for changes, and in the systematic analysis of the opportunities such changes might offer for economic or social innovation.*[13]

Both innovating and theology are essentially sense-making efforts. Combining them into an integrated effort seems like a reasonable, if not practical, thing to do. Such combination and integration might take the best sense-making practices from both in order to find better ways of making sense of change than either one could do on its own.

MORE THAN PROCESSED INFORMATION

Even without an explicit theological perspective, many continue to describe how we make sense using an information-processing metaphor. Such a model assumes that we first sense what is going on around us, and even within us, from a diverse array of sensors—eyes, ears, nose, tongue and tactile nerve endings distributed throughout our bodies. Then we process the electrochemical signals these distributed sensors deliver to the brain, sometimes consciously, sometimes not. This processing many call cognition, which is not only affected by the signals it receives from sensors, but also from stored signals that come from memory, hence recognition.

13. Drucker, *Innovation and Entrepreneurship*, 34–35, italics in original.

Using the operations of a computer to characterize how we make sense is understandable. The dominant imagination can't help but be influenced by the pervasiveness of computational devices and repeated declarations that we are living in the information age and operating in the knowledge economy. Digital choreographies of electrons do show some analogous affinities for the electrochemical firings of synaptic structures in our brains.

However well it works as a metaphor though, it just doesn't sound all that plausible. The realities of how we make sense are more open-ended, social and organic than the rather closed, individual and deterministic processes programmed in computers. Describing what happens in our brains when we make sense as information-processing is seductively familiar but intuitively troubling, and quite possibly dangerously inaccurate.

The information-processing analogy breaks down like other mismatches between the metaphors we use to name complex systems and the nature of those systems. The metaphors may be familiar but they don't quite fit. Russell Ackoff points to these mismatches as seductively misleading classifications. For Ackoff the critical variable for classification is choice,[14] a variable that is particularly relevant in making sense of change. Theology can help us understand and even clarify the importance of choice in making sense.[15]

Ackoff suggests four types of systems, classified by where choice shows up within these systems. The four he names as deterministic, animated, social and ecological. A system that has no choice, either in its constituent parts or as a whole—like automobiles, fans, and clocks—is *deterministic*. A system wherein the parts have no choice but the whole does—animals, humans and other living organisms—is an *animated* system. Systems that have the capability of choice in both parts and as a whole—like organizations, communities or whole societies—these are *social* systems. And finally, systems where the parts are capable of choice but the whole cannot choose, these systems are ecologies or *ecosystems*.

When we use a deterministic metaphor (e.g., computer) to describe an animated system (e.g., sense-making) we mismatch the metaphor with the reality it is intended to describe. These mismatches produce less

---

14. Ackoff, *Re-Creating the Corporation*, 21.

15. Moser, *Elusive God*, 55–60.

than desirable results.[16] The way we make sense as an individual—to the extent that we really make sense alone—is more of an animated or social system than it is deterministic. The way we make sense as an organization is more of a social system than it is deterministic.

The information-processing metaphor for sense-making assumes not only that there is sense to be made from the information processed. It also assumes that what is meant by information is commonly understood. Both of these assumptions simply don't bear the weight of closer examination.

Look more closely at what is meant by information. In the late 1980s Milan Zeleny and Russell Ackoff contributed to what has now become a standard way of differentiating data, information, knowledge, understanding and wisdom.[17] It is commonly referred to as the "information hierarchy." All levels of the hierarchy are involved in making sense.

Twenty years after Ackoff's earliest version of the hierarchy he reexpressed his original with characteristic clarity. Here is how he described the hierarchy:

> There are five types of content in the human mind: data, information, knowledge, understanding, and wisdom. They form a hierarchy: information is more valuable than data, knowledge more valuable than information, understanding more valuable than knowledge, and wisdom more valuable than understanding. Nevertheless schools and organizations of all types tend to focus on the lower-valued aspects of mental content (especially information) rather than on the more highly valued understanding and wisdom.
>
> *Data* consists of symbols that represent properties of objects and events. For example, street addresses designate locations using numeric and alphabetic symbols. Inventories consist of numbers attached to various items identified alphabetically. These too are data.
>
> *Information* consists of data that have been processed to be useful. They are related much as iron ore is to iron. Very little can be done with iron ore (data) but once it is converted to iron (information) it has very many uses. Information is contained in descriptions, answers to questions that begin with words such as who, what, when, and how many.

16. Ibid., 30.

17. Ackoff, "From Data to Wisdom," 3–9; and Zeleny, "Management Support Systems," 59–70.

Knowledge as know-how is contained in instructions, answers to questions that begin with "how to." It is one thing to know in what city some activity is located—information—but another to know how to get there—knowledge. It is one thing to know that an automobile can carry you from one place to another—information—but another to know how to get there—knowledge.

It is yet another matter to know why a person wants to go there. Explanations are contained in answers to questions beginning with why. They provide *understanding*.

Data, information, knowledge, and understanding all can contribute to the efficiency with which we can pursue objectives; with whether we do things right.

Wisdom, on the other hand, is concerned with effectiveness, whether we do the right thing. Wisdom is contained in evaluations. It provides a person with a willingness to make short-term sacrifices in order to make longer-term gains.

There is a significant difference between doing something right and doing the right things. The more efficiently we do the wrong thing, the "wronger" we become. When we correct an error committed in pursuing the wrong thing, we become "wronger." If we commit an error doing the right things and correct it we become "righter." Therefore, it is better to do the right thing wrong and correct it than to do the wrong thing right.[18]

Outside the company of God, without a theological perspective this hierarchy is left unframed. *In* the company of God the hierarchy is framed with and by the purposes of God and the recognition of our own limitations. The Apostle Paul made this observation so concisely and beautifully in his first letter to the Corinthians.[19]

In a mere thirteen verses Paul frames what we in the information age and knowledge economy so often leave unframed. Paul frames it with the purposes of the company of God—to love—and with the reminder that all our data, information, knowledge, understanding and wisdom is partial and incomplete. In fact, even our sensing is "in a mirror," not a window. We are constantly distracted by the reflection of our own image, our own interests and our own identities. And not only is it a mirror, it is "dim." In the Greek the word "dimly" actually means riddle. The English word for it is enigma—"a perplexing mysterious, or unexplained thing."[20]

18. Ackoff, *Differences*, 54–55.

19. 1 Cor 13.

20. *New Shorter Oxford English Dictionary*, s.v. "enigma."

Early in his first letter to the church in Corinth Paul takes on both the top and the bottom of this information hierarchy. Paul says that some—the Greeks—desire wisdom while others—the Jews—desire data.[21] But both wisdom and data, and all that is in between, are framed by the wisdom of God at the top and bottom of the frame. The enigma[22] in the center of the frame is the mysterious reality of the sense made in Christ crucified. This center is a "stumbling block" and "foolishness" to those who place their bets on data and human wisdom, whose information hierarchy is left theologically unframed.

This is not to imply that content up and down the information hierarchy is senseless and without value. It is to say, however, that what we know and understand, and the data and information that feeds both, is always partial and incomplete. It is also to say that when our incomplete understanding and wisdom is framed by the purposes of the company of God, this incompleteness is not the handicap it is when we try to make sense without a theological perspective, especially when aiming to create new value for others.

NOT JUST IN THE BRAIN

Many cognitive scientists assume that the brain is where all the "processing" or sense-making occurs. "Cephalocentric" is what neurologist Frank Wilson calls this prevalent but mistaken assumption.[23] Wilson makes a persuasive case for a more distributed sense-making. Wilson contends that not only the hands but the whole body is engaged in making sense. It doesn't all happen in the brain.

Making sense is not merely some cognitive processing function that occurs in cortical matter where data feeds are processed, inputs from sensors are compared with retrieved patterns stored in memory, and thought outputs are produced. Rather

> both the desire and the capacity to learn are present in all of us, and both are difficult (though not impossible) to extinguish. Both grow, take shape, and continually reinforce one another through the action of the many seen and unseen hands that will touch us, move us, guide us, challenge us, and protect us for as

21. 1 Cor 1:22.

22. Wink, *Human Being*, 19–34.

23. Wilson, *Hand*, 295 ("sense-making" added).

> long as we live. The desire to learn is reshaped continuously as
> brain and hand vitalize one another, and the capacity to learn
> grows continuously as we fashion our own personal laboratory
> for making things,[24]

and for making sense as well; with brains, yes; but also, hands; ours, others and God's.

Wilson and others[25] will not let us rest comfortably imagining that we make sense like computers process information. The image of the detached, objective scientist, while potent and pervasive, is no longer tenable either as description or prescription for making sense.[26]

Making sense is in the *making*. This is not confined to cognitive processing in the brain but involves where and how we interact, engage and "interface" (to borrow a word from systems thinking) with the social and physical world around us. We may be able to imagine ourselves as distinct and detached individuals. But while we may be able to imagine this, reality will not let us escape being a participant in our particular social and physical environments.

Theology has known this for sometime. It's in the truth of what's called the *imago Dei*—the image of God. We first encounter the *imago Dei* very early in Scripture. In the first chapter of the first book it shows up as a foundational assumption of sorts. We are made in the image of God. And the only image of God we have at that point in Scripture comes from the previous twenty-five verses. The image is of a God who makes or creates, including making sense. If we are made in God's image, then we too are not only God's creations—God's creatures. We are creators ourselves, or at least co-creators. This image of God is an inescapable characteristic of who we are.

We create. We make sense, sometimes well and sometimes poorly. We do this in the *making*, whether it is making the sense we are able to make, or in enacting and forming that sense in relationships, products,

---

24. Ibid.

25. Weick, *Sensemaking in Organizations*, 44.

26. The Heisenberg uncertainty principle in quantum mechanics and the related observer effects in physics no longer allow us the option of being "uninvolved." In 1927 Werner Heisenberg first proposed (and it was subsequently confirmed) that there is a fundamental limit to the precision with which certain pairs of simultaneous physical properties at the quantum level can be known. What Heisenberg proposed for quantum dynamics was an observer effect that also applies to other areas of physics—that the observer alters what is observed.

policy, processes or problems solved. This is not only what we do. It is who we are.

This starting assumption may itself prove to be central to innovation theology. In fact, it may turn out to be what living a meaningful life requires of us—creating new value for others. If so, this implies that innovating is not some optional activity, but an essential act of living a life of meaning and purpose.

If there is any element of truth to this, then the sense we make about sense-making itself will recognize the inescapability of our entanglement with our own environment. This is a difficult thing for those of us who have grown up in what is an individualistic and self-centered culture. Imaging ourselves not as the center of our own lives but non-centric parts of a wider social and physical fabric doesn't come easily to us. Thinking of ourselves as supporting cast members rather than the central character feels strange. However, it is likely closer to the truth of the social and physical fabric of reality itself. It is certainly more aligned with a theological perspective.

A MODEL

When we make sense of change the sense we make will remain significantly handicapped without the influence of a theological perspective. As a result, a model is in order.

First, projecting sense-making on the "bigger screen" of how organizations make sense can help us visualize sense-making better than what may happen inside an individual where sense-making is more compact, integrated and autonomous. Such a projection also accounts for the social influences that are undoubtedly at work. The model comes from my experience with organizations' attempts to not only make sense of external changes but to convert the sense made into new value for others.

Picture three interoperating subsystems—sensing, interpreting and remembering—along with an ample set of feedback loops that enable these subsystems to interoperate. Many organizations have some form of these capabilities, often implicit and ungoverned. But whether explicitly managed or not, these capabilities directly influence the adaptive capability of the organization to respond to its external environment.

Sensing. Having multiple and varied sensors is essential. In an organization these sensors are people (not so much devices), each attuned to different interests, sources and frequencies. People who are naturally forward thinkers[27] may have their own way of taking in information, the most classic and well-known classification for which may be the Myers-Briggs Type Indicator. A variety of sensors brings robustness to an organization's ability to sense its environment. Who these forward thinkers are is very important. Not everyone is. The mix can be deliberately balanced or biased, depending upon the inclinations of the organization.

For example, if the immediate task is to overcome the organization's own blind spots or identify threats or opportunities, then diversity is essential. On the other hand, if the task is more oriented to preempting an organization's own autoimmune responses to change, then a sufficient representation of senior executives and resource stewards among the forward thinkers will be important.

Interpreting. Having some kind of mechanism that periodically brings inside what is sensed on the outside is necessary. Bringing outside forward thinkers together to creatively and collaboratively make sense goes a long way toward reducing perceived ambiguities, if not uncertainties. The results of such conversational collaborations are both interpretive *and* generative. These collaborations produce both shared meaning and common commitment in response to change. Conversations like these, whether formal or informal, turn out to be essential for creating new value. The sense made often describes both the foreground and the background—the context from which value derives.

While the metaphor of central processing may be useful to describe this interpreting subsystem, it is too computational. This processing should include rigorous analysis to be sure. But by no means should it be left to analysis alone. Analytical, interpretive *and* generative thinking are essential. This is why a computational (information processing) model misses the point. Sense-making can certainly start with observations which lead to discovery. However, sense-making must also engage in invention.[28] Both discovery and invention are essential to making sense.

Remembering. What is remembered and how it is remembered is essential to making sense as well. What an organization remembers will significantly influence the sense it makes but also what it senses to begin

27. David Kelley, founder of the design firm IDEO, refers to these people as "T" types: individuals who have, because of their position, experience or both, a broad perspective and an ability to go deep into the details of at least one relevant specialty.

28. Lester and Piore, *Innovation*; Weick, *Sensemaking in Organization*, 87, 91, 185–87.

with. The organization's memory may itself be comprised of three different types: traditional, short-term and future. Think of these as different types of pattern banks.

Traditional memory stores all types of routines and knowledge bases that could be regarded as important parts of the organization's intellectual assets. Like the autonomic memory in a human, what is in this memory is well known and understood by years of repeated experience. This memory can produce orthodoxies and filters that prevent new signals from even being recognized as signals. However, there is much knowledge contained in this kind of memory as well.

In *short-term memory* are recent experiences the organization has that have been formally reviewed for lessons learned. There is also likely much tacit knowledge adjacent to short-term memory that could be converted into an explicit form and included in this short-term memory. Often the contents of this memory include recent successes and failures and even hypotheses regarding the root causes.

In *future memory* are scenarios—narratives that are plausible and provocative—of what may and could occur but has not yet happened. These scenarios represent glimpses into the external landscape of the organization's future that differ from the organization's projected trajectory. Without this third type of memory the other two will eventually turn core capabilities into core rigidities.[29]

Recognition operates with all three of these memories and plays a special role for enabling sensing, interpreting and remembering to interoperate effectively. It is by recognizing not only past but also future patterns that sensors (people) are encouraged to attend to what they might otherwise regard as "noise" without the pattern having been explicitly expressed.[30]

For recognition, Karl Weick speaks about what he calls "minimal sensible structures." These are many and varied but each provides a past frame into which we naturally and often unconsciously place cues from our present experience.[31] Meaning is made when we are able to construct a relation between a frame we have used in the past and a cue we experience in the present. This is what "connecting the dots" means.

29. Leonard-Barton, "Core Capabilities and Core Rigidities," 111–25.

30. A prototypical story of Royal Dutch Shell's scenario-enabled ability to anticipate OPEC before any of the other oil companies illustrates the practical benefit of scenarios. See also Schwartz, *Art of the Long View*, 53–56.

31. Weick, *Sensemaking in Organizations*, 111.

Frames have their own vocabularies. These vocabularies name cues arising in our current experience. According to Weick, types of frames include vocabularies of society (ideologies), of organizations (operating assumptions or givens), of work (paradigms), of coping (theories of action), of predecessors (tradition) and of sequence and experience (stories).

Theology appears to offer a rich set of minimal sensible structures for our sense-making. We need look no further than the stories, images, parables, poetry and songs of Scripture. Look deeper, however, and a theological perspective may offer even more than some additional sense-making structures. Given how theology incorporates not only tradition and story but also ideologies, assumptions, paradigms and theories of action, theology offers "master" sense-making structures. I don't believe it an exaggeration to say that, for Christians the gospel narrative is *the* sense maker. It has the ability to help us describe and prescribe or to frame, if you will, our present experience of change. It offers us ways to make sense that are perhaps more robust than any other minimal sensible structure alone.

A theological perspective, however, can become a closed conformance to orthodoxy rather than an open appreciation of what is experienced. When this happens, theology loses whatever humility it might have had, and the truth becomes a fixed proposition without life. In these instances, the vocabulary of the frame excludes rather than includes, narrows rather than expands, and constrains rather than liberates, the sense-maker. We force-fit the new realities of change into black and white distinctions that preserve the frame more than accept and appreciate the reality experienced. This turns sense-making into control taking. And it seldom works for very long, especially with change and innovation.

Despite this risk, sense-making with a theological perspective is more practical and encouraging than without one. With a theological perspective the demands of our current projects and the continuity of our own narratives relax their collective grip on what is relevant. Something, or more properly some One, has taken their place.

In the company of God the need to establish, build and maintain our individual and social identities has been satisfied. In the company of God we already have an identity—we are beloved children and voluntary servants. Anything else related to who we are is merely interesting, not essential. In the company of God our current projects are no longer just *our* projects. They are projects of a company. If we sense that one or more of those projects doesn't seem to fit in the company of God, then such a project may be a candidate for termination or dissolution.

In the company God, our own narrative is really only meaningful in the context of the greater narrative of the company. There are not only others but the Other participating and contributing with us in the progress and completion of these projects. It is not up to us alone. As a participant and contributor to that narrative, we no longer need to be anxious.[32] Without these identity needs, misaligned projects, and independent narratives all clamoring for our attention, the sense we make of change is less apt to be distorted. We are freed to sense and appreciate the new realities of change on its own terms, not ours.

Some might imagine that such a perspective would narrow our choices and restrain our thinking. Quite the contrary, a theological perspective should not constrain us. When in the company of God we are freer—"emancipated," to use Walter Brueggemann's term[33]—to sense, interpret and remember with less distortion from the needs of our own identity, the demand should our own projects and the leading roles in our own narratives. We are instead liberated to sense what is real, to interpret what is true and to appreciate where we might contribute in a supporting role to the larger, broader and deeper narrative beyond our parochial interests.

When our identity needs have already been met as children in, servants of, and heirs to, the company of God, we are freed from needs for attention, credit or acclaim. Such needs skew our sensing, interpreting and remembering. With conscious confidence in the projects in which we are engaged, we are freed to give it our all—whatever the project—because we believe these projects are contributing to a greater purpose.

Of course, this is all well and good in theory. Putting it into practice is an imperfect, two-steps-forward-one-step-back kind of experience. Turning toward and tuning in to that which we give our attention requires turning away from and tuning out the rest. This is especially the case when there is so much vying for our attention. According to some, the most important function of attention is our ability to screen out rather

---

32. Matt 6:24–34.

33. Brueggemann, *Practice of Prophetic Imagination*, 21–24.

than take in.[34] How do we choose what and who to tune out? How do we know what is and is not relevant, especially when responding to change?

In the company of God, sensing the movements and contrasts in change becomes less the quick and anxious classification of "friend" or "foe" and more a seeking of what rings true, appears beautiful and proves loving. Where we direct our eyes, ears, taste, touch and smell is not toward what satisfies our aesthetic sensibilities, appetites for personal satisfaction, or longing for our own comfort and security. Rather, our senses tune in to where there is hatred, injury, doubt, despair, darkness and sadness as the company's purpose is to sow love, forgiveness, faith, hope, light and joy.[35] In the company of God, interpreting is less about gaining control of the situation or insulating ourselves from it, and more about consoling, understanding and loving, certainly more than being consoled, understood or loved. And in our remembering in the company of God, we are more likely to find meaning and purpose when we forget ourselves, more likely to forgive when we know what it feels like to be forgiven and more likely to awaken to a new life when we have experienced the death of our old selves.

CONCLUSION

Confucius had this to say about making sense: "I hear and I forget. I see and I remember. I do and I understand."

Making sense of change requires us to dive in, despite uncertainty and ambiguity. It is an *act* more than cognition or recognition of faith. Innovating itself is a form of making sense of change. Innovators embody the sense they make of change into new forms of value for others.

The one creating the new value and the one for whom the value is created must both recognize the sense made, to be sure. It is not merely a private or personal sense-making adventure. And the sense innovating makes is subject to various challenges, including what else is on the agenda of the organization doing the innovating. In fact, the choice whether to aim resources at innovating in the first place is a function of whether the sense the organization finds in change points to a value worth pursuing. This chicken-or-egg kind of question often can't get past the calculus of controllers with MBAs.[36]

34. Davenport and Beck, *Attention Economy*, 58.
35. From the St. Francis Prayer.
36. Denning, "Surprising Reasons."

Likewise, theology is a form of making sense. It does not explicitly aim to create new value for others nor embody that value in forms that manifest both sense and value to others, at least the way innovating aims to. However, the extent to which theology is uninterested in what is valuable or forgets the needs and vocabulary of its beneficiaries—both lay and clergy alike—is the extent to which theology will find itself wandering in the dry and desolate wilderness of irrelevance, or like Jonah, crouched under the skimpy shade of a fading fig tree of propositional and doctrinal language.

Native to making theological sense is an understanding of God's interests—the purposes, movement and operations of the company of God. Native to making sense in innovating efforts is an understanding of what makes for new value. The former tends to source much of its sense-making from what God has done in the past (hindsight). The latter tends to source its understanding from new realities emerging in the present (insight). Both, however, are keenly interested in where these realities are headed (foresight).

These sense-making sources are hardly incompatible. When brought together, these two make for a larger, more versatile set of tools with which to sense, interpret and remember. Together they promise a more practical way of creating new value for others, particularly in the company of God.

CONVERSATION STARTERS

1. Where is the scriptural narrative more useful in helping us make sense of change?

    (a) What biblical narrative arcs (e.g., captivity, wilderness wandering, conquest, exile, etc.) are most appropriate for describing our current context(s)? Why?

    (b) Does the use of more than one arc to describe current contexts lead to a more practical understanding for creating new value?

2. How does identity anxiety—racial, gender, national, economic, ethnic, etc.—stand in the way of our freedom to make sense of change and create new value for others?

8

Make Meaning *Before* Money

Why do you spend your money for that which is not bread,
and your labor for that which does not satisfy?[1]

THE DOTCOM BUBBLE BURST in the years 2000–2001. Four years later entrepreneur and start-up investor Guy Kawasaki found himself speaking to an audience gathered by the Stanford Technology Ventures Program. He told them to make meaning before making money.[2]

Kawasaki explained, "If you make meaning you will probably make money. But if you set out to make money, chances are you will neither make money nor meaning." Kawasaki went on to situate meaning in one or more of the following: increase the quality of life for others, right a wrong, or prevent the end of something good.

If the entrepreneurial effort does not have something to do with at least one of these, then perhaps the entrepreneur should reconsider.

Absence of meaning surely contributed to a few burst bubbles in 2000 and foreshadowed Kawasaki's counsel. Though it may not always be followed, the advice reflects a growing desire on the part of many to do well by doing good. Social venturing, B corporations, and even many for-profit ventures express interest in both cause *and* commercial success.

1. Isa 52:2.
2. Guy Kawasaki, "Make Meaning in Your Company," Stanford Technology Ventures Program Educators Corner, School of Engineering, Stanford University, October 20, 2004, https://www.youtube.com/watch?v=lQs6IpJQWXc.

Lack of meaning is not the only cause of punctured bubbles. It is also the lack of value, perhaps even more so. The products and services many dotcom companies envisioned left promised value unrealized. As much "vaporware" as software was developed, due in part to what Gartner Inc. now regularly tracks and calls the hype cycle.[3] Hype cycles continue to demonstrate that meaning is often *conceived* before any money is really made.[4] Value can never be created without a customer, client or beneficiary recognizing and validating it by the exchange of their cash or by the outcomes achieved for the cause.

Kawasaki is right, but only partly. Both meaning *and* value are at the heart of making sense of change, especially the kind that leads to innovation. But in the process we can end up either creating meaning without value, or creating value without meaning.

Meaning made *without value* ends up being a private matter. Certainly I can make sense of change for myself only. Personal meaning may improve my ability to navigate in a chaotic and nonsensical world, or it helps me to get along with others. But it remains psychological or emotional, confined to private and personal realms. It lacks public or shared value. When private meaning trumps public value, people isolate and insulate themselves. And when making money for ourselves trumps the making of meaning and value for others, the future of the other is sacrificed at the altar of our own individual interests. Sooner or later, however, our own private interests prove parochial, insufficient and of limited meaning, particularly when compared to the greater meaning and purpose found in creating value for others.

Value *without meaning*, on the other hand, confines value to a financial frame. Money may be made to be sure, but whether meaning and value accompany this money-making may not be so obvious. When money is made without meaning, both our understanding of value and efforts to create it remain acquisitive, transactional, and closely associated with only what can be quantified, measured and monetized.

Making money is more a *result* than purpose of any commercial enterprise.[5] Failure to distinguish between result and purpose continues to lead many astray. In fact, when pursuit of financial performance comes

---

3. "Hype Cycle" is a branded graphical presentation used by the Gartner Group—an information technology research and advisory group.

4. "Making money" should not to be confused with receiving investors' money.

5. Drucker, *Management*, 60, 61.

at the expense of purpose, it can be an early indicator of the decline to come.[6]

The following looks at what a theological perspective brings to meaning, value and money and how each influences the other. It is especially interested in the *making* of each, given how often the money overshadows the other two. Bringing a theological perspective to our understanding of meaning, value and money reintegrates an understanding of value that all too often becomes disintegrated, delaminated and compartmentalized. In fact, this essay proposes that theology offers perhaps the best means for us to return to a more holistic notion of value—an integrated view that is not possible through economics, ethics, or their combination alone.

Said differently, making sense of change and creating new value for others relies to a great extent on our ability to connect the dots. We are more likely to select substantive dots to connect and connect them in ways that make deeper meaning—a sense that matters—when we do so in the company of God. In the company of God the dots that matter and the connections made are more likely to enable the new we create for others to be meaningful, substantive and valuable. In the company of God we have both the criteria for selecting the dots that matter and the guidance to shape the character of their connections. In the company of God, both dots and their connections are "rooted and grounded in love."[7] Put cryptically, in the company of God plumb lines[8] will precede top lines and bottom lines, which benefits everyone.

What then makes for meaning? What is meaningful and how do we discern the more from the less meaningful, not just in the privacy of our own minds and hearts, but in public arenas as well?

MEANING

In understanding what makes for meaning, the hard physical sciences may have less to contribute than do the softer sciences of philosophy and theology. Gordon Allport defined meaning in a nutshell: "He who has a why to live can bear with almost any how."[9]

6. Collins, *How the Mighty Fall*, 54.

7. Eph 3:17.

8. Amos 7:7–8.

9. Frankl, *Man's Search for Meaning*, 12.

Allport's inspiration came from Victor Frankl who survived what would have been unbearable for most of us. As a prisoner of the Nazi concentration camp at Auschwitz, Frankl found himself "stripped to naked existence," losing his father, mother, brother and wife to the same concentration camp system in which he found himself. But even in these circumstances Frankl found meaning in his devotion to something (or someone) greater than himself.

First published in 1946, the book's popularity sent it through multiple printings. In Frankl's own preface to the 1983 edition, he looks back on the book's success and offers readers this suggestion:[10]

> Don't aim at success—the more you aim at it and make it a target, the more you are going to miss it. For success, like happiness, cannot be pursued; it must ensue, and it only does so as the unintended side-effect of one's personal dedication to a cause greater than oneself or as the by-product of one's surrender to a person other than oneself.

A cause greater is at least one of the dots that must be connected to other dots if meaning is to be made. Such a dot is teleological if not theological. It is a "super dot" that ties together threads of meaning, purpose and value implicit in other dots and connections.

What is meaningful is valuable and what is valuable is meaningful. If we are going to make meaning before money[11] then sooner or later we need to understand value. Value is variously understood but it is always derivative of purpose.

Change stimulates sense-making in both individuals and organizations. And when we find ourselves trying to make sense of change, not only for ourselves but also for others and indeed *with* others, we are unlikely to get very far without an adequate understanding of what we often assume we understand—*value*.

VALUE

The word derives from the French word *valoir*, from the Latin *valere*, meaning "be strong" or "be worth." In English, connotations vary depending on whether the word form is a singular noun, a plural noun or a verb.

10. Ibid., 16.

11. Money is often confused with value, though it is really a means of exchange, a medium of storage (for exchange value), and a standard of equivalence.

As a singular noun, equivalence is the connotation first noted in the dictionary: "that amount of a commodity, or medium of exchange, considered to be an equivalent for something else or a fair or satisfactory equivalent or return."[12] For example, when we say "that's good value for the money" we deemed it worth the cost incurred, whether in money, time, attention or devotion. Equivalence, however, is chronically vulnerable to *equivocation*, particularly if there is no common standard or criteria by which equivalence is determined.

As a plural noun the connotation shifts to moral matters. Even such a slight change—the simple addition of an "s"—illustrates how ready we are to divorce the moral from the economic. Such a divorce may comfort us with a convenient compartmentalization, but it leaves us lounging on the couch of moral relativism. What is right and fitting for one context may not be for another.

As a verb ("to value" something or someone), the act of appraisal is front and center. Without some common standard, however, every appraisal remains an estimate at best and equivocation at worst. When we value something or someone we cannot escape *evaluating*. As evaluators we put ourselves in the judgment seat. Is this person, place or thing worth the expense of our money, time, attention, or devotion? When we value someone (even ourselves) or something, we typically endow the person, place or thing with a worth that is greater than another. Comparative logic is difficult to avoid. *Discrimination* is unavoidable.[13]

Upon what basis do we evaluate? Theology has much to say about this basis. Economics tends to avoid the question, if it can. Ethics is hard-pressed to avoid relativism. Many will insist that a category error is being made when economics and ethics intersect. Many would prefer that economic value remain unrelated to ethical value and vice versa.

This separation, however, may not hold up when closely scrutinized. Simply from a theological point of view, to imagine that God's interests are confined to moral not economic matters is in effect putting limits on God's interests. To suggest that God is not interested in how evaluations are conducted is clearly as untenable as is the absolutist position that God judges everything and everyone harshly.

---

12. *New Shorter Oxford Annotated Dictionary*, s.v. "value."

13. In contrast is the repeated biblical imperative to "show no partiality" found in Luke 20:21; 1 Tim 5:21; Acts 10:24; and Jas 2:1–13.

VALUE LAYERS

Topsoil, subsoil and bedrock present a useful way to think about value. Common expressions like "deeper meaning" or the "real value hidden underneath" suggest that, like soil, value is layered as well. Like layers of soil, the layers of value lack sharp, well-defined boundaries between them, and no one layer alone is sufficient for life and growth. All are necessary and work together. In fact, meaning and value come from the integration among and between the layers. Even bedrock influences subsoil. Soil scientists refer to the influence of the bedrock as "parent material."

What grows is nourished by soil that holds its roots. What is growing and how fast is more visible at the topsoil layer, for sure. But what is more difficult to see is what goes on just under the surface, where nutrients make themselves available to seeds germinating before breaking through the top soil.

This is the case for value as viewed by individuals, organizations, communities or whole societies. The top layer of value—markets—is typically where value is seen and recognized. The origins of value, however, germinate from the subsoil and bedrock underneath. When it comes to understanding the structure of value, no one layer alone is sufficient, for growth and life.

Following this analogy, value can be described as having three basic layers: the transactional (topsoil), the instrumental (the subsoil in the middle) and the intrinsic (the underlying bedrock). Each deserves consideration.

"Exchange" or "market" value are terms economists use to refer to the topsoil of *transactional value*. Equivalency is their primary concern, based on quantitative and monetary standards agnostic to context. Examples include the exchange of an employee's experience for pay in an employment agreement, or a box of cereal on the grocery shelf exchanged for cash at the checkout counter. Equivalency lasts only for relatively short periods of time, given various other forces affecting fluctuations of transactional value.

The subsoil of *instrumental value* is interested in the function or purpose of the product, system or program. "Means value" or "value-in-use" are other designations for instrumental value. Estimating the value at this layer is context dependent. The particular context in which the thing is used or the person is employed determines its value. For example, the value of a pizza cutter in and of itself is not much, except when it is used to cut a freshly baked pizza. Its value is realized as and when it is used, less the costs associated with storing it, cleaning it and even using it. The use context determines the value at this layer. At this middle layer value is often assessed in terms of *practice* or application. At this layer, value is often calibrated in terms of measurable *performance*. In fact this layer could also be called the performance layer where value and performance is more easily seen, measured and compared.

The bedrock of *intrinsic value* represents what is important regardless of use, context or equivalency. Intrinsic value is typically considered a moral or ethical standard or virtue, like trustworthiness, justice, love, kindness, and honesty. "Intrinsic" suggests that the value comes from within. It is inherent to the thing or person, regardless of external conditions. Intrinsic value is qualitative more than quantitative and persists across varying contexts and conditions. Likewise at this layer, value is often defined as a *principle*—what is true and valid regardless of the contextual differences.

These three layers of value are often viewed as separate—even mutually exclusive—and often applied differently, depending upon whether people or objects are the focus of attention. Typically classical economics separates transactional and instrumental value from intrinsic value. Economics justifies this by claiming that economics is primarily interested in the transactional or instrumental values of goods rather than people. Economics typically absolves itself of concerns regarding intrinsic value, leaving these concerns to ethics. This effectively excludes ethical considerations from economic analysis, all because intrinsic values are regarded as something different and disassociated from extrinsic ones and vice versa. This disassociation leads to a persistent "de-lamination" of value.

The persistence of this de-lamination may reflect the absence of a theological perspective. Bring theological perspective to these layers and fresh questions arise. Might the widening gap between the accumulating wealth of the one percent and the declining wealth of the rest of us be symptomatic of this de-lamination, particularly when the financial economy becomes increasingly disassociated from the real economy? Can substantive value or meaning be created in a transactional layer alone? Mustn't such meaning also penetrate into and through the instrumental layer and to intrinsic value as well, if it is to matter?

De-lamination may be cognitively convenient by keeping things categorically neat and tidy. In reality, however, the three are inseparable. For example, commercial organizations concern themselves with both transactional and instrumental value and yet must comply within the constraints of intrinsic values. If they ignore intrinsic value, they risk erosion of societal and customer trust. Without this connection to intrinsic value the company can be out of business in very short order. Remember the world's largest accounting firm, Arthur Anderson? When it lost the trust of society and clients it vanished in less than a year.

This de-lamination may also infect nonprofit organizations that we imagine are more concerned with intrinsic value. However, to the extent that these organizations ignore the subsoil and topsoil of instrumental and transactional value—measurable impact, outcome and effectiveness—these organizations risk losing contributions from current and future donors, not to mention the trust of the communities they serve.

Who is to say that what we are engaged in can't carry intrinsic, instrumental and transactional value at the same time? The more meaning we make, the more value layers this meaning will penetrate and intersect. Isn't this typically what we mean when we admiringly attribute something with a deeper value—a value that money can't buy? This is what we are invited to do when in the company of God.

If we are to make meaning before money, if we are to make sense of change and create new value for others, surely one or more of the dots that we connect will need to be found in the subsoil of instrumental value if not the bedrock of intrinsic value. The "good soil" Jesus referred to in his parable of the sower[14] is likely a soil of all three layers.

When all the dots we find to connect originate from the topsoil of transactional value alone—represented by quantitative data or so-called "big data"—the value we create and the meaning we make will be thin at best and likely short lived.[15] This echoes Jesus' own interpretation of the parable of the sower.[16] The soil of the hard path invited the tweeting birds to come along and eat them up. The soil of the rocky ground had insufficient depth. Scorching sun withered the little sprouts quickly. The seeds that fell among thorns were choked by "the cares of the world and the lure of wealth" such that they yielded nothing. It is only in the good soil of instrumental and intrinsic value that seeds can bear fruit and yield "in

14. Matt 13:3–34; Mark 4:3–32; Luke 8:5–15.

15. Meadows, *Thinking in Systems*, 194. Meadows made the observation that numbers are the least effective basis upon which to intervene in a system, from which could be inferred that numbers are the least effective "dots" to start with in making meaning in response to change.

16. Matt 13:4–7, 22–23.

one case a hundredfold, in another sixty, and in another thirty." It matters where the dots come from.

With this layered view of value in mind we can look more closely at how meaning can be made and value can be created.

WHICH DOTS TO CONNECT

"Connect the dots" is an apt expression for making sense of change. It also describes something most of us can do.

That most of us can do this turns out to be a very good thing, given how necessary it is for making sense. However, our increasingly connected era seems to be giving us more dots to connect and even more ways to connect them. "We're going to find ourselves in the not too distant future swimming in sensors and drowning in data," observed Lt. General David Deptula in 2010.[17] The sea of sensors and the flood of data are slated to rise even more with the emerging "Internet of Things." Will this be another flood of biblical proportions—this time a flood of data?

Making meaning and money depends as much upon the dots we select as it does on the character and quality of the connections we make. Selecting may be what we still have to learn. As dots and ways to connect them proliferate, the dots we choose and how we connect them will become only more important. Our cultural atmosphere is already drenched with data and saturated with unseen signals crisscrossing the atmosphere and incessantly skipping between cell towers. With all this connectedness, some are asking whether we are really communicating anything or not, and if we are, is the content of our communications meaningful or not. Is all this connective capacity and capability leading us to more, better or deeper meaning and value?

MIT's Sherry Turkle believes not. Turkle observes that all this connectivity is causing us to expect more from technology and less from each other. Citing analysis of data from over fourteen thousand college students over the past thirty years Turkle suggests we are "connected as we've never been connected before, and we seem to have damaged ourselves in the process."[18] She points to the disturbing findings from a University of Michigan's Institute for Social Research study:

17. Magnuson, "Military 'Swimming in Sensors.'"

18. Turkle, *Alone Together*, 293.

> Since the year 2000, young people have reported a dramatic decline in interest in other people. Today's college students are, for example, far less likely to say that it is valuable to try to put oneself in the place of others or to try to understand their feelings. The authors of this study associate students' lack of empathy with the availability of online games and social network. An online connection can be deeply felt, but you only need to deal with the part of the person you see in your game world or social network. Young people don't seem to feel they need to deal with more, or over time they lose the inclination. One might say that absorbed in those they have "friended," children lose interest in friendship. . . . Their detachment is not aggressive. It is as though they just don't see the point.[19]

Making sense of change is not about more and faster data. It is about making meaning. It is about trusting our abilities to perceive, decipher what dots to connect and creatively connect them in coherent and compassionate ways. This is what it takes to make sense, meaning and ultimately new value for others in response to change. Technology can help us make the connections, at least initially. But something besides technology will be necessary to make sense, meaning and value from the connections. In the company of God, this something just may be theology more than technology.

CONNECTING DOTS

Connecting the dots is not just a familiar expression. It's a familiar experience. But to understand how meaning is made and value is created in the act of connecting dots we need to get behind the colloquial expression. How does connecting the dots create the content and form of meaning and value?

Karl Weick, and others, explain it this way: meaning requires three things—a past "frame," a present "cue," and an association between them.

> The lack of prototypical past moments . . . can prolong the search for meaning. Frames tend to be past moments of socialization and cues tend to be present moments of experience. If a person can construct a relationship between these two moments, meaning is created. This means that the content of sense-making is to be found in the frames and categories that summarize past

19. Ibid.

experience, in the cues and labels that snare specifics of present experience, and in the ways these two settings of experience are connected.[20]

A past frame, a present cue, and an association between the two, these form a "minimal sensible structure" which is what we create when we make sense of change. It also shows up in creating new value for others. Minimal sensible structures may come in enmeshed multiples as well; like Edwin Friedman's "interlocking emotional triangles,"[21] these minimal sensible structures comprise the fabric of the meaning we make to navigate life, private and personal as well as public and societal. All this is but a more technical way of describing what most of us are quite familiar with already.

Not all dots, of course, are equal. Neither are all connections. The minimal sensible structures connect different dots in different ways. The meaning that can be made and the new value that can be created from connecting the dots is a function not only of the number and nature of the dots that are connected, it is also a function of the strength of the connections themselves. When we bring a theological perspective to the dots, frames and the connections, the minimal sensible structures we create take on a deeper meaning. With a theological lens the dots we pay attention to, the connections we draw and the frames we use will more likely seek transformational rather than transactional value.

Remember the workbooks in early elementary school instructing us to connect the dots? Who among us hasn't had an experience of penciling lines between sequentially numbered dots on a page? Drawing lines between numbered dots gives us the simple pleasure of watching a form emerge. When the form begins to emerge we experience the pleasure of a modest "aha" experience. A piece of the puzzle falls into place. Dots connect. Meaning is made, or perhaps more accurately, discovered. What we couldn't quite see before, now we can see more clearly, at least in part.

Three decades of facilitating creative problem-solving and invention sessions have left me with the conviction that everyone has the ability to connect the dots. It is an individual competence, enhanced by collaborating with others, to be sure. But as an individual skill it is innate in us all, regardless of how well or poorly we may assess our own connection-making competence.

20. Weick, *Sensemaking in Organizations*, 111.

21. Friedman, *Failure of Nerve*, 204.

When making sense of substantive change we naturally look for a "deeper meaning." The phrase suggests that meaning resides under the surface. It presumes that what we see and experience on the surface is only a part of the story. We assume the real or underlying meaning—the sense we make of change—comes from a root cause under the surface. The same can be said for value. Meaning is never far from what people regard as the *underlying value*.

Where this habit of mind and heart comes from may not be all that clear. Parents see it early when their child gets to the point of repeatedly asking "why?" Perhaps children are simply demonstrating a fresh fascination with infinite regression. Parents will at some point run out of time or patience and answer with a final, "I don't know," or, "Because I say so," or, "Because it just is."

Certainly there are different attitudes toward this habit of looking for the deeper meaning and underlying value. Many of us are content to remain close to the surface finding sufficient meaning there. Others of us have a longing to go deeper. Even among those who long for deeper meaning there are different degrees of depth that prove satisfying. Some won't stop digging for a deeper meaning until they hit the bedrock of intrinsic value or even the hot molten core below it. For others it may be entirely sufficient to stop digging when they discover something practical that works for their immediate need.

Regardless of our own propensities and patience, the connections we make will need to find dots at deeper layers than at the layer of topsoil alone. If we make sense only at the transactional layer of value we may make money but it will be without much meaning.

MONEY WITHOUT MEANING

No one literally "makes money" of course, except for the central banks or national treasuries, at least as and when nations choose to increase their country's money supply. Businesses and individuals do not "make" money unless they are counterfeiting. It is interesting, though, how often we use this expression even as a synonym for "making a living." Suffice it to say, money is deeply entangled in our patterns of thought, speech and behavior, so much so that it may be impossible to see it for what it actually is.

Money itself is unique among other commodities. It is a means of exchange, a common standard for comparing values and a means of storing value which when stored can generate more money through interest. Because of these attributes—especially the combination of these attributes—money easily becomes not only de-laminated from the other layers of value. It can become its own layer of value. As and when it disengages from the instrumental or intrinsic layers of value, money becomes its own power and principality and a very powerful one at that (though not particularly principled).

When our intent is to make money regardless of the sense, meaning or value, a longing remains unsatisfied, even when plenty of money is "made." This unsatisfied longing is a sign and symptom of the absence of meaning at the transactional and instrumental layers. A sense of meaning and purpose greater than ourselves is missing, as may be the incarnation of this value at the instrumental layer.

Transactional value alone can be like empty calories. There is energy there to be sure, energy that can be derived, converted and stored. However, there is little nutrition and by itself, it represents an unsustainable, unhealthy diet.

As it turns out, there are many ways to make money other than making sense, meaning or new value for others. These other ways may be increasing in number and even in their respective ability to make money without meaning: selling short, trading in derivatives, collecting interest and all other forms of speculation, to name a few.

Idolatry is theology's term for making money without meaning, at least one type of idolatry. It is a particularly prevalent, persistent and ancient one. Idolatry can be a loaded word without an ear tuned to theological concerns. Like "sin," it waves a big red flag. From a secular viewpoint idolatry would not even come to mind. It doesn't even show up unless we include a theological frame in our sense-making.

The interest theology has here is as much practical as it is doctrinal, especially in the context of sense-making and value creation. Avoiding illusions and delusions that plague making sense of change and creating value is essential. Idolatry is illusion and delusion, and theology's concern with idolatry can be quite practical. There are at least two reasons for this.

The first is that technically idolatry is showing devotion and ascribing meaning to some thing (or some one) that doesn't deserve it. Practically, idolatry is accompanied by emotional obsession and cognitive compulsion. Both misdirect time, attention and devotion, not unlike the emotional obsessions that accompany physical addiction.

The desire for more is at the heart of this idolatry. Jesus gave it the name Mammon—a quirky Aramaic expression—which is often translated "wealth." Wealth suggests accumulation. Jesus made it clear that in his opinion Mammon is always in direct competition with God for our time, attention and devotion. Mammon vies with God to be our master. Neither can be truly a master if we try to serve both simultaneously.[22]

Accumulation, and especially accumulation far beyond what one needs, is the illusory power animating and enabling money to become the idol that it can so easily become.

The actual idolatry here, however, is the time, attention and devotion in the pursuit of "more." In the parable of the dishonest manager[23] this form of idolatry is linked to capacity, even more than the nature of the content filling that capacity. It's about having more than is necessary. Or as Matthew puts it, storing up treasure where moth and rust consume and thieves break in and steal.[24]

While Mammon may be the idolatry, money is the idol. As an idol it can take on various forms: coin, paper or electrons. But as an idol it has no reality beyond what it represents—a means, medium and standard. Nor is money by itself the root of evil.[25] Idols are by definition man-made, empty. Their reality is illusion. Idols have little if any intrinsic value, except perhaps for the gold from which they are made. The meaning they hold is totally imputed to them, endowed by the misdirected longings of those who give the idol their time, attention and devotion. While idol*atry* is the undue devotion to accumulation—wanting more than we really need—money is the *idol*, one with a potency that may be increasing.

In his book *Theology of Money* Philip Goodchild observes that in the modern world the limitations of money have been overcome by the perception of money as valuable in and of itself. No longer is money seen as simply a means of exchange, medium of storage and standard by which to compare values. Money has taken on its own power, a power that competes with the power of God. Goodchild puts it this way:

22. Matt 6:24 and Luke 16:9, 11, 13.

23. Luke 16:1–13.

24. Matt 6:19–20.

25. 1 Tim 6:10—"the *love* of money is the root of all kinds of evil."

Where God promises eternity, money promises the world. Where God offers a delayed reward, money offers a reward in advance. Where God offers himself as grace, money offers itself as a loan. Where God offers spiritual benefits, money offers tangible benefits. Where God accepts all repentant sinners who truly believe, money may be accepted by all who are willing to trust in its value. Where God requires conversion of the soul, money empowers the existing desires and plans of the soul. Money has the advantages of immediacy, universality, tangibility, and utility. Money promises freedom and gives a down payment on the promise of prosperity.[26]

Money is a potent, prevalent and persistent idol. As an idol money may have become more powerful than other idols in its rivalry with God.

The second reason to invoke the notion of idolatry is to differentiate money and its accumulation from the positive intent of God. In doing so, we must clarify just what that positive intent is.

If God truly has our best interests at heart, then the prohibition against idolatry is as much a function of God's concern for what is good and healthy for us as it is a function of divine jealousy. Making money without meaning—without instrumental or intrinsic value, or both—is not healthy for us, whether we are thinking of the health of individuals, organizations or society as a whole. When meaning is confined to the transactional layer, what takes precedence is what we can "get out of " life, experiences or relationships. It remains a thin topsoil sure to dry up and erode before too long.

The idolatry of accumulation has a close association with the transactional layer. This layer is comprised of outcomes and outputs. It is the easiest to measure and count. But just because it can be counted—whatever it is—doesn't necessarily mean it counts. "The paradox of accounting is that it directs attention to what is counted rather than to what matters."[27] What matters is that which demands our time, attention and devotion, which the human sciences of wealth ignore. The science of wealth only studies the outcomes of economic activity. "The investigation of the powers and principles by which time, attention and devotion are distributed should belong, by contrast, to the discipline of theology."[28]

26. Goodchild, *Theology of Money*, 11.

27. Ibid., 24.

28. Ibid., 7.

Devotion to accumulation is measured quantitatively often to the exclusion of qualitative considerations. This leads to all sorts of distortions in what is regarded as meaningful and valuable. Transactional value trumps intrinsic value or becomes so divorced from any recognizable connection with intrinsic value that we lose our grounding in what really matters. The sense made in these more surface contexts may indeed create monetary wealth, but it is hollow not hallowed. It may exist in some fashion, but it remains without meaning. It provides security without substance, solutions without sustainability.

Many individuals and organizations with established revenue streams often become obsessed with the metrics of what is valuable. They are governed by a transactional mind-set (e.g., accounting, metrics, quantifications). They often look to markets and transactions for ways to accumulate or save rather than commit and create. But it is in spending—especially time, attention and devotion—and from intrinsic value that new value is created and meaning is made.

Making meaning is much easier when we know what makes for meaning to begin with. When we already have a sense for what is meaningful and what is not, then we are already part of the way there. Not knowing what makes for meaning is equivocation. Here is where theology offers tremendous practical advantage over purely secular perspectives. In the company of God, plumb lines precede top lines or bottom lines. A primary goal of theology is to keep the plumb lines front and center.

MEANING WITHOUT VALUE

Making meaning without value may be less pervasive. But it is just as debilitating a misdirection of energy. If the dots that resonate with intrinsic principles do not link with dots in some context of practice, any meaning that might be made will likely remain as empty and lifeless as an idol.

Principle must find its form in practice. The language of invention calls this "preferred embodiment" or "the reduction to practice." The language of theology calls this incarnation or the "scandal of particularity." But whether we are using the idioms of invention or theology, the type of connection is the same. It is a connection that crosses the imaginary boundary between theory and practice, between the ideal and the real, between intrinsic value in the context-less realm of principle and the instrumental value of a specific context and practice.

Meaning without value may be produced in a consumer economy more often than we care to admit. How much is difficult to say. In part, the amount may be manifest in what percent of the overall economy is engaged in activities related to advertising and promotion. What the Philadelphia retailer John Wannamaker said years ago still seems to hold true: "Half the money I spend on advertising is wasted and the trouble is that I don't know which half."

But whether in marketing, producing or innovating, value is not the neat and tidy concept accountants might like us to believe it is. Nor at the other end of the continuum is value resident in the pristine ideal ethicists might secretly want us to think it is. It's really much more fuzzy than that.

What or who is important and valuable to one person may not be to another. Neither economics nor ethics can completely escape erosions into relativism and even subjectivism.

A recent attempt to escape this relativism is Robert and Edward Skidelsky's book *How Much Is Enough: Money and the Good Life* (2012). From an economic and philosophical perspective the Skidelskys propose a rough set of universal and indispensable intrinsic values.[29] There are seven: health, security, respect, personality,[30] harmony with nature, friendship and leisure. Living a life that realizes all of these is what it means to live the good life, at least in the view of this economist and his philosopher/ethicist son. To be fair, the Skidelskys recognize the difficulty in realizing these intrinsic, principled and "pure" values in the real world. But what seems to interest the Skidelskys are the potential conflicts between these values, rather than the embodiments of these values themselves.

Theology has an essential contribution to make here. Theology is much more familiar with the paradox at the center of the idea that God "scandalously" choose to show up in local and particular circumstances and that when God is involved (when is God not?) both the specific and the universal are also. Philip Goodchild expresses it this way:

> Theology, concerned with the ultimate criteria of life, is the most fundamental and radical inquiry. It attempts to discern

---

29. Skidelsky and Skidelsky, *How Much is Enough*, 150–67.

30. Ibid., 160–61. Here the Skidelskys suggest independence sufficient for choice-making.

how truth, goodness, and life come to be constituted. It offers to the world a vision of life interpreted according to the richest categories of meaning. It has the duty to invest life with the deepest layers of spiritual wealth—that is, it has to determine what is the nature of true wealth. This is the vocation for theology, whether Christian or not, and it is the most fundamental inquiry, whether pursued by believers, nonbelievers, or no one at all. Worldly wealth, which can only mean exchange value in terms of money, is to be judged against a new revelation of divine power.[31]

Goodchild goes on to suggest that theology is uniquely positioned for the task of evaluating all values,[32] which is nothing less that what Jesus saw himself doing. His central message is "repent, for the kingdom of heaven is at hand," essentially a reevaluation of what and how we value what is meaningful.

Businesses and organizations often relegate ethical issues to matters of compliance. Theology, on the other hand, if it steps up to its vocation, will strike at the root of both an organization's purpose and strategy, the way it operates to produces value and the value it produces. Theology asks whether this value is worth producing, not because money is to be made, but because meaning, sense and intrinsic value for people's lives are at stake.

The last parable Jesus tells in Luke's gospel is a direct challenge to the propensity of making meaning without value.[33] In this parable a leader goes out of town on an extended trip. Before leaving he calls together his direct reports and gives each varying amounts of money with which to trade during his absence. Upon his return he asks, quite naturally, how each performed with what each had been entrusted. The ones to whom he had entrusted more came back with returns of ten and five times earnings, performances that garnered each of them even more favor, trust and responsibility.

In contrast was the one who returned only what he had *preserved*. He had "given back" only what the leader had given him, largely out of a conserving fear and narrow ignorance of the leader's own intention and commitment. Jesus concludes the parable with a rather harsh, "I tell you, to all those who have, more will be given; but from those who have nothing, even what they have will be taken away." Such is the fate of the

31. Goodchild, *Theology of Money*, 4.

32. Ibid., 5.

33. Luke 19:1–27.

organization that remains in its own comfort zone of preservation rather than innovation.

The last one put what he received under the mattress. He remained in the pristine and private layer of intrinsic value, principled but essentially afraid. He kept it to himself and unlike the others, took no risk in deploying what he had been given. The result was valueless meaning, lifeless existence and even further loss of what little he had been given.

Socrates famously claimed the unexamined life is not worth living. To this Socratic truth might be added the unengaged life is not worth examining. A purpose greater than ourselves cannot remain in some abstract, un-deployed state of isolation, preserved and conserved. Even a principled dot with meaning and purpose will die the death of irrelevance without being connected to a particular place, person or thing in a specific context—in other words, without committing to practice.

All this reflects John Gardner's[34] observation that "the society which scorns excellence in plumbing as a humble activity and tolerates shoddiness in philosophy because it is an exalted one will have neither good plumbing nor good philosophy; neither its pipes nor its theories will hold water." With no pipe between layers of intrinsic and instrumental value, genuine meaning, sense and value are difficult to discern and make. Making sense that means something to another ushers us directly into the instrumental value layer—the middle layer—where all value and meaning is shaped by the local context.

MAKING IT IN THE MIDDLE LAYER

If the meaning we make matters to others—ourselves and even with God—then the making of it will command our time, attention and devotion. It will require us to show up, pay attention and give ourselves to the particularity of the local circumstances of a specific context, including its people, place and circumstances.

Such commitments do not come easily to individuals and organizations defining themselves only by the transactional topsoil. The specific and local is uninteresting to those invested in scale or leverage. These are concerns native to the quantitative. In fact, when we are at the layer of topsoil, meaning has already been made. At this layer meaning and value is now being distributed, extended or extracted.

34. Secretary of Health, Education and Welfare in the Johnson Administration.

The *making* of meaning however, occurs at the middle layer—the layer of practice—where concerns are qualitative and relational more than quantitative and transactional. Isn't this what Jesus points to in his attention to the one lost sheep, not being satisfied with the ninety-nine who are not lost?[35] Clearly there is a view of value here beyond the numbers.

In the context of commercial organizations, profits are the signs and symptoms that new value for others *has been* made. The making of it happens at a different level altogether. This distinction caused Clayton Christensen to counsel innovators in their attempts to make meaning to be patient for growth and impatient for profits. Profit is a more reliable indicator of new value for others than growth in the commercial sphere.

If what Christensen suggests is true, then entrepreneurial success stories based on exponential growth, like Facebook and Twitter and others, might give us pause to carefully examine whether their meaning and value links to anything deeper in the intrinsic layer of value. The slogan "think globally, act locally" might be amended with "start locally." Similarly, for a nonprofit organization the outcomes and impacts are signs that meaning has been made but the making of it happens at the instrumental layer.

The intent here is not to disparage outcome or its limited orientation to value. There is nothing inherently wrong with scalable initiatives, just as there is nothing inherently more righteous or redemptive about them. The intent rather is to suggest that meaning and substantive value is more likely to be made at the middle layer and that this middle layer is first and foremost governed by local context. This is the "scandal of particularity." The more classical theological principle is incarnation.

The principle of incarnation for theology, embodiment for patenting and particularity for the globally minded, is as much paradox as it is scandalous. Paradox is always problematic for those inclined to logic, rationality or reason. The biblical witness is scandalous however, in its narrative and poetic retelling of Israel's tumultuous and far-from-stable relationship with God. It bears witness to a God who is not confined to human logic, reason or even some Aristotelian or Platonic standard of rationality. God is free to do as and when God pleases. Otherwise God would not be God. If it is God's choice to commit to a specific time and place, to a specific people, even display what might otherwise be considered to be a discriminatory (though perhaps purposeful) choice of some

35. Luke 15:1–7.

rather than others, while simultaneously loving and committing to all, then who are we to suggest otherwise?

Of course, we do suggest otherwise, and often. As and when we do, we reveal only our own presumptions and bias for neat and tidy logic more than revealing anything about God. This divine reality—an embarrassingly persistent contradiction to our penchant for thinking *we* are God's agents and understand God—is what Walter Brueggemann calls the "agency of *God.*"[36]

The idea of divine agency is also a scandal, at least to the educated, sophisticated and enlightened. It is the idea that God not only exists, but is willing, able and active in intervening in particular and local affairs, not according to our standards of coherence and logic and presumptions about phenomenology, but from God's standards of faithfulness, righteousness, loving kindness and mercy. God seems to choose to act and invites us to act in particular contexts, each with its own purpose. This is the franchise, territory or domain, if you will, of the company of God, the reign of God on earth.

This middle, instrumental layer is where meaning is made and new value is created for others. This has not completely escaped the awareness of worldly companies sensitive to the vulnerabilities of trying to survive in an information and knowledge economy. In the book *The Knowledge Creating Company*, Ikujiro Nonaka and Hirotaka Takeuchi proposed that it is not what a company knows that creates wealth.[37] Rather, it is the company's ability to *create new knowledge that matters*—i.e., knowledge that carries instrumental value. This ability turns out to be the real source of wealth creation, not simply knowing something. As a result, much of Nonaka and Takeuchi's attention is given over to how knowledge that has value is created.

They describe a set of four different processes all of which share conversion, interestingly enough, as the essential process. All four of these conversion processes represent instances of dot-connecting and dot-converting. The four conversions are socialization, externalization, combination and internalization.

Socialization consists of tacit-to-tacit conversions of knowledge. For example, when two practitioners get together and talk shop and one or both of them get an idea they go and use. *Externalization* consists of

---

36. Walter Brueggemann's comments made at the Fuller Forum (spring 2015) "Justice, Grace and Law in the Mission of God."

37. Nonaka and Takeuchi, *Knowledge-Creating Company*, 3–7, 56–94.

tacit-to-explicit conversions of knowledge. For example when an expert commits his or her know-how into an explicit expression in writing, a presentation or some codified form. In the process of expressing this kind of knowledge there is often new knowledge created. I have witnessed this new knowledge creation repeatedly as inventors come to a new awareness of their own invention when they work with a patent attorney who puts it on paper in drafting a patent application. *Combination* consists of explicit-to-explicit conversions of codified or published knowledge. For example when one discipline's codified knowledge links up with another's codified knowledge in another field as in the case of interdisciplinary studies. *Internalization* consists of the explicit-to-tacit conversions of codified knowledge into an act or routine of a practitioner in action.

New value comes from these conversions of understanding, in context and on purpose. Seeing and recognizing new value is more about redrawing contextual boundaries and reframing content and less about calculating outcomes with precise metrics. The one who sees value where others do not is the one French economist J. B. Say first named an entrepreneur. The entrepreneur is one who takes a low value material—a material that others reject because of its commonness—and brings it into a higher value use.[38] The entrepreneur doesn't change the properties of the material. Rather, the entrepreneur sees in the material a contribution it can make to a specific context and purpose. Context sculpts value. There is no value without context.

What looks like a reversal of the relative value of a material, from worthless waste to a key ingredient, is not a transformation of the material by any supernatural or transubstantial magic. Rather, it is the introduction of a context to the material, or perhaps the reverse, the introduction of the material to a context.

Many successful companies make the mistake of looking for large opportunities, believing that by analysis they will be able to spot such large-scale opportunities. They ignore the reality that what becomes large first starts small, even at first, rejected. "The stone which the builders rejected has become the head of the corner. This is the Lord's doing and it is marvelous in our eyes."[39]

38. Drucker, *Innovation and Entrepreneurship*, 21.

39. Ps 118:22–23.

The rejected stone of Psalm 118, quoted not only in the gospels of Matthew, Mark and Luke,[40] but also cited by Peter,[41] the rock upon which Jesus said he would build his church—the "get-behind-me-Satan" rock whom Jesus rejected, the rock that denied Jesus three times, and the one who apparently had his own challenges with emotional self-regulation.

Does the gospel really mean to say that it has a bias for inferior quality materials and broken rocks? Does it really mean to say that the kingdom of God is constructed and built not only with low value material but even with material that has been rejected, discarded, considered waste? Is the gospel some kind of spiritual recovery, reuse, and recycling program?

All of this should give us a big pause regarding what (and who) we regard as valuable, how we assign value and the ways we measure it. The value scheme of the world resides on a different base than the value scheme of the gospel.

Both times Jesus refers to the rejected stone come in narrative contexts in which scribes and Pharisees question his authority. The scribes and Pharisees want Jesus to claim his authority. But instead, Jesus asks them a question regarding *their* authority, promising to reciprocate an answer to their question once they answer his.

Why the cat and mouse game here around the question of authority? I sense that Jesus knew that real authority is not claimed. It is recognized. Similarly, real value is not claimed or assigned. It is recognized. This is not only a spiritual truth it is an entrepreneurial reality. When value is assigned from the top down rather than recognized from the bottom up, the value is transactional and performance oriented. It tends to be imposed.

This does not imply that the desire to perform is not important nor a worthy goal. However, the motivation to improve our performance, as worthy as that may be, is less likely to create new value for others. It may improve the numbers and relative value may increase. But when we start from the transaction layer it tends toward repetition and imitation rather than innovation and the creation of new value. If we are looking for substantive dots to connect and we look for them in the numbers, we will always be looking in retrospect. Retrospect might promise us the benefits of hindsight, including a level of precision. But it will always be the "hinds" we are sighting. Making sense of change that leads to creating

---

40. Matt 21:42; Mark 12:10; Luke 20:17.

41. Acts 4:11 and 1 Pet 2:4–7, citing Isa 28:16.

new value for others necessitates foresight. Theology might call it ends oriented, or even eschatological.

STARTING BELOW BEDROCK

This brings us to the question of where to start. Where do we begin the search for dots to connect? If it is not from the transactional level, then should we start with dots that are instrumental or intrinsic? Or should we be starting from some other place?

If we enter the instrumental value layer from a starting point of intrinsic value we are more likely to make meaning and create new value for others that matters. When principle motivates and animates practice, from the bottom-up so to speak, we are more likely to make deeper meaning and create new value that is more substantive. Peter Drucker named the most reliable places to start as "the unexpected" and "incongruities."[42] Theology might use different words, like "wonder" and "injustice," respectively. Regardless of the words used, they point to the same places to start. Bedrock.

Starting the search for dots in the bedrock is no mean feat in a pluralistic, multicultural world, even with a theological perspective. Once we start looking for dots at the intrinsic layer of value the search can quickly turn into a wandering in the wilderness of equivocation. Competing mind-sets, ideologies and traditions, religious, cultural or otherwise, not to mention moral relativism, infect this bedrock of value and principle, particularly in a world that espouses different views on what these principles are, not to mention how these principles are understood.

Extend the soils analogy deeper still and we find a hot, molten core—as much energy as matter—under the layer of bedrock. Without a theological acknowledgment of this single core, the bedrock will remain a shifting foundation layer—tectonic plates of intrinsic value subject to different cultures, frames and points of view.

Underneath this bedrock, however, is a deeper single core that theology acknowledges as the source of all meaning and value. This single core, of course, is God. This single core may have been what Jesus spoke of as the sum of all the commandments and ordinances—to love God and neighbor as yourself.[43] All other values—intrinsic, instrumental and

---

42. Drucker, *Innovation and Entrepreneurship*, 35.

43. Lev 19:18; Matt 19:19; 22:39; Mark 12:31–34; Luke 10:27; Rom 13:9; Jas 2:8.

even transactional—are derivations or corruptions of this one core. This core is pure generative energy emanating outward, generous, creative and creating. The molten core under the bedrock is the hot love of God.

As it emanates and extends outward with centrifugal expansion it will encounter crusted expressions of bedrock, often viewed as fixed, propositional and permanent. From the point of view of the core, however, the bedrock principles—commandments or short lists of intrinsic value—appear as hardened but brittle legacies where the hot energy of love has cooled and left a residual crust.

However, when we begin to look under the bedrock, we discover that value is more likely to come from what is "rooted and grounded" in love.[44] It emerges not from the transactional layer of value, but from what supports intrinsic and "living" value.

CONCLUSION

Making meaning before we attempt to make money will invite criticism from the skeptic. The skeptic imagines it naïve to think that if you build it they will come.

Naïve though it may be, if you don't build it, they certainly will not come. The notion may be naïve but its alternative is despair, passivity or both.

The starting point for any creative act, whether on the part of the artist or the entrepreneur, is not money-making but meaning-making. This starting point will of necessity accept the very real risk that the meaning made may not make any money.

> The artist who hopes to market work that is the realization of his gifts cannot begin with the market. He must create for himself that gift-sphere in which the work is made, and only when he knows that work to be the faithful realization of his gift should he turn to see if it has currency in that other economy. Sometimes it does, sometimes it doesn't.[45]

The innovating organization that tries to make meaning and create new value for others cannot escape this risk either. But the organization that tries to avoid the risk at all costs, that seeks to save its own life, just may lose it.

44. Eph 3:17.

45. Hyde, *Gift*, 279.

CONVERSATION STARTERS

1. How can biblical theology help reintegrate (or "re-laminate") the de-lamination of meaning from value, and value from money?

2. What are the principles (vs. prescriptions) biblical theology can provide to innovation leaders to help them avoid the temptations of the quick fix?

3. Does microfinance represent an authentic innovation that is more transactional than relational? Does it represent the exception that makes, breaks or nullifies the rule?

9

Coincidence
God's Way of Staying Anonymous

Enlarge the site of your tent,
and let the curtains of your habitations be stretched out.[1]

IF WE HOPE TO make sense of change then we have to pay attention to
the evidence it presents. The same holds true for creating new value for
others.

Whether input or feedback, evidence provides both initial stimulus
and ongoing guidance for our sense-making and value creation. If the
sense we are able to make and the value we are able to create[2] ends up
substantial and sustainable, attention to the evidence will have played a
major role.

This is not as easy as it may seem. What kind of evidence we give our
attention to and conversely what evidence we choose to ignore makes a
difference. Too often we ignore evidence that deserves our attention and
attend to evidence we could or should otherwise ignore.

Attitudes and orientations toward certain kinds of evidence may
shape the kind of sense we make as much or more than the evidence

---

1. Isa 54:2.

2. Not necessarily for God's creating. Theology's concept of creation *ex nihilo*—that
God creates out of nothing while our creating is out of something—differentiates human from divine creativity.

itself. As a result, our evidentiary attitudes and orientations are worth a closer look, which is what this essay proposes to do.

Focusing on what is important requires us to filter out what is not. Attention spans are limited. When change is what we are trying to make sense of, we will not necessarily know what evidence to focus on and what to filter out. Learning to discern what is signal and what is noise comes slowly with experience, patience, and in practice with others. But even with practice we cannot escape a dilemma: the more attention we give to some evidence the less we give to other. Our attention is limited even with the help of others.

Signal and noise are not the only evidentiary differences. Evidence comes in different types as well, and sense-making can inadvertently discount types that upon second thought, we might want to reconsider.

Evidence that most of us give priority to are events experienced firsthand, reports from others with supporting data, of course, and truth claims that sound reasonable. Without at least one of these we will likely remain skeptical, or ignore it altogether. Firsthand experience, the reports of others and truth claims constitute what Paul Moser refers to as *spectator evidence*. Most call this kind of evidence empirical, the type we can see with our eyes and sense with the other nerve endings. This kind of evidence does "not demand that its recipients yield their wills to the source of the evidence."[3]

When God is included in our assessment of the evidence, however, and especially when God may be the *source* of the evidence itself, then we must include a kind of evidence that *does* make such demands. Take for example the "lone moral reformer who, having had his or her own will morally corrected via conscience, speaks against societal racism or some other widespread injustice."[4] Moser includes the prophets, Jesus and Mother Teresa of Calcutta in the list of individuals whose own lives present a kind of evidence that "serve as ways for God's will to challenge and to redirect us non-coercively, if we are suitably receptive."[5]

Bringing a theological perspective into our sense-making and innovating requires us to attend to evidence that is not confined to empirical criteria alone. We will also need to include evidence that speaks to the conscience.

3. Moser, *Elusive God*, 46, 52.
4. Ibid., 54–55.
5. Ibid.

What follows proposes that this evidence tends to come to us by way of an anonymous God,[6] who presents us evidence in change that may not confine itself to our typical standards of verifiability. Attending to this kind of evidence enables us to take a broader view of the "neighborhoods" in which we make sense. It deepens our interest in the welfare of the neighbors who live in these neighborhoods. It may be the kind of evidence missing in many innovating attempts. It may be one reason why the failure rate for innovating has remained so high for so long.

In short, this essay reexamines our habitual dismissal of coincidences because they lack an apparent causal connection. Reconsidering this bias will broaden our field of view and deepen our awareness. The sense we can then make of change and the new value we can then create for others ends up more aligned with the purposes of the company of God. In other words, we will make better sense and create more substantive value for others with broadened and deepened attention to the evidence that addresses our conscience, collective and individual.

First, however, we need to consider how change itself shapes and presents evidence before considering how we orient our time, attention and devotion to it.

MORE THAN ONE KIND OF EVIDENCE

Change literally means the emergence of difference, the substitution of one thing for another or the following of one thing after another.[7] The emergence of difference assumes some prior continuity. For change to show itself, some experience of the continuous must precede it. "Continuity" comes from the Latin combination of *con* ("together with") plus *tenere* ("to hold"). Change is a difference in what *was* holding together but now, for whatever reason, is not.

Likewise, the evidence of change manifests itself through contrasts, a word that comes from another Latin combination of *contra* ("against") and *stare* ("stand"). Change *stands against* continuity. As such, change is incongruous and often unexpected, frequently disruptive. Contrasts come as negative to those emotionally and cognitively wed to the continuity of their lives. Conversely, contrasts may come as positive to those for whom the continuity of their lives has become oppressive. But whether

6. Or at least a partially known and partially knowable God.

7. *Shorter Oxford Annotated English Dictionary*, s.v. "change."

negatively resisted or positively received, contrast is what attracts our attention.

Often what we thought was *status quo* turns out to be neither *status* nor *quo*. A contrast reveals either what we imagined to be continuous is no longer the continuity (*status*) we imagined it to be, or we are no longer in the safe, known and secure position in which (*quo*) we imagined ourselves, or both.

Contrasts are essentially borders and borders reside in between two sides: the old and the new, the familiar and the strange, the dark and the light. Contrasting borders can be sharp, high resolution, black and white distinctions. Perhaps more often they are subtle shades of grey. But whether distinct or nuanced, the contrasts of change raise an immediate question: whether the continuity we imagined we were "in" was mistaken.

Perceived contrasts present themselves in spectator evidence, whether directly perceived or indirectly received. To confirm the veracity of the contrast we subject it to standards and methods of empirical evidence. The *source* of this evidence, however, and its trustworthiness are often unexamined. The "authority" of the source, the fidelity of the means through which the evidence comes, and the methods by which we validate it remain entangled.

Theology, however, will add another kind of contrast—a different type of evidence—one that we might *directly receive*. This kind of evidence is what classical theology calls revelation. Paul Moser calls this "authoritative" or "volitional"[8] evidence—a kind of evidence that is tuned to a frequency of a person's will and influences directly what one chooses to do as a result. After all, we are not just beings who observe, think and feel. We are beings who also choose and do. Rather than simply being tuned to the frequency of a person's senses, volitional evidence is tuned to the frequencies of willingness. Instead of evidence for the mind to consider, this kind of evidence is for the heart to absorb. When absorbed by the heart both heart and mind may be transformed. This is the kind of evidence that can change what we value and ultimately decide to do, and specifically what we decide to change in our own way of living and being.

Spectator and propositional evidence is the kind of evidence we subject to either empirical methods, rational argument or both. In so doing we come to believe that we objectively assess this evidence from a detached point of view. It is perceptual and cognitive. Volitional or

8. Moser, *Elusive God*, 32–82.

authoritative evidence, on the other hand, addresses the conscience. It invites a change of heart. It speaks to us as beings who decide and act, not merely as beings who think and feel. This applies as much to individuals as to organizations.

This evidence issue is not a new problem. Even the disciples wrestled with it. Pulling Jesus aside they asked him privately what evidence to look for. He replied, "Many will come in my name and say, 'I am' (or 'I am he') and they will lead many astray. When you hear of wars and rumors of wars, do not be alarmed . . . this is but the beginning of the birth pangs."[9] When the scribes and Pharisees asked him for a sign, Jesus was less charitable. "An evil and adulterous generation asks for a sign but no sign will be give to it except the sign of the prophet Jonah."[10]

The Apostle Paul had to deal with the evidence issue as well. The issue surfaced early in the development of the Corinthian church. In Paul's response he identified three different kinds of evidence. Speaking from his own direct experience as a Jew and Pharisee, as a Roman citizen (and fluent with the Greek language and culture) and as someone whose own life had been radically changed. "For Jews demand signs and Greeks desire wisdom, but we proclaim Christ crucified, a stumbling block to Jews and foolishness to Gentiles."[11] In contrast to empirical evidence (signs) and reasoned argument (wisdom), Paul points us to a third way of knowing—volitional knowing. This kind of evidence is very different from the signs of Jerusalem or the philosophy of Athens,[12] mind-sets that seem to prevail even today.

Richard Niebuhr described this kind of evidence as revelatory in that it "illuminate[s] other events and enable[s] us to understand them."[13] Revelatory evidence makes our individual and collective past(s) more intelligible than before. It enables us to remember what we would prefer to deny or forget, to appropriate a broader field of view and deeper sense of meaning and value, and to discern in our present moment a more confident sense of reality.

9. Matt 24:3–8; Mark 13:3–8; see also Luke 21:7–11.

10. Matt 12:38–42; Luke 11:29–32. Repentance (*metanoia*—changing your way of knowing) is an essential dimension of this sign, as is the fact that the unfavored Ninevites were the ones who repented, not Israel.

11. 1 Cor 1:22–23.

12. Moser, *Elusive God*, 158.

13. Niebuhr, *Meaning of Revelation*, 80.

This revelatory evidence is not fully confined to matters religious, doctrinal or scriptural, but turns out to be "a starting point for the interpretation of past, present and future history [that] is subject to progressive validation."

> The more apparent it becomes that the past can be understood, recovered and integrated by means of a reasoning starting with revelation, the more contemporary experience is enlightened and response to new situations aptly guided by the imagination of the heart, the more a prophecy based on this truth is fulfilled, the surer our conviction of its reality becomes.[14]

Through authoritative, volitional or revelatory evidence we can "discover what is implicit in our lives and will become explicit."[15] It is just this conversion of implicit to explicit that proves seminal for not only making sense of change but for innovating.[16]

Ikujiro Nonaka and Hirotaka Takeuchi made the prophetic observation—still ignored by many today—that it is not what a company knows that enables it to sustain its success and to innovate. Rather, it is the company's ability to create new knowledge, particularly knowledge that is valuable to the other, that leads to innovation. This ability to create new knowledge occurs when implicit knowledge converts into explicit and back again into implicit knowledge.[17]

Implicit or tacit knowledge is the kind of informal and hard to codify knowledge carried by skills or craft captured in the term "know-how." It is embodied in the "feel" of the craftsman, a feel that has been hard won through years of experience in a variety of different conditions and situations. It cannot be written down anywhere in any complete kind of way. When this kind of tacit knowledge is expressed through the breath required by the spoken word, often in the context of collaborative problem solving with others, this knowledge mixes with the tacit knowledge of others and in the process, new knowledge and new value is conceived.

Therefore, while change may be something we can anticipate and predict, at least in part, it is often not until we experience directly its evidence and contrasts that we awaken to do something, even if only to

---

14. Ibid., 97.

15. Ibid., 95.

16. Nonaka, *Knowledge-Creating Company*, 64–67.

17. Ibid., 9.

make sense and respond. One current example might be the delays in our collective response or nonresponse to climate change.

The empirical or spectator evidence of climate change is mounting, as is the volitional evidence as well. This change is one case—albeit a massive one—wherein God is likely speaking to us all, directly, empirically *and* volitionally. Incumbent interests will cause blindness and deafness to deny the change and often will argue on empirical grounds alone. But our refusal to see in these changes massive opportunity to create new value for others may not be confined to the visual or auditory impairments of incumbency. It may also have to do with what theology calls idolatry.

COGNITIVE IDOLATRY

Looking back on his own life, a self-effacing friend of mine recently remarked, "I think my education has exceeded my intelligence." Something other than the obvious humility struck me in my friend's observation. It was the simple differentiation between education and intelligence.

More often than not we assume that education and intelligence go hand in hand. Writing about literacy, Walter Ong[18] made the profound observation that just because someone comes from a culture without a written language doesn't mean that they lack intelligence. "Illiterate" technically refers to someone without the ability to read, not without the ability to sense, think or make sense.

Given that we live in an information-intensive and literate society, "illiterate" has unfortunately come to connote unintelligent, uneducated and lacking. But not so fast, Ong reminds us. Just the opposite could be the case. Someone who cannot read or lives in a culture without a written language, though rare, can exhibit extraordinary intelligence. It is entirely possible that even those of us with plenty of education, including those of us with an overabundance of verbal and written skills, can easily fool ourselves into mistaking our literacy as demonstrable proof of our intelligence.

Equating education with intelligence, or intelligence with literacy, is a symptom of what can be called cognitive idolatry.[19] "In cognitive idolatry, we deny, if implicitly, God's supreme authority in commending ways

18. Ong, *Orality and Literacy*, 171–72.

19. Moser, *Elusive God*, 101.

of knowing God's reality."[20] God may not choose to reveal God's intentions in ways that conform to our cognitive criteria and preferences. God is free to reveal God's realities as and when God chooses. God remains unrestricted by our own rules and standards, including our notions of what makes for relevant and valid evidence.[21] Such is, by definition, the perfect freedom of One for whom all things are possible.

Our habitual and often immediate dismissal of coincidences is one way cognitive idolatry operates. Those who study complex systems, however, see coincidences differently. Students of systems dynamics view coincidences as potential occurrences with causality masked by the complexity of the system itself. Such appears to be without a direct cause and may, indeed, not have a direct cause. However, it may have a cause that is simply unknown. Carl Jung observed as much when he said "that because the statistical method shows only average aspects, it creates an artificial and predominantly conceptual picture of reality. That is why we need a complementary principle for a complete description and explanation of nature."[22]

The possibility of such an explanation of nature, however, was dimmed considerably by Ahlston Chase's account of the origins of the endangered species act (known by many as the "spotted owl" controversy).[23] When Chase's account was published the book garnered strong negative reactions from virtually every side of the controversy—conservationists, lumber companies, policy makers and radicalized eco-terrorists. This book is worth reading if only for the way in which it challenges so many of our embedded assumptions.

Chase was able to skewer the stubborn "truth" of what we imagine to be the "natural ecosystem." Chase observed that the very notion of ecosystem is derivative of mathematical modeling. In reality nature is wild, volatile and impossible to predict. Presuming that we know what its "health" should look like, assumes we know the whole system and

---

20. Ibid., 102.

21. While Anselm resolved what appeared to be a dilemma by concluding "faith precedes understanding" (or "I believe in order that I may understand"), faith and theology are not so inseparable. Faith (believing) may represent volitional knowledge and theology (reason) the rational reflection upon faith. The relevance of both for innovating is certainly worthy of a more careful sorting.

22. Jung, *Synchronicity*, 61.

23. Chase, *In a Dark Wood*. Chase's account is part investigative journalism, part philosophy, and part ecological policy critique.

understand how it is supposed to operate. This is a classical symptom of idolatry—taking the position ourselves of the One who alone has this knowledge. While we would like to think that nature is really an ecosystem and in fact we call it "ecology" and declare we know what makes for a healthy ecosystem, Chase suggests otherwise.

What Chase examined in the realms of biology, ecology and public policy, Jung explored in the realms of perception and psychology.

> The modern discovery of discontinuity (e.g., the orderedness of energy quanta, of radium decay, etc.) has put an end to the sovereign rule of causality . . . synchronicity is no more baffling or mysterious than the discontinuities of physics. It is only the ingrained belief in the sovereign power of causality that creates intellectual difficulties and makes it appear that causeless events exist or could ever occur. But if they do, then we must regard them as creative acts, as the continuous creation of a pattern that exists from all eternity, repeats itself sporadically and is not derivable from known antecedents.[24]

Jung took direct aim at our cognitive idolatry, the golden calf of which is the controlled experiment. The controlled experiment, Jung said,

> consists in asking a definite question which excludes as far as possible anything disturbing and irrelevant. It makes conditions, imposes them on Nature, and in this way forces her to give an answer to a question devised by man. She [nature] is prevented from answering out of the fullness of her possibilities since these possibilities are restricted as far as practicable.[25]

In other words, bias is built into the design of a controlled experiment the moment the conditions are controlled.

Jung approached coincidence with great caution and only after repeated experience of the phenomena. Late in his career he choose to make a full and complete explanation. "In most cases these were things which people do not talk about for fear of exposing themselves to thoughtless ridicule."[26] Jung frames coincidence this way:

> The discoveries of modern physics have, as we know, brought about a significant change in our scientific picture of the world, in that they have shattered the absolute validity of natural law

24. Jung, *Synchronicity*, 101–2.

25. Ibid., 35.

26. Ibid., 4.

and made it relative. Natural laws are *statistical* truths, which means that they are completely valid only when we are dealing with macrophysical quantities. In the realm of very small quantities prediction becomes uncertain, if not impossible, because very small quantities no longer behave in accordance with the known natural laws. The philosophical principle that underlies our conception of natural law is causality. But the connection between cause and effect turns out to be statistically valid and only relatively true for explaining natural processes and therefore presupposes the existence of one or more other factors which would be necessary for an explanation. This is as much as to say that the connection of events may in certain circumstances be other than causal, and requires another principle of explanation.[27]

This other principle of explanation is, of course, what theology has traditionally called revelation. Revelation is typically, if not always, God's free choice. It is up to God where, when, how and even how much God chooses to show us of God's intent (and presence and character, if God so chooses). God is by definition, not under any constraint, least of all, any cognitive constraint we might impose.

In revelation there is always something more than a miraculous or coincidental occurrence. There is also what Moser calls a *noncoercive* invitation to enter into a relationship with God—to join in with the company of God. This is not a neutral event that is observed from the sidelines. Rather, it is a disturbing and transformative experience if the revelation is accepted and received. It changes the intentions, reorients the values and "converts" the recipient who opens herself to the truth and reality of the occurrence.

The noncoercive character of coincidence is consistent with a primary characteristic of a loving God. This is a characteristic that does not impose or coerce a man or a woman, and perhaps even a community or an organization, into the company of God. Unlike most earthly companies, in the company of God we are invited and voluntarily join. This makes the relationship with God and with others in God's company qualitatively different. If there were any imposition or coercion, as there is in most other companies, the relationship would be less voluntary, chosen and free.

27. Ibid., 5.

We are certainly free ourselves to reject the evidence of God's revelation to us, whether it is a coincidence, miracle or however we might choose to categorize it. Such rejections of the evidence have been going on well before René Descartes located skepticism in the mind.[28] In fact, Jesus expressed his own skepticism about the effectiveness of miraculous evidence without a readiness, willingness or longing in the heart of the recipient. His skepticism is central to the parable in the Gospel of Luke about Lazarus and the rich man. The story concludes, "If they do not listen to Moses and the prophets, neither will they be convinced even if someone rises from the dead."[29] The Gospel of John chronicles the same kind of skepticism as well, recounting what Isaiah recognized centuries before: "Although he [Jesus] had performed so many signs in their presence, they did not believe in him."[30]

In this respect we really are our own worst enemies, victims of our own cognitive idolatry. In its various forms, our cognitive idolatry causes us to rule out evidence that we should not ignore. Like most other forms of idolatry, it seduces us into believing we are in a position to judge what is, or is not, right and true.

BEYOND COGNITIVE IDOLATRY

How do we get beyond this addiction-like tyranny of causal evidence and cognitive idolatry? How do we engage the heart in sense-making and creativity, not just the mind?

A short answer may be to pay attention when the heart resonates with what mind is ready to dismiss. Accidents we may ignore. Incidences we may overlook. But coincidences may be too precious to deny.

A more considered answer suggests that we can get beyond our cognitive idolatry and our widespread worship of causality when we seek evidence neither in the signs of Jerusalem nor the wisdom of Athens but rather in the truth of the Anointed One, crucified.[31]

---

28. The legacy of Descartes' famous "I think therefore I am," intentionally or unintentionally left us seemingly locked into assuming that we think with the mind—what Frank Wilson refers to as an "encephalocentric" and incorrect assumption about cognition, i.e., that it all happens in the brain. Wilson, *Hand*, 295.

29. Luke 16:19–31; and Isa 6; 44:18.

30. John 16:37–40.

31. 1 Cor 1:22–23.

> Through the cross of Christ we gain a new understanding of
> the present scene; we note relations previously ignored; find
> explanations of our actions hitherto undreamed of. Deeds and
> sufferings begin to compose themselves into a total picture of
> significant action in which the self no longer occupies the cen-
> ter. We now begin to comprehend the tragedy of contemporary
> life as a connected, unified affair in which one act succeeds an-
> other by a moral necessity in view of the great divine, dominat-
> ing purpose.[32]

Niebuhr suggests revelation is not confined to matters of personal
piety nor communal religious practice. Rather, it should be used as the
center of our efforts to make sense of change and create new value for
others. The life and death of Christ *as a parable and an analogy* can separate out the signal of what matters from the surrounding noise of our
present circumstances. Without this filter, our imaginations can hide
from us what we are and obscure what we are doing.[33]

"'Father, forgive them, they know not what they do,' is applicable to
us in every moment."[34] Using the life and death of Christ in this way not
only reveals what is signal. It transmits this signal through the mind to
the heart. It is no longer some distant past or multisyllabic doctrine, but
an arrow that pierces the heart and changes it, and so begins a process
of converting the whole person to a greater purpose in a broader, more
inclusive neighborhood with deeper, more satisfying meaning. It is not
just a detached, dead proposition. It becomes a central, living, moral and
personal reality. "Thus the heart reasons with the aid of revelation,"[35] and
in so reasoning it makes sense of change through love—of God, of neighbor, and even of enemy.

Niebuhr's recognition of the revelatory potency of parable and
analogy resonates with what studies of creative problem-solving have
chronicled for some time. Evidentiary research has long been aware of
the near universal ability of people to use metaphor and analogy in both
generative and descriptive efforts. Metaphors enable connections that
retrospectively make sense and prospectively generate conceptions of
new value.

32. Niebuhr, *Meaning of Revelation*, 90–91.

33. Ibid., 89.

34. Ibid., 91.

35. Ibid., 96.

Ironically it is when we find ourselves in the role of knowledgeable experts that we tend to neglect the qualitative, playful and affective richness of metaphor and analogy. Demonstrating our technical knowhow as "experts" we tend to favor the quantitative, serious and rational. However, when experts are mixed with non-experts and both are invited to use metaphor, parable and analogy, fresh connections to describe the problem and generate fresh solutions spontaneously emerge. Experts themselves—even scribes and Pharisees—can escape binding confinements of their own expertise to pursue substantive new meaning and value.[36]

In preparing and facilitating invention and creative problem solving sessions I have seen fresh connections enabled by metaphors uncover additional dots to connect. More often metaphors, parables and analogies serve to help experts make sense from new connections they were not able to see without them. Sometimes the metaphors and analogies stimulate potent new ideas. In most cases, however, it was the metaphor, analogy or parable that invited experts to go beyond their empirical, rational and constrained thinking.[37]

Repeated experience of this pattern over the years has left me with the conviction that when experts are able to go beyond the conventional boundaries of their discipline's current accepted canon, they see qualitatively and aesthetically something in their mind's eye that they—as only experts can—recognize as beautiful. Beauty attracts both their attention and their devotion. And from both attention and devotion, fresh meaning is made and new value is invented, even before the experts can find the words to describe what they are seeing in their mind's eye. When they do, they invariably turn to a metaphor or analogy to describe what they are seeing.

Theology comes with a host of metaphorical and analogical images, particularly as and when these metaphors and analogies come from the life, death and resurrection of Jesus. Given theology's subject matter, it cannot escape this kind of thinking. Theology is also familiar with making connections across well worn mental and emotional divides. This may be because of the mystery that is at the heart of all theology.

W. J. J. Gordon observed that a good descriptive metaphor has a quality of

36. Gordon, *Synectics*, 92–102.

37. Ibid., 103–14.

> mystery about it as it postulates similarities between apparently
> unlike things, and as it illuminates and excites in the confusion
> of our impressions by simultaneously suggesting an identity and
> a separateness. . . . The impression of mystery may derive from
> the fact that a metaphoric sort of activity operates not only on
> conscious but also on preconscious and subconscious levels.[38]

This all may be very interesting, but does it make any practical difference in making sense of change, making meaning and creating new value for others?

There are at least two practical implications. One is the importance of creative collaboration among and between deep experts from diverse disciplines. Such collaborations are increasingly required for making sense of complex, dynamic and intensifying change and its commensurate urgency for creating new value. The other is that the freshness and originality of connections made will shape the character of the sense we make and the substance of the new value we create for others. Without the metaphoric, parabolic and analogical beginnings, we are hopelessly saddled with digital, binary and quantitative connections, the sense and value we make from which is neither new nor substantive.

Gordon's observation of the mystery in metaphor, and Niebuhr's inclusion of parable and analogy as carriers of revelation, point to how metaphor, parable and analogy penetrate both mind and heart and connect the two. Beyond the evidentiary and practical, however, the elusiveness of God remains, and remains a bit of a mystery itself. The potency of this mystery and its presence in coincidental evidence is worth a closer look.

GOD'S ANONYMITY

Why does God appear so intent on remaining so mysterious, elusive and even anonymous? Even Jesus appears scrupulously shy of claiming the identity so many wanted to ascribe to him. What's going on here? Why would God be so inclined toward such an anonymous posture?

Might it be because God's love for God's creation and creatures is as noncoercive as it is unconditional? It does not *impose* itself or *compel* the objects of its desire to conform, accept or even respond. Instead, it invites, attracts and creates space for us to choose, to volunteer, to consciously step into the company of God on our own. If it were otherwise

---

38. Ibid., 114.

the resulting relationships in the company of God would be disingenuous, constrained and anything but free or loving. Isn't the inviting,
noncoercive character of metaphor, parable and analogy the same kind
of attraction? Each seems an animating and roomy space in which to
breathe, think, feel, explore, wonder and discover, and to do so with each
other. The attracting rather than promoting, noncoercive orientation of
God aligns well with God's tendencies toward anonymity.

But why would God choose to remain so anonymous? At least two
reasons are worth considering.

One may have to do with the combination of the perfect freedom
and perfect love of God. God, by definition, is perfectly free to do as God
sees fit.[39] God is unconstrained by our cognitive rules, our empirical tests
of causality or our controlled experiments. Along with this perfect freedom is perfect, noncoercive love. God's love is freely given to us in such
ways as to attract rather than promote, to invite rather than coerce, to
give us the ability to respond, even to reject God, rather than mold us into
preprogrammed robots. Genuine love "must take the risk of rejection,
because it refuses to depersonalize any responsible person with dominat-
ing coercion of that person's will regarding the reception of love."[40]

This combination of God's perfect freedom and perfect love seems
better served by a posture of anonymity than it does by fixing God with a
name. If God were to be totally transparent, exclusively named, with only
one name and only one correct pronunciation, that name would surely be
misused—a violation of the third commandment—it would likely set up
an idol in the name itself. An individual name, even its correct pronunciation, carries more coercive power. God's apparent desire seems to be
to invite rather than compel us into a co-creative relationship. If we were
to be coerced into such a relationship with God the relationship would
be more of a transaction than a covenant, more deal than communion.

God seems to prefer us to enter the relationship on our own. The
implication of this noncoercive love puts the emphasis squarely on free
choice, God's and ours. This freedom to choose, if a genuine choice, includes the option to refuse. Considering our individual and collective
past manifests all manner of refusals, it is remarkable that God apparently continues to choose to be in relationship with us. This certainly

39. The word "God" is itself a relatively anonymous word. "God" is more of a designation than a name.

40. Moser, *Elusive God*, 63.

speaks more to the love and graciousness of God than it does about the character of humanity.

The second reason God might choose to remain anonymous may grow out of God's years of experience with human tendencies toward control. By remaining anonymous, God preempts our ability to contain and control God, despite the persistence of our attempts to do so. Idolatry is but one type of this tendency, albeit a significant one.

Might it be that *we* have the need to name, a need that God may not share?[41] True, God brought every living creature to the man "to see what he would call them and whatever the man called every living creature, that was its name."[42] But the Creator is not one of the creatures. The extent to which we ignore the difference between our taxonomic needs and the possibility that God's taxonomic needs are different, already satisfied or non-existent altogether, is the extent to which we unwittingly attempt to push God off his throne and sit in it ourselves. Besides, names do not capture everything about who or what is named.

Thus far I have only appealed to reason, though speculatively, as to why God might want to remain anonymous. Surprisingly enough, Scripture also strongly suggests that God may have inclinations toward maintaining God's anonymity.

One of the more seminal biblical passages that speaks of this divine inclination is God's reply to Moses' request for some evidentiary authorization—some name, proof and set of credentials—to present to a skeptical Pharaoh and an equally likely skeptical Israelite nation (Exod 3). This request of Moses appears entirely reasonable. Moses has just received God's set of instructions: go to the corporate boss Pharaoh and tell him to release his entire labor force and turn these people over to you (Moses), who, we may recall, is a fugitive and wanted man. Yeah, right. It doesn't take much imagination to give God's request a low probability of success. Moses simply anticipates the most likely question the people God will ask: "Who do you think *you* are?" In fact, Moses asks pretty much this question of himself: "Who am I that I should go to Pharaoh and bring the Israelites out of Egypt?"

God's response is revealing, as it always is, not only for what it says but for what it doesn't say. "I will be with you." From God's point of view this is really all Moses needs, though God goes on to offer a sign that it is

41. While God has many titles, a title is not a name.

42. Gen 2:19–20.

"I who sent you": an after-the-fact kind of *non-sequitur* proof that "you and the Israelites will worship God on this mountain." Huh? This was not likely all that satisfying or reassuring to Moses. It is easy to see why Moses goes on to ask for a little bit more by way of credentials—evidence of both authorization and authentication. So Moses lays out before God the likely "if/then" scenario: "If I (Moses) come to the Israelites and say to them, 'The God of your ancestors has sent me to you,' and they ask me, 'What is his name?' What shall I say to them?"

This seems an entirely reasonable request based on an entirely probable scenario. But God's response is stunningly elusive. "I am who I am," or as some translators prefer, "I am what I am" or still other translators suggest, "I will be what I will be." God's response even eludes consensus among the translators! Again, this is not exactly what Moses was looking for. But God, sensing Moses' disappointment, goes on to say, "Thus you shall say to the Israelites, 'The Lord [in the Hebrew YHWH meaning "to be"], the God of your ancestors, the God of Abraham, the God of Isaac, and the God of Jacob, has sent me to you: This is my name forever, and this my title for all generations.'"

This is truly remarkable, not only for God to say, or not say, about God's own name. It is remarkable to have such a seminal story included in any religion's own scripture. Not only is this not a name in the conventional sense of what we normally think of as a proper name. It is a revelation that God may choose to have no name. It shouldn't go unnoticed that this story is told in the authoritative writings of all the Abrahamic religions—Christianity, Judaism and Islam.

We might think with Jesus Christ this divine anonymity was broken. In a way, it was and is, but perhaps not completely. Consider the indirections and evasive shyness in response to direct questions that kept coming to Jesus about his identity. Those who ask range from John the Baptist to Pilate and many in between.

When John the Baptist sends his own disciples to ask, "Are you the one who is to come, or are we to wait for another?" Jesus response is to point to the evidence: "Go and tell John what you hear and see: the blind receive their sight, the lame walk, the lepers are cleansed the deaf hear, the dead are raised and the poor have good news brought to them."[43] Then of course there is this enigmatic encounter between Pilate and Jesus

43. Matt 11:2–6; Luke 7:18–23.

that speaks loudly of the deafening restraint of Jesus. He refuses to acquiesce to Pilate's or anyone else's definition of Jesus' identity:

> Then Pilate entered the headquarters again, summoned Jesus, and asked him, "Are you the King of the Jews?" Jesus answered, "Do you ask this on your own, or did others tell you about me?" Pilate replied, "I am not a Jew, am I? Your own nation and the chief priests have handed you over to me. What have you done?" Jesus answered, "My kingdom is not from this world. If my kingdom were from this world, my followers would be fighting to keep me from being handed over to the Jews. But as it is, my kingdom is not from here." Pilate asked him, "So you are a king?" Jesus answered, "You say that I am a king. For this I was born, and for this I came into the world, to testify to the truth. Everyone who belongs to the truth listens to my voice." Pilate asked him, "What is truth?"[44]

Jesus' interaction with Pilate is echoed in what the prison warden says to the prisoner Luke, played by Paul Newman in the movie *Cool Hand Luke*. "What we have here is a failure to communicate."

This evasive shyness about his own identity is no more evident than in Jesus' unambiguous willingness to identify himself as the Son of (the) Man—perhaps the most enigmatic if not anonymous self-reference.[45] Coupled with Jesus' ambiguous shyness regarding his identification with the title Son of God, anonymity is a part of Jesus' image of himself.

ANONYMITY ON PURPOSE

So what? What does the anonymity of God have to do with the evidence of change, our making sense of it and ultimately, our ability to create new value for others?

An answer resides in the consistent pattern that occurs when God breaks anonymity and reveals a broader, deeper and greater reality. Theophany is the technical term used to categorize instances of divine appearance. Most biblical theophanies evoke a predictable response sequence: first there is fear followed immediately by a divine voice saying "fear not." Then God breaks out of hiding to reveal God's reality, existence, presence, character and intent.

---

44. John 18:33–38.

45. Wink, *Human Being*, 113–47, 259.

Why is this, particularly if God is a compassionate God, slow to anger and abounding in steadfast love?[46] Might it have less to do with God than it has to do with the cognitive, moral and volitional asymmetries between God and humanity—the gap between the divine and human realities?

Might the anonymity of God have more to do with the condition and states of mind, heart and will of the one receiving the revelation than it does with the One who is on the giving or revealing end? Paul Moser puts it this way:

> The matter of knowing God's reality, then, becomes as much about us as potential recipients as about a perfectly loving God's contribution by way of non-coercive self-revelation. We thus need to consider, with due resolve and honesty, whether we are genuinely willing to be known, and thereby transformed away from selfishness, by a perfectly loving God. If we aren't, then we ourselves could be a sizeable obstacle to our acquiring some purposively available evidence of divine reality.[47]

The anonymity of God may be but the necessary consequence of God's radical and perfect freedom, and coincidences are but noncoercive signs that God has already taken the initiative, acting already in the changes that come to us as an invitation, waiting for our response.

Coincidence as evidence of divine reality and activity turns out to be a very effective partner in maintaining God's anonymity. Coincidences have the distinct character of *attracting* our attention rather than demanding or forcing it. Coincidence invites us to "turn aside and look at this great sight."[48] We can always ignore it and refuse to turn aside because we are too busy or have to keep the schedule for our next appointment (whether we are appointed or not). Unlike causes or correlations, coincidences have the distinct advantage of immunity from imposing or promoting themselves on our attention. It is as if God prefers to whisper to us—as in the still, small voice that came to Elijah—rather than shout at us.[49]

The new value we create for others may not reside in what we say or what we produce as much as it is in what the other hears and receives.

---

46. Exod 34:6; Num 14:18; Ps 86:5, 15; 103:8; 145:8; Joel 2:13.

47. Moser, *Elusive God*, 119.

48. Exod 3:3.

49. 1 Kgs 19:11–13. The NRSV's translation is "sheer silence" instead of the RSV's "still small voice."

This is but the tangible realization of whether and how we show up with love *for the other*, even our enemies, not for ourselves or our own interests.[50] Ultimately we make sense of change and create value for others embodied in what we co-create—whether through words on a page or in products or services we invent and reduce to practice. But the value is never in the embodiment alone. It is realized only when the value is received.

In other words, until the words are read, products and services used and the intent is absorbed and integrated into the life of the other, only then is the benefit to the other, the love of the other, realized. There is no sense we can make or value we might create without it being first seen, experienced and received. The love *expressed* in the particular form of the value itself may be no different than the original Source who *impressed* this love into a form to begin with. Incarnational theology is never very far from revelation theology, and will likely never be very far from innovation theology.

RESPONDING WITH THE HEART

Awareness of our bias for the causal, empirical and rational is one thing. Getting over it is quite another. Tuning into evidence resonant with the frequencies of the heart does not come so easily, particularly when our minds are so active and perhaps educated beyond our intelligence.

Even when attuned to these heart frequencies we can experience resistance, rejection and more bad news rather than good. What is it that can help us pay more attention to the language and evidence the heart attends to, and attune ourselves the purpose, presence and movement of God's company?

Seeing through our previous denials, facing more clearly and directly our own mistakes, accepting the emotional deflation that goes along it and taking full responsibility for it is not something many of us are inclined to go out and seek. However, when it comes *to* us, it is a way of learning that impresses us more deeply than other ways. This way of learning and knowing is contrition. Other ways do not seem to penetrate as deeply as contrition, nor evoke the change of mind and heart that contrition does.

50. Phil 2:4.

Contrition[51] is the perceptual, emotional and cognitive means through which our minds and hearts change. Such change is the consistent theme that runs the length and depth of the prophetic tradition, from Isaiah, Jeremiah and most of the others, all the way through to the fulfillment of this tradition in Jesus' concise summary of his own purpose: "repent for the kingdom of God is at hand." This repentance (*metanoia* in the Greek, literally meaning "to change our knowing") is essential for making sense of change and for creating new value for others.

Isaiah's own personal and direct experience of contrition is one of both purgation and vocation all wrapped up at the same moment:

> In the year that King Uzziah died,
> I saw the Lord sitting on a throne, high and lofty; . . .
> And I said:
> "Woe is me! I am lost, for I am a man of unclean lips, and I live among a people of unclean lips; yet my eyes have seen the King, the Lord of hosts!"
> Then one of the seraphs flew to me, holding a live coal that had been taken from the altar with a pair of tongs. The seraph touched my mouth with it and said:
> "Now that this has touched your lips,
> your guilt has departed and your sin is blotted out."
> Then I heard the voice of the Lord saying,
> "Whom shall I send, and who will go for us?"
> And I said, "Here am I; send me!"[52]

What comes next is not what we, or Isaiah for that matter, might expect: a Cassandra-like prediction that Isaiah will speak a truth that no one will hear.

> And he said, "Go and say to this people:
> "Keep listening, but do not comprehend; keep looking, but do not understand."
> Make the mind of this people dull, and stop their ears, and shut their eyes,
> so that they may not look with their eyes, and listen with their ears, and comprehend with their minds, and turn and be healed.[53]

51. Another Latin combination meaning "to bruise."

52. Isa 6:1–8.

53. Isa 6:9–10.

Why would God go to all the trouble to forgive and painfully purify Isaiah and then give the prophet the dismal task of telling the truth to those who refuse to accept or understand it? Why would a loving God, consistently interested in Israel's change of heart and mind, seemingly cause Israel to harden its heart and close its mind? Is this divinely dictated hardening of Israel's heart simply a clear repudiation of any possibility of "cheap grace"?[54]

Noteworthy here is the presence of the same resistance that shows up in the message and mission of Jesus. All four gospels directly quote Isaiah's prophecy of resistance,[55] or what Walter Brueggemann calls the nonresponsiveness of a people "deeply narcoticized not only by chemical dependence, but by a host of numbing dependencies: poverty and wealth in the extreme, brutality, militarism [and] self-indulgence."[56]

Cognitive idolatry is deeply entrenched and not easily broken. The Gospel of John hints at the root cause of this idolatry this way: "for they loved human glory more than the glory that comes from God."[57] Even Isaiah himself raises an understandable, albeit humble, query about God's intentions:

> Then I said, "How long, O Lord?" And he said:
> "Until cities lie waste without inhabitant, and houses without people,
> and the land is utterly desolate;
> until the Lord sends everyone far away,
> and vast is the emptiness in the midst of the land.
> Even if a tenth part remains in it, it will be burned again,
> like a terebinth or an oak whose stump remains standing
> when it is felled." The holy seed is its stump.[58]

This last fragment in the final verse holds out only the thinnest thread of hope: seed of new life from a black charred stump. It is a seed of hope that only the One for whom all things is possible might fulfill. There is little, if any, hope that might come from human wisdom or cognition to be found in this stump.

54. "Cheap grace" is the reception of God's love and forgiveness without the experience of God's judgment.

55. Matt 13:14–15; Mark 4:12; Luke 8:10; John 12:37–43.

56. Brueggemann, *Isaiah,* 1:63.

57. John 12:43.

58. Isa 6:11–13.

Jeremiah seemed even less hopeful:

> For from the least to the greatest of them, everyone is greedy for unjust gain;
>> and from prophet to priest, everyone deals falsely.
> They have treated the wound of my people carelessly
> saying, "Peace, peace," when there is no peace.
> They acted shamefully, they committed abomination;
>> yet they were not ashamed, they did not know how to blush.
> Therefore they shall fall among those who fall.[59]

When we do not "know how to blush" it is difficult to learn. Perhaps this is but another way of expressing that the fear of the Lord is the beginning of wisdom.[60] But in the verse that immediately follows Jeremiah's warning there is a word of grace, invitation and promise:

> Stand at the crossroads, and look, and ask for the ancient paths,
> where the good way lies; and walk in it, and find rest for your souls.[61]

However, this word of hope doesn't last long. Before the same verse is finished Jeremiah reminds us that the denial persists: "But they said, 'We will not walk in it.'"[62]

Contrition is the necessary experience—the narrow gate—that takes us through the threshold, away from our cognitive idolatry and into the company of God. Contrition gets us from merely knowing with our minds and perceiving with our senses to a wider knowing and deeper understanding that comes from the heart, where love is reflected and responds in making sense of change and creating new value for others. The Psalmist expresses it perhaps the best:

> The sacrifice acceptable to God is a broken spirit;
> a broken and contrite heart, O God, you will not despise.[63]

---

59. Jer 6:13–15.

60. Job 28:28; Ps 111:10; Prov 1:7; 10:9; Eph 5:17.

61. Jer 6:16.

62. Jer 6:16.

63. Ps 51:17.

LOVING TRUMPS KNOWING

Attention to the evidence is essential for creating the *knowledge* necessary for making sense. Attention to the evidence is essential for cultivating the *love* necessary for creating new value.

This may be one reason that typical failure rates for innovating efforts are as high as some report them to be. Too many innovating efforts rely on either one or the other, not both. It is not just a matter of knowing or being the smartest one in the neighborhood. Nor is it just a matter of loving, or being the most mindful and empathetic listener in the neighborhood. Both knowing and loving are required for making sense of change and creating new value for others. But if there is one that is more important than the other, it is surely love.

Paul recognized this when he said, "Knowledge puffs up, while love builds up."[64] Paul didn't leave it to that sound bite alone. He went on to say, "Anyone who claims to know something does not yet have the necessary knowledge; but anyone who loves God is known by him." Cognitive idolatry is all about being right, which, it turns out, is less important than being loving, even in making sense of change and especially in creating new value for others. I learned this the hard way many years ago.

When I was seven years old, my family returned to Washington, DC. The year was 1959. The family naturally returned to the church in which my parents had been active before moving away from Washington. This was New York Avenue Presbyterian Church, located two blocks from the White House. "New York Ave," as it was called by its members, proudly kept President Lincoln's pew prominent in a large sanctuary, sized to fit the storied Peter Marshall with whom my parents had played bridge when they first attended in the late '40s. Back then my parents had been swept up in the piety inspired by the charisma and Scottish brogue of this famous preacher.

However, when they returned ten years later, times had changed, and so had they. Church, at least this church, was a place for social action. The politics of civil rights and war protests came up alongside the piety of worship and Bible study. Mother marched in Selma and demonstrated against the Vietnam War. Dad served on the board of the Washington Council of Churches. Through my parents' activism the church began to look like an exciting, edgy kind of thing to be involved in. It was all about

64. 1 Cor 8:1–2.

"loving your neighbor," even your enemy neighbor. It was where the action was. As kid growing up, I just assumed this was the norm.

Unconsciously I carried this assumption with me, all the way to that small church in North Carolina, where I found myself at the end of the decade of the '70s, freshly ordained, ready to do what I thought was "church"—the edgy kind of thing where the action was. The Presbyterian church there was comprised of about a hundred souls. Almost as soon as I arrived, I looked around for the closest "institutional neighbor" for this little congregation to love. The neighbor turned out to be a youth detention facility, part of the Department of Corrections for North Carolina. Of course the church I was serving was entirely white, while 80 percent of the "residents" of the Department of Corrections in North Carolina were at the time African American.

When I broached the "love our neighbor" initiative with the lay leaders of the church, the reactions and responses were, how shall I say, "mixed" at best. Few, if any, were enthusiastic about the prospect of any kind of ministry with or for the youth in the detention facility. One of the leaders—who ultimately left this little congregation in protest—begrudgingly said, "We'll worship with them but we won't eat with them"—a deeply unfortunate reflection not only of the one who expressed it but of the integrity of our worship.

My righteous imagination (and indignation) kicked in. For several weeks I passionately preached from the Old Testament prophets—Amos, especially—and selectively extracted the pointedly inclusive sayings of Jesus from the gospels. Ultimately the poor little church reluctantly went along, following their young, protesting pastor into a ministry of loving our closest institutional neighbor. But the delicate balance between maintaining the peace, purity and unity of the church—the essence of a vow I had taken when I was ordained—was hardly maintained. Purity, perhaps, at least from my perspective; but peace and unity were left to fend for themselves.

The struggle within this unsuspecting congregation left me depleted, disappointed and resigned to the likelihood that the currency of trust and understanding required of a pastor might be more forthcoming in a congregation farther north. So I eventually went north to a larger congregation, one more open and willing to take on love-your-institutional-neighbor kinds of initiatives, or so I thought. There, with some distance and time I did some soul-searching about the experience I had left in the Bible Belt. I came to a lesson repeatedly confirmed in a whole host of various times and places since then. The lesson is really very simple: *it is more important to be loving than right.*

This contrition I had to come to on my own, though it is a lesson that I was not the first to learn. The Apostle Paul himself came to it as an-always-right, smartest-guy-in-the-room kind of Pharisee. He was stopped in his tracks on the road to Damascus. Paul's former bias for cognitive intelligence was shattered. He came to see his own experience of knowledge puffing up in contrast to love building up. And he came to express this same understanding in his letter to the church at Corinth, a church populated with a few too many who were a bit too full of themselves:

> If I speak in the tongues of mortals and of angels, but do not have love, I am a noisy gong or a clanging cymbal. And if I have prophetic powers, and understand all mysteries and all knowledge, and if I have all faith so as to remove mountains, but do not have love, I am nothing.[65]

CONCLUSION

Persistent and chronic failure in making sense of change and creating new value for others is really nothing new. Even Jesus warned of various false prophets whose veracity and trustworthiness is only revealed in the integrity of the fruit they bear.[66] Knowing this could evoke one of two reactions.

One is a resignation. Many leaders resign themselves to the apparent fact that any future success in making sense of change and creating new value will be short-lived, if ever it lives to begin with. Sense and value are just too circumstantial and dependent upon too many unfathomable factors beyond our control or knowledge.

The other is a willful response—a testosterone-laden insistence to "just make it happen." This kind of response ends up elevating sheer persistence to a virtue, whether it is called for or not. After all "if at first you don't succeed, then try, try again."

For most of my professional and personal life I have been both a spectator and participant in these two mind-sets. I suspect I am not alone. Looking back on myself as both spectator and participant leads me to Einstein's famous observation that we cannot hope to solve difficult

65. 1 Cor 13:1–2.
66. Matt 7:15–20.

problems with the same thinking used to create them. Such wisdom is helpful in suggesting where not to look for solutions. However, it is not very helpful for directing us where to look. We must look elsewhere for that. In fact, we must broaden our field of view and deepen our sense of what makes for value. We must use both mind and heart and look for both empirical and volitional evidence.

Self-interests and cognitive idolatry can so easily creep back into our hearts and minds. It is much easier to *say* "let each of you look not to your own interest, but to the interest of others" than it is to practice it, fully and completely. "What's in it for me?" is a very difficult question to shake off. This is especially true for commercial innovators. But it can also be true for charitable foundations demanding certain performance outcomes of their recipient nonprofits, not to mention individuals just trying to make sense of change and do something valuable in response.

However, where ever the fruits of our sense-making and creative efforts are substantive and sustainable, these fruits will likely come from simply showing up for the other, like God shows up for us, noncoercively, anonymously, working not for our own interests, but for the purposes of the company of God.

CONVERSATION STARTERS

1. Where and how might biblical theology find its prophetic and pastoral voice(s) in speaking grace to a knowledge, information and performance economy?

2. Can biblical theology make its contribution to innovating more effective by honoring God's anonymity? What does it look like to honor God's anonymity?

3. Do STEM-enabled innovations reflect the interests of the company of God? How? How not?

10

Humility

A Practical Necessity That Takes Practice

The pride of everyone shall be brought low.[1]

CHANGE SOMETIMES PRESENTS REALITIES about which we can make little or no sense. Changes can be so large, dramatic, sudden or strange that making sense of them is difficult if not impossible.

The inability to make sense of what happened at Sandy Hook Elementary School is one example. On December 14, 2012, in a quiet town in Connecticut, a troubled Adam Lanza killed his mother before laying siege to the school. There he gunned down twenty children, six more adults and then himself. Making sense of this incident still eludes us.

If anyone was in a position to make sense of the tragedy it was Andrew Solomon. His book *Far from the Tree* had been published just months before. The book is about parents whose children are profoundly different from other children, even to the point of senselessly destructive behavior. Solomon published an attempt to make sense of the tragedy at Sandy Hook about two years after, being the only one to interview Peter Lanza, the father of the killer, Adam. But as Solomon himself admits, his attempt was unsuccessful.

1. Isa 2:17.

Terry Gross interviewed Solomon shortly after the account of his failure was published in the *New Yorker*.[2] I happened to hear the interview on the radio. It was Solomon's response to Gross' question that caught my attention.

> *Gross:* Now that you have interviewed Peter Lanza do your conclusions [from *Far from the Tree*] change at all? If you were writing *Far from the Tree* now, would you say anything different at the end of the book?

> *Solomon:* I think this story illuminates the complex idea that diagnosis, which we think of as so useful, may actually be an impediment to insight. . . . For many people diagnosis is a huge relief. . . . It is something that you want. But this experience teaches me a diagnosis can be incredibly helpful and it can be incredibly dangerous.

> *Gross:* So after writing this article, you have a lot more insight. We all have a lot more insight into what happened. But we're all still left with a lot of mystery.

> *Solomon:* I think it's an essentially mysterious event, and I think it will always be a mysterious event. I wish that I could have uncovered a logic in it, but the logic eluded me, as it's eluded everyone who's looked at it.[3]

Despite the horrific events at Sandy Hook Elementary, and not withstanding his own investment in making sense of this horrific event, the honesty of Solomon's admission is striking.[4] His humility is as noteworthy as his observation about the dangers of diagnosis. Perhaps they are one and the same. *Diagnosis may be an impediment to insight.*

Even for less dramatic, tragic or senseless events, our diagnoses can prove lacking and at times, dangerously so. Logic, narrative or explanation eludes us. The matter remains open. There is no final insight, no conclusion, and no resolution. Admitting that our diagnosis masks as

---

2. Solomon, "Reckoning."

3. Transcript of interview of Andrew Solomon by Terry Gross, "For Sandy Hook Killer's Father, Tragedy Outweighs Love for His Son," Fresh Air, National Public Radio, March 13, 2014.

4. And seemingly missed by Terry Gross, as evidenced in the way she asked her second question.

much as it reveals, ignores as much as it acknowledges, points to the necessity of humility.

What follows looks at what humility brings to making sense of change. It proposes that humility actually makes more sense in our sense-making than the alternatives. These alternatives typically impose on reality rather than expose or explore. Humility keeps us open to the more that will be revealed rather than closed by our own ideological prejudices. It keeps us attentive to bottom-up plausibility more than top-down predictability. And it keeps us willingly induced to love more than quick to deduce ourselves right.

Without humility, making sense of change can easily inflate and elevate the sense maker. With self-inflation we lose a sense of proportion essential for making sense and perceiving value. With elevation we end up looking down, judging and imposing order, structure and meaning. Imposition conforms to the imposer more than to the evidence emerging from the experience. Without humility we can easily lose perspective and distort any sense there is to be made.

In and of itself humility may be morally virtuous and emotionally prudent. But in the context of making sense, it plays a pragmatic role. Without humility the fidelity between perception and reality becomes prematurely fixed. The space we leave for the presence of God narrows. Humility is a practical necessity when it comes to making sense of change.

But humility takes practice, a lot of practice. This is especially the case for those of us prone to seek certainty, clarity and closure. When we experience the exhilaration of having made some sense, such an experience can easily seduce us into believing that we have finally figured it out. But a gap will always remain between what is real and true and how we understand and express that reality and truth. With humility, however, the gap can become a wellspring of renewal, but only just so long as we remain engaged, enter that gap ourselves and persist in our efforts to make sense and create value for others.

Without humility the gap easily ends up being denied, or its dimensions underestimated. When we mistakenly imagine we have closed the gap finally, completely and with certainty, at that precise moment we have begun to close not only our minds but our hearts as well. We end up leaving little room to account for the free movement and surprising presence of God. Such mistaken certainty is a symptom of brittle fundamentalism and closed-minded fanaticism knotted more to ideology than provisionally coupled with reality, a reality that is always changing. In short, humility is necessary in sense-making because any sense we make can only be provisional and temporary, partial and incomplete.

This may be disappointing news to those who are otherwise heavily invested in being right, accurate or precise. However, knowing the sense we make is only temporary and partial is no reason for resignation or despair. Nor is it any reason to stop trying to make sense—as if we could stop anyway. Nor is it cause to retreat into some passive observer role, waiting to see what will develop before engaging in and with the new realities change brings to us. Rather, it is simply to acknowledge that making sense of change, particularly when the aim is to create new value for others, is precarious without some modicum of humility. This is especially the case when making sense of change does not come easily and we are tempted to make judgments rather than sense.

JUDGING

Quickness in assigning change as either "good" or "bad" is symptomatic of a deep-seated habit. The habit is to judge rather than appreciate the new realities in change.

Consider the following parable social psychologist Richard Nisbett uses to illustrate our tendency to judge. It's an ancient Chinese story about an old farmer whose only horse ran away.

> Knowing that the horse was the mainstay of his livelihood, his neighbors came to commiserate with him. "Who knows what's bad or good?" said the old man, refusing their sympathy. And indeed, a few days later his horse returned, bringing with it a wild horse.
>
> The old man's friends came to congratulate him. Rejecting their congratulations, the old man said, "Who knows what's bad or good?" And, as it happened, a few days later when the old man's son was attempting to ride the wild horse, he was thrown from it and his leg was broken.
>
> The friends came to express their sadness about the son's misfortune. "Who knows what's bad or good?" said the old man. A few weeks passed, and the army came to the village to conscript

all the able-bodied men to fight war against the neighboring province, but the old man's son was not fit to serve and was spared.[5]

Quickness to judge change as good or bad is a habit peculiar to Western mind-sets and relatively absent in Eastern ways of making sense, according to Nisbett.[6] Eastern sense-making assumes change is constant and that to make sense of change requires one to be cognizant of the opposite of what appears to be true now. A Westerner, on the other hand, will just as likely assume that what appears to be the case cannot simultaneously hold the opposite. In the case of change, whatever the new realities change presents for the Western mind are likely to be either good or bad, not both. For the Eastern mind-set, they can be both good and bad, and if so, then there is not much to gain in assigning the labels "good" or "bad" to any change.

A nonjudgmental attitude toward change is not the exclusive monopoly of an Eastern mind-set, however. Early in the book of Genesis, just after God forms man "from the dust of the earth," God plants a garden in Eden with trees that are not only beautiful to look at but good for food.[7] This includes, of course, the tree of life and the tree of the knowledge of good and evil. The stage is set. Then God puts man in the garden to till it and keep it. And the very first thing God says to man is, "You may freely eat of every tree of the garden; but of the tree of the knowledge of good and evil you may not eat, for in the day that you eat of it you shall die."[8] We all know what happened after that.

Even from a theological perspective (and even Western Christian mind-set), the intended state of mankind is more appreciative than judgmental. Judgment—ours then God's—comes in after the fall. Or perhaps judgment *is* the fall. Humanity is not intended, qualified or knowledgeable enough to judge what is good or bad. What precipitates the fall—and why it is a "fall" to begin with—is that humanity over-reached. We elevated ourselves higher than our capabilities. And from such an elevated altitude we inevitability end up looking down on others, exercising judgment, something mankind has not the knowledge, perspective or capability of doing. This overreach has been a root cause of much injustice, violence, unrest and unhappiness.

5. Nisbett, *Geography of Thought*, 12.

6. Ibid., 13.

7. Gen 2:4.

8. Gen 2:17.

The problem of exercising judgment is not confined to Genesis. Take a look at Jesus' interaction with a rich and devout man.[9] Jesus has a remarkably reflexive reaction to the deferential salutation of the wealthy but earnest seeker. The rich and devout man "runs up to Jesus and kneels before him" and asks, "Good Teacher, what must I do to inherit eternal life?"[10] Jesus' first reaction is to ignore the question by asking one of his own: "Why do you call me good? No one is good but God alone."

Jesus' response to a seemingly reasonable if not courteous question appears a bit extreme. That he responds to a question with a question and a sharp correction is curious.[11] What is it about "good" that garners such a critique from Jesus? Is Jesus shunning any and all judgments that fall into the dichotomous classifications of good and bad? If this were the only passage we had to go on it might be a reasonable inference. There are others places where Jesus does not hesitate to assign "good" and "bad" to certain behavior and even people, however.[12] No, Jesus is not advocating some kind of moral blindness. At the very least Jesus seems to be challenging the deferential salutations of the rich and devout young man.

The story ends with the famous, haunting conclusion that it is harder for a rich man to enter the kingdom than it is for a camel to go through the eye of a needle. Jesus lifts this lesson up for his disciples who are standing to the side observing this interaction wondering, "Who then can be saved?" If this successful and devout man (not unlike some of our fabulously rich and successful entrepreneurial heroes) will find it harder to be saved than a camel going through the eye of a needle, who, if any, can be saved? To which Jesus replies with a tautological reminder about the nature of God: "For mortals it is impossible, but for God all things are possible."[13]

Paul also had a problem with the assignments of "good" and "bad," and suggested our proneness to these distinctions is a much a function

---

9. Matt 19:16–26.

10. Mark 10:17–31; also Matt 19:16–30 and Luke 18:18–30.

11. In Luke's version (Luke 18:18–30) this exchange is virtually the same. In Matthew's version (Matt 19:16–30), however, Jesus' responds, "Why do you ask me about what is good? There is only one who is good." Matthew's rendition deflects focus on Jesus and leaves it more ambiguous. However, all three versions capture Jesus' reaction to the seeker's presumptive use of the word "good."

12. *TDNT*, s.v. "agathos" (good). See also Matt 5:45; 12:33–37.

13. Matt 19:26.

of sin as of anything else.[14] Though seemingly innocent or polite, assigning goodness or badness to people, places and even things appears to be beyond our ability, authorization or pay grade. This lack of authorization hardly stops us however.

In the days immediately following the 9/11 attacks with the repeated images of the World Trade Center's twin towers collapsing, I remember reflexively wincing when the president unambiguously declared Iran, North Korea and Iraq the "axis of evil." My wince felt unpatriotic, even disloyal. So I didn't say anything. It was a reflex. I didn't choose the feeling. It just came. Perhaps it was the same kind of visceral response Jesus seemed to have when anyone, particularly anyone with even a modicum of power over others, assigns "good" or "bad" status, especially with an unwavering degree of finality and certainty.

Think of the way Jesus handled the situation of the woman caught in the act of adultery.[15] The scribes and Pharisees kept pressing him for his opinion, looking for his explicit concurrence with their prior judgment. This is not unlike what happens in any so-called political "discussion" these days. There is no interest in substantive views, just agreement or disagreement. "We don't care what you think, just whose side are you on?"

Jesus finally chooses not to "side" but to respond, "Let anyone among you who is without sin be the first to throw a stone at her." Of course, they all went away, leaving just Jesus and the woman remaining there together. And Jesus asks, "Has no one condemned you?" to which she replies, "No one." And then Jesus says plainly, "Neither do I condemn you. Go your way, and from now on do not sin again." All of this, along with our quickness to spot specks in the eyes of others while ignoring the log in our own,[16] should give us significant pause. Contrary to persistent and prevalent habits of contempt, we are in no position to diagnose who or what is innately bad or good. The essence of humility may be the absence of this habit.

So where does this habit come from? Why is it that, despite the explicit counsel to "judge not" and the repeated experience that when we do, we ourselves end up doing the very thing we accuse others of doing, we find it so difficult to kick the habit? Is it a part of our neural circuitry as

---

14. Rom 7:7–13.

15. John 8:1–11.

16. Matt 7:1–5.

some cognitive scientists and behavioral economists suggest?[17] Or might the cause be the idolatry of maintaining our own status and identity? A theological perspective might suggest so.

Idolatry may sound like an old-fashioned and even loaded word. But from a theological point of view, idolatry is a central and persistent problem infecting otherwise healthy relationships between God and mankind. Its infectiousness spreads to our relationships with each other as well. Its forms are many and varied, and like adaptive bacteria constantly morphing in its resistance to antibiotics, forms of idolatry keep changing. But whatever the form, idolatry is simply misdirected devotion and concern.[18] Idolatry elevates to ultimate what should remain penultimate.

Idolatry is not to be confused with apostasy (abandonment or renunciation of faith), heresy (misguided doctrine or belief) or blasphemy (impious irreverence). The dictionary might call it "excessive devotion."[19] It can be defined as "a worship of a god that mankind creates instead of worshipping the God who created mankind."[20] Paul Tillich saw it as "being ultimately concerned with that which is not ultimate."[21]

The specific idolatries that threaten our efforts to make sense of change are the idolatries of identity, knowledge and progress.[22] Whether the sense we make of change threatens or advances our own individual or corporate identities, confirms or challenges our own accumulated knowledge, or accelerates or slows what is considered progress, the sense made must and should remain for the time being, not permanent, ultimate or unconditional. If the sense we make becomes any more than temporary, penultimate and conditional—which often happens in fanaticism, fundamentalism and among the ideologically orthodox—we will inevitably and simply stop making sense. This is of course impractical and insane. Making sense in the company of God, then, has the practical benefit of avoiding such erosions of sanity. Any innovation theology that offers practical guidance will be especially alert to these forms of idolatry. Humility is simply good practice.[23]

17. Kahneman, *Thinking: Fast and Slow*, 89–97.

18. Horden, "Idolatry," 165.

19. *New Shorter Oxford English Dictionary*, s.v. "idolatry."

20. Hordern, "Idolatry," 165; and Tillich, *Systematic Theology*, 3:355.

21. Ibid.

22. Idolatries of knowledge and progress are addressed in other essays.

23. The idolatry of knowledge is addressed in the essay "Coincidences: God's way of staying anonymous."

IDOLATRY OF IDENTITY

The idolatry of identity may manifest in the brand-building efforts of organizations, corporations, nations, denominations, and in some cases, even individuals. Brand has become virtually synonymous with identity. The time, effort and resources spent promoting organizational identity are staggering. The efforts are visible just about everywhere you look.

Organizations regard their brands and associated identities as one of their primary assets, justifying massive investments in advertising and promotion to support and spread their reputation. Brand identity, brand values, brand equity: these idols have become preoccupying for many, even to the point where spending on the brand eclipses investment in the substance and value the brand is built upon. Shouldn't it be the other way around?

The idolatry of identity is equally prevalent within individuals as well. Until recently one's admission of "shameless self-promotion" was considered a confession. In this Facebook era, self-promotion looks more like the accepted, even expected, norm.

Idolatry of identity infects how we perceive and think. It is particularly problematic when it comes to making sense of change. Karl Weick considers identity a "core preoccupation in sense-making."[24] In his survey of the sense-making literature, Weick points to our persistent "preoccupation" to establish, build, and maintain identity. This preoccupation influences all aspects of the way we make sense, largely due to the very human habit of seeking a positive affective state about our selves, the persistent desire to perceive ourselves as competent and effective, and the desire to sense and experience coherence and consistency.[25]

"Preoccupation" is itself a symptom of idolatry, perhaps even a synonym. And while there are many possible idols causing many different kinds of idolatry, the idolatry of identity is one that leaves insidious distortions on how we make sense of change. To put it simply, we are constantly and cognitively, both in our reason and emotions, getting in our own way.

When identity needs preoccupy, they infect the way we make sense of change. The ignition that starts the sense-making process may reside in any one of our five senses. But after it is ignited, cognition and recognition quickly follow. All remain vulnerable to missed signals, misperceptions

24. Weick, *Sensemaking in Organizations*, 20.

25. Ibid.

and biased interpretations. Sensed ignition is prey to all sorts of perceptual illusions, not to mention selective perception and "blind spots" where we do not see what is right in front of us. Cognitions are likewise riddled with all sorts of curious, paradoxical and unconscious biases,[26] not to mention prevailing paradigms or mind-sets. Recognitions are subject to much the same battery of distortions. We can be as selective in our memory as we can be in what we perceive with our senses.

Preoccupation with our own identity will preempt any other object of our perceptions, attentions or devotions. This preoccupation conspires with the habit of judging something or someone as friend or foe, good or bad, threat or opportunity, depending upon how it intersects with establishing, maintaining or growing our identity. This idolatry of identity reflects Charles H. Cooley's famous "looking-glass self," the widely accepted notion in social psychology that our identity is to a large degree a product of how we imagine others see us. The Apostle Paul may not have had Cooley's theory in mind when he said, "now we see in a mirror, dimly,"[27] but Paul was not unaware of the same problem.

Idolatry arises in part from what often feels like the absence of God, the cause of which we attribute to God rather than ourselves. When we have not made sense of the new realities change presents us, we can easily assume God has left the scene, rather than the more probable alternative, that it is we who have left God's scene. And in God's misperceived absence, just as nature abhors a vacuum, so we abhor the vacuum and fill it in with something other than God. Leading the parade of candidate vacuum fillers is our selves, reputation and identity.

"Who am I?" is the question so often asked by both individuals and organizations. And when asked in the vacuum—in the perceived absence of God—the question keeps getting asked, despite the fact that theologically it has already been answered. With a theological perspective, the question is not "Who am I?" Rather, the question is "*Whose* am I?" And theology answers that we are God's creations, children and servants. Accepting these identities frees us to attend to what is happening, to what God's intentions are as they emerge.

Of course, many of us don't like that answer. We would prefer a more elevated answer, one with a bit more altitude, status and height. And when we don't like the answer, when being a creation, child or

---

26. Piattelli-Palmarini, *Inevitable Illusions*, 31–44.

27. 1 Cor 13:12.

servant of God doesn't fit our self-concept, well, then we return to our self-made identity.

The result of this idolatry, as with most forms of idolatry, is a lack of humility in the very way we make sense of change. After all, from the ignition of what we sense in our perceptions through the cognition of our thoughts and feelings extending into the recognition that relies on our memories, we are at the mercy of volatile, partial and error-prone sense-making "equipment."

OPEN-MINDEDNESS TO EMERGING TRUTH

Most definitions of humility frame it as a quality or disposition; an attribute of character or moral virtue embodied in an individual. Humility certainly is all this. But for making sense of change and for creating new value for others we need a definition tailored to the purpose.

Open-mindedness to emerging truth, even and especially a truth that we would rather not acknowledge, might be such a definition. Defining humility this way explicitly acknowledges the constancy of change and the unavoidable reality that "now I know only in part."[28]

"Emerging truth" of course implies that more will be revealed. It also assumes that I won't have "the truth, the whole truth and nothing but the truth," and if I think I do, then I have lost what little bit of humility I may have had. "Emerging truth" might sound too equivocal for some who believe the next step after equivocation is cynicism and cynicism is but a half-step closer to despair. This is certainly not the intent. Rather, "emerging truth" acknowledges the likelihood that we will see and learn more, and in this sense humility is a step toward hope.

Hope without humility can easily devolve into unrealistic expectations, cognitive arrogance or naïveté. Humility without hope can easily degrade into a passive acquiescence. "Emerging truth" acknowledges the received wisdom that the description is never the described;[29] that there will always be a gap between how we describe and understand the truth, particularly living and life-giving truth, and the fullness and reality of that truth, whatever and Whoever that is.

28. 1 Cor 13:12.

29. The full quote from Jiddu Krishnamurti is: "The description is not the described; I can describe the mountain, but the description is not the mountain, and if you are caught up in the description, as most people are, then you will never see the mountain." Krishtamurti, *Impossible Question*, 190.

Less obvious is what is implied in "mindedness." Both thought and feeling, cognition and affection are inseparably coupled not only in our minds but in our brains as well, as an increasing number of cognitive and neuroscientists are realizing. In fact, some go so far as to say that we are more feeling beings who happen to think than we are thinking beings who happen to feel.[30] In this sense, I could have said "open-heartedness to the emerging truth," but this feels a bit contrived. "Mindedness" seems to fit when the context is making sense of change, so long as we include both perception and feeling in cognition.

Perhaps the key to this definition of humility is "open." "Open" may be the easiest word to understand but the most challenging part of this definition to practice. There are degrees of openness, from wide on the one hand, to "left ajar" on the other. But whatever the size of the opening, and however easy it may be to adjust its width, "closed" is clearly contrary to humility.

"Open-mindedness to emerging truth" sounds like a reasonable working definition of humility. But putting it into practice when in the middle of our efforts to make sense of change and create new value for others, is another thing altogether. To keep a mind open, especially our own, is not such an easy thing to do, particularly when we are out of alternatives, time or both and have to make a choice.

Competence, capability and capacity[31] each come into play and work together in attempts to make sense of change and create new value for others. Humility, it turns out, is a practical necessity in all three. When present and practiced, humility enables many practical benefits in making sense of change. It lets the "air" out, so to speak, when we are too full of ourselves. It decreases the intensity of our need to be recognized. It opens us up to realities we might otherwise deny. It weakens our individual tendencies to prejudge. It even increases the freedom to choose

---

30. Taylor, *My Stroke of Insight* (TED Talk).

31. Competence, capability and capacity are often used interchangeably. However, it may be helpful to differentiate them. By "competence" I mean to suggest the possession and practice of sufficiently functioning and applicable knowledge, strength and skill. Competence is an individual skill. "Who knows how?" is a question asked about having the right competencies. By "capability" I mean to suggest an interpersonal and collaborative process or ability, typically facilitated by sufficient trust. It is what effectively uses and combines diverse points of view, experiences and expertise. "How can we get done what we need to do?" is a question asked of capability. "Capacity" is volumetric, and means the power to hold, receive or accommodate. Capacity is about amount and questions related to it are typically on the order of "Do we have enough?"

and respond. Among all these benefits though, the most important may be the way humility modulates the inflationary effects of identity needs. Creating new value for others in response to change requires us to perceive value clearly, without inflating or deflating it. Humility keeps our perceptions proportioned, especially about ourselves.

Beyond these practical benefits, looking at humility as an individual *competence*, a prerequisite for collaborative *capability* and as spare *capacity* will help us not only see humility's virtue. It can help us see its value, especially for making sense of change.

A PERSONAL COMPETENCE

Appreciating new realities on their own terms comes first in making sense of change. Practicing humility as a competence means giving our full attention to what change is presenting to us without imposing our intentions or pretensions. When we impose our intentions on what is new and emerging we can too easily use an old sense to frame and fit a new reality. This *imposes* more than *exposes*. When we do this we substitute intention for attention.

Some might call this "top-down" thinking, more intended to extend a past reality than attend to a new one. "Top-down" thinking comes from an elevated altitude, likely the legacy of our own identity needs, status or position. None of us, however, can honestly claim such a position when making sense of change. The altitude at which any of us reside is nowhere near the top to warrant "top-down" thinking.

Was this what Jesus meant when he said, "Truly I tell you, unless you change and become like children, you will never enter the kingdom of God"?[32] Another exemplary reference to children is in Mark's gospel, where Jesus says, "Let the little children come to me; do not stop them; for it is to such as these that the kingdom of God belongs. Truly I tell you, whoever does not receive the kingdom of God as a little child will never enter it."[33] It is to such as these that the kingdom *already* belongs. Contrary to the disciples who, like anxious parents, attempt to restrain and contain their otherwise curious and trusting children, Jesus points

---

32. Matt 18:3. The verse that follows in Matthew is also suggestive: "Whoever becomes humble like this child is the greatest in the kingdom of heaven" (Matt 18:4).

33. Mark 10:13–16.

to children as the example. Do children innately know how to give their attention without the distorting effects of intention?

Neurologist Frank Wilson goes so far as to suggest that as very young children, all of us have a built-in competence of intention-less attention. We are born not only with a natural curiosity, but also with a co-evolutionary partnership between the hand and the brain. According to Wilson, "A baby's instinctive attraction to movement, followed by the impulse to reach and then to grasp (catch), is one of the earliest maturational imperatives in the human nervous system."[34] The humility of a child may be our more natural condition.

For years I have facilitated small groups of engineers, physicists and scientists collaboratively inventing. Playful inventors will often enter the conceptual field of the problem being solved from the "inside out." They have learned to do this by imagining themselves "inside" the inanimate object or system. They mentally "miniaturize" themselves and place themselves within the imaginative space within which they are attempting to invent. This enables them to view the system with a specificity, intimacy and empathy that is not possible from a more distant and detached "outside in" point of view.

This skill requires a freedom to leave the security of one's own detached and hard-won expert status to take up a new position and point of view without a professional identity. With such freedom inventors who have learned how to do this change their way of thinking and their point of view. When this practice is done collaboratively, results can be as potent as they are surprising. Conceptual dimensions, structures and inter-relationships begin to become apparent which were not otherwise "visible" from the outside looking in, or from the top down. This practice requires an intellectual playfulness and humility[35] that may be essential for creating new value for others.

Humility just may be our more natural, created and intended position. Humility always means lower rather than higher. A humble point of view enables one who chooses this perspective to *under*stand—to stand under rather than over—what or who is perceived. *Over*-standing is a chronic threat to our ability to sense and perceive. Humility is not only up-close and personal. It is also choosing to position your self so as to

34. Wilson, *Hand*, 103.

35. See the current research and discussions on intellectual humility at St. Louis University and Fuller Theological Seminary, supported by a Templeton Foundation grant.

look up rather than down. Just as pride and over-standing go hand-in-hand, so humility and understanding are mutually reinforcing.

Humility is as much about the proper *altitude* as it is about the proper *attitude*. As a competence it is relative, relational and regulatory. Humility is *relative* in the sense that it seeks a position lower than something or someone else. The Latin root is *humus*, which literally means ground, earth or soil. Humble is the relative position of the creation to the one who created it, the creature to the Creator. Humility is *relational* in its social and moral connotations. It is a deferential, subservient and respectful orientation to others, particularly others of higher rank. Humble is the relational posture of a servant to the Master. Humility is *regulatory* in the sense that is it unpretentious and resists the natural inflationary, or in some cases deflationary, tendencies of the self.

Psychological attitudes toward the "self" are often prevalent in descriptions of humility. For example, one of the more popular definitions of humility is "not thinking less of your self but thinking of yourself less."[36] This definition has a certain appeal. "Thinking of your self, less" infers a greater interest in some one or some thing other than one's self. It connotes a relational, respectful orientation to others and a restrained and proportionate emotional maturity. As such, humility is certainly a disposition more confidently ascribed to others than assigned to ourselves. It is difficult to spot humility when you are looking in the mirror.

But there is an inherent deficiency in this psychological definition. The self remains center stage, in the foreground and quite possibly even in an elevated position. With a theological perspective, however, it is a given that God occupies center stage and with God in the more prominent position the self, identity, or ego, is relegated to a supporting role. In fact, theology's view of humility will go even further. For theology, humility may be even more than just a moral virtue. It may be a necessary condition of what it means to be a living being.

As creations of the One who formed us from the dust of the ground and breathed into our nostrils the breath of life we became living beings.[37]

---

36. Lewis, *Mere Christianity*, 191. What Lewis did say that was similar is in the chapter entitled "The Great Sin" (pride): "Do not imagine that if you meet a really humble man he will be what most people call 'humble' nowadays. . . . He will not be thinking about humility; he will not be thinking about himself at all." The exact wording can be found in a discussion about community, interestingly enough, in Warren, *Purpose Driven Life*, 148.

37. Gen 2:7.

Psychology starts with the self. Theology, in contrast, starts with dust and breath, the breath of God. Before we are a "self" with our own individuality and identity, we are "God's breathed-on dust."[38] *Humus*, earth. Humility is our natural created condition.

We tend to forget this, of course, and our amnesia doesn't make much sense, given that as "God's breathed-on dust" we are "purposed" and permitted so much. We are made from the beginning to care for the garden God put us in. We no longer have to ask what purpose and meaning there is to our lives. We have a "massive, genuine permit" to share in the whole goodness of creation—"you may freely eat of every tree of the garden, except of the tree of the knowledge of good and evil."[39] Yet we also must honor the limits of our competence, or to "resist the kind of ambition that seeks to make us like God."[40]

The prophet Micah echoed the same sense of what is required of a creature, servant and child of God: "do justice, love kindness, and walk humbly with your God."[41] This is nothing less than the way God created us. It's when we overreach and elevate ourselves that we start making less sense.

When it comes to making sense of change and especially to creating new value for others, humility is frequently forgotten, seldom considered and often left unpracticed. The consequences are quietly and consistently disastrous. When humility is forgotten, unconsidered and unpracticed, our perspectives become elevated, our interests become self-centered and theology fades into psychology, leaving us hard pressed to think of ourselves less, when the only real way to do that is to think more of the other and the Other in the other.

AN ORGANIZATIONAL CAPABILITY

Humility can also be a prerequisite for collaborative capability—a process that effectively brings together diverse people, perspectives and expertise to make better sense and value for others. For two (or more) heads to *be* better than one, some humility needs to reside in each head.

---

38. Brueggemann, *Remember You Are Dust*, 81.

39. Gen 2:17.

40. Brueggemann, *Remember You Are Dust*, 81.

41. Mic 6:8.

First, humility acts as a necessary "lubricant" for collaboration, especially when the collaboration is between diverse experts. Little if any collaboration is likely without it. Most any kind of effort requires mutual respect, generosity and an initial assumption of trust among the collaborators. In order to establish respect, generosity and trust, each individual must exhibit some humility to even enter much less participate. Should but one individual sincerely believe that others—some or all—are unnecessary, then such an individual will see no reason to collaborate. Likewise, when organizational or legal requirements insist on the assignment of individual credit or inventorship, as in organizational compensation policies and patent system demands, this lubricant can run low or wear out completely. People start thinking about the "credit they deserve" and take their individual eyes off the collective ball.

Second, making sense of change and creating new value for others often represent "tough problems," some even call them "wicked problems."[42] These kinds of challenges by their very nature require diverse perspectives, different areas of expertise and the participation of those with different experiences.

Each of us alone, no matter how well read or widely experienced, will make sense in a different way than another. We can make better sense—like the parable of the seven blind men each touching the same elephant and describing the elephant in different ways—with the perspective and methods of others, not just our own. More diverse viewpoints will likely lead to deeper understanding and appreciation. The challenge is to bring those diverse views together. This is where humility comes in.

Third, both making sense and creating value require a willingness to revise. Revisions come easier when we have sufficient humility to regard our own understanding as provisional. Sense-making is inherently iterative. We have to keep doing it. Examples of this come from both psychotherapy and creative problem solving. In therapy, most therapists will begin the conversation assuming the "presenting problem" is not the "real problem." In creative problem solving there is an analogous assumption: the first definition of the problem is the "problem-as-given" or PAG. Somewhere along the line this PAG will, with sufficient understanding from diverse perspectives, transform into a PAU—the "problem-as-understood." Others call this "reframing." I have witnessed this transformation many times and when such transformations occur, they come

42. Rittel and Webber, "Dilemmas," 155–69, and "Tackling Wicked Problems."

with a flood of new ideas, even "breakthroughs." Without some degree of humility, some open-mindedness to the emerging truth, these transformations come more slowly and with stronger resistance.

We are simply more effective, give more of our attention and have more attention to give, when we are not thinking of ourselves at all, but totally given over to the task, challenge or problem at hand. And when there is a prospect that a deeper, more complete understanding can lead to better progress toward a solution, the service becomes more important than the server. The servant is less concerned with his or her own status and more interested in doing what is called for, including the will of the One doing the calling. This is the essence of being a servant, a good and faithful servant.[43] In fact, where the Gospel of Matthew suggests that being a child gives us more ready access to the kingdom of God, the Gospel of Mark points to the role of the servant—"the servant of all."[44]

Isn't this practice of humility what Jesus pointed to in the first of his unambiguous denunciations of the scribes and the Pharisees?[45] "They do all their deeds to be seen by others." Sounds like the idolatry of identity. "They love to have the place of honor at banquets and the best seats in the synagogues, and to be greeted with respect in the marketplaces, and to have people call them rabbi. But you are not to be called rabbi, for you have one teacher and you are all students . . . nor are you to be called instructors, for you have one instructor. The greatest among you will be your servant. All who exalt themselves will be humbled, and all who humble themselves will be exalted." It's as if Jesus is simply stating of law of moral physics or reminding us of an inescapable law of spiritual gravity.

Humility as a prerequisite for collaborative capability is a practical necessity. When practiced rather than codified, humility enables us to make better sense with others and create more value for others. Shunryo Suzuki, the late founder of the Zen Center in San Francisco, said as much when he concluded his famous *Zen Mind, Beginner's Mind*, in this way: "We must not be attached to America, or Buddhism, or even to our

43. From its many and various citations in both the Old and New Testaments, including the particularly poignant Servant Songs in Isaiah (Isa 42, 44, 49 and especially 52:13—53:12) the theme of servanthood is a significant theological theme relevant to both an individuals and organizations.

44. Mark 9:33–37.

45. Matt 23, esp. vv. 5–12.

practice. We must have a beginner's mind, free from possessing anything, a mind that knows everything is in flowing change."[46]

A SPARE CAPACITY

Humility can also be viewed as having sufficient spare capacity for making sense and innovating. Humility is to *have* capacity, not be *at* capacity. Being at capacity, to be stretched beyond your limits, brings along with it an inability to flex, adjust or adapt. You are just "filling orders," or "reacting to what comes next" rather than choosing what ought be to next. If we are so preoccupied that we have no capacity left, we are unlikely to even sense what is changing, much less make sense of it. Our minds can effectively close when we are so full of our selves or our own intentions that we have little "opening" left for anything or anyone else.

Simply being busy may not be normally associated with a lack of humility. However, letting others know just how busy we are is often worn as a badge of self-importance. Or when we overestimate the capacity we think we have, we can find ourselves trying to pour five gallons into a one-gallon container. Some of us do this more often than we care to admit.

Pride is inherently inflationary. It swells. When we exceed our capacity we can easily lose sight of our own natural limitations and leave little room for others (and the Other) to play a role or even have a presence. This will distort our sense of proportion. A sense of proportion is crucial for seeing the value we are ultimately trying to create.

With capacity on hand, we have room to moderate and modulate. This is what is meant by "staying within yourself," or "knowing your own limits." As open mindedness, humility implies not only that the door to our mind is open. It also implies that there is room to enter as well.

Humility holds a central place in theology, though at times poorly practiced. One of the earliest theological attempts to make sense of this essential disposition and practice is expressed in the difficult but not impossible idea of "emptying oneself." This expression is found in the Apostle Paul's letter to the church at Philippi. Biblical scholars are generally in agreement that Paul is quoting one the earliest creeds. Paul put this creed in the context of his exhortation to the Philippians to have "the same mind" in their sense-making, urging them to take a shared altitude as much as a shared attitude in their sense making efforts. Here's what he wrote:

46. Suzuki, *Zen Mind, Beginner's Mind*, 178.

Do nothing from selfish ambition or conceit, but in humility regard others as better than yourselves. Let each of you look not to your own interests, but to the interests of others. Let the same mind be in you that was in Christ Jesus,

> who, though he was in the form of God
>
> did not count equality with God
>
> as something to be exploited (or grasped),
>
> but emptied himself,
>
> taking the form of a slave,
>
> being born in human likeness.
>
> And being found in human form,
>
> he humbled himself
>
> and become obedient to the point of death—
>
> even death on a cross.[47]

Emptying ourselves, of our selves, our concerns for establishing, maintaining and building our identity or our "containers" as Richard Rohr labels it,[48] makes the space necessary for making sense; not only making sense of our lives, but of the new reality change brings. Rohr reminds us "one of the best kept secrets, and yet one hidden in plain sight, is that *the way up is the way down*. Or, if you prefer, *the way down is the way up*."[49] This way down—the emptying rather than filling—is not just apparent to Rohr, but to others like Peter Senge and Otto Scharmer who are among those thought leaders engaged in making sense of large scale change and transformation.[50]

Without emptying our "containers" we remain so full of our own intentions that we will have little capacity to recognize others and their intentions. Changes that signal the possibilities in the intentions of others will likely go unnoticed or denied. If we are going to make sense of change, we will need some spare capacity. Spare capacity comes not from filling but by emptying. Jesus compared the publican to the Pharisee[51] and the prodigal son to his elder brother[52] to remind us that it is those

---

47. Phil 2:3–8.

48. Rohr, *Falling Upward*, xviii.

49. Ibid., xvii, italics in original.

50. Senge, *Presence*, 218.

51. Luke 18:9–14.

52. Luke 15:11–32.

who are full—whether of things or themselves—who have the most difficulty in making sense of change and contributing to new value to others.

A PRACTICE THAT TAKES PRACTICE

Knowing and remaining within our own limits is both necessary and practical, when making sense of change and creating new value for others. This seems to hold true for both individuals and organizations. Pushing your own limits may be admirable at times. But to push them consciously you first need to know where those limits reside. Pushing limits is typically applicable to contexts wherein efficiency more than effectiveness is the concern. When attempting to make sense of change, effectiveness (doing the right thing) is more important than efficiency (doing things right).

As many economies continue to shift from manual labor to knowledge work, knowledge workers are expected to yield greater and greater levels of productivity. The constraint, we are led to believe, is no longer time but information. Give knowledge workers more and better information and they will produce higher and higher yields merely by adding their creativity.

There is some truth to this. But it may not be all the truth. As productivity curves plateau and economists continue scratching their heads about this,[53] doing things more efficiently doesn't necessarily mean we are doing the right things. "With knowledge alone we can increase the efficiency of a system but not its effectiveness," Russell Ackoff reminds us.[54] "An increase in effectiveness requires understanding, but even understanding is not sufficient. We must be aware of why the system does what it does and whether it ought to be doing it." Understanding is about why the system behaves as it does. Wisdom is about whether the system's intentions are worthy or not.

Quests for improvements in efficiency are narrower in scope than quests for effectiveness. The value from increased efficiency is incremental, rarely new and often benefits the server more than the served. Making sense of change and creating value for others is more about effectiveness—an effectiveness that starts with enough humility to admit that we do not know but need to learn. And this kind of learning typically

53. Aeppel, "Why Is Productivity Slowing Down?"

54. Ackoff, *Re-Creating the Corporation*, 123.

comes through direct experience, showing up, and being fully present. In other words, it requires practice.

Practice starts with the humble assumption that I don't really know but I am open to discover. "I've come to believe that learning is the essential unit of progress for startups," says Eric Reis.[55] Learning is unlikely to occur without having some open-mindedness (humility) to begin with. Learning comes from direct experience, from the bottom up. It requires an intimacy with the "data" that may only be possible through direct, unmediated participation and personal presence. This is the kind of feedback you can trust, a trust that builds with successive iteration. More and better sense is likely to be made from engaged, repetitive experimentation than detached, one-time planning, especially if the aim is to create new value for others. In other words, it requires practicing humility.

This point is often missed by impatient leaders and organizations obsessed with efficiency. Direct experience seems to be required to confirm with confidence we are making the kind of sense that leads to new value for others. Instead of trying to impose clever ideas to make sense of change and create new value, Reis suggests we try out a "minimal viable product" so as to produce validated (by experience) learning, from the bottom up. This is what is meant by "lean" at least in the context of innovation.[56]

CONCLUSION

We are more able to make sense of change and the new realities it brings when questions and concerns about our own identities are at rest.[57] Theology gives us reasons to rest by reminding us that we are children, servants and creations of God, even "God's breathed-on dust." To the extent we embrace this identity is the extent to which we are truly free to attend to these new, change-born realities without interference from our own anxious need to establish a personal place, purpose and presence. In the company of God our anxiety about identity is put to rest.

---

55. Reis, *Lean Start-Up*, 49.

56. Use of the term "lean" may confuse more than clarify. "Lean" suggests efficiency to some. What Reis and others intend, I believe, is emphasis on the bare minimum to be tested through direct experimentation.

57. Heb 4:1–13.

As creatures, children and servants of God our lower position offers us a perspective that looks up rather than down—not only to God, but to others. As the Apostle Paul would have it, "do nothing from selfish ambition or conceit, but in humility regard others as better than yourselves. Let each of you look not to your own interests, but to the interests of others."[58]

Theology suggests that not to answer "who am I?" may be as grounding, nourishing and life giving as to answer it. Seeking identity in role, profession, geography, ethnicity, gender, wealth or reputation, pales in comparison to accepting ourselves as creatures, children and servants of and in the company of God, which ultimately frees us to make sense and create new value for others.

With change comes realities that are new, unfamiliar and abnormal, at least in the context of the routine flow of our lives. Humility may be less of a choice and more of a necessity. But it is not without its practical benefits. Beyond the typical connotations of moral virtue, humility slows and even "lows" us down. As the Psalmist recognized,

> Though mountains shake . . . and waters roar . . .
> Though nations rage, the kingdoms totter, . . .
> Be still and know that I am God.[59]

Stillness can only enhance the fidelity of our perceptions of change. When standing still we are more likely to see what we otherwise miss, understand what we otherwise *over*-stand and more likely to make a sense that leaves room for the free movement and loving presence of God. God is doing for us what we cannot do for ourselves. With the practice of humility we are more likely to avoid the glance that turns out to be wisdom's enemy.[60]

Sooner or later, assuming we are not in total denial or petrified in total delusion, the truth will emerge. It always does, eventually. When it does, it sets us free,[61] which of course is not always a comfortable or comforting thing. With freedom comes responsibility, choice and the need to keep making sense of the change that itself keeps coming. Whether we think we want it or not, the truth that returns us to freedom will appear

58. Phil 2:3–4.

59. Ps 46:2, 3, 10.

60. The poet Ezra Pound is attributed with the aphorism "Glance is the enemy of wisdom."

61. John 8:32.

as much, if not more, a freedom *for* than a freedom from. And when that happens, we are on our way to creating new value for others.

At first glance, this might cause some to disengage, withdraw and even give up. If we cannot make sense of the realities change presents to us, how can we expect to contribute, much less to understand, to say nothing of creating new value for the other? A second look, however, can carry a potential reorientation of our entire perspective. It puts us in touch with how much knowledge there is and how little of the total we each have been exposed to. It puts us in touch with how short the shelf life is of any sense we are able to make. But it does not have to lead to disengagement or giving up. Quite the opposite, it leads to the realization that we cannot stop engaging, even if we wanted to, when in the company of God. Given that change doesn't stop, neither can our efforts to make sense of it.

CONVERSATION STARTERS

1. Can biblical theology contribute more effectively to the practical necessity of avoiding "contempt prior to investigation"?

2. Should the primary purpose of innovation theology be to create a safe, neutral and generous space where people, places and ideas are encouraged to create new value for others?

3. Should innovation theology avoid condemning or condoning specific innovations and/or the technology applied by them?

The Company of God

11

This Company Has No Exit Strategy

Never again shall all flesh be cut off by the waters of a flood.[1]

THE LONE INNOVATOR OR sole entrepreneur is more fiction than fact. Heroes may dominate our innovation narratives but the realities of innovating take place in the company of others.

Look closely at the actual birth experience of companies. What we find are relationships. In the field of commercial innovations think Hewlett and Packard, Walt and Roy Disney, Gates and Allen (Microsoft), Jobs and Wozniak (Apple). In the field of social innovations think Millard and Linda Fuller and Clarence Jordon (Habitat for Humanity) or Bill W. and Dr. Bob (Alcoholics Anonymous). As much as we would like to believe the lone and heroic narrative of the individual entrepreneur, the reality is less about single parenting and more about high-trust relationships that broaden into the collectives we call companies. Companies do not guarantee success, of course. But entrepreneurial failure is likely without them.

Companies can hold our respect for their responsiveness. Others warrant our disdain for their bureaucracy. One might employ us, while another we might wish to work for. Some stretch across the globe while others remain local. Whatever their business and wherever they operate, companies seem as necessary and prevalent as they are useful.

---

1. Gen 9:11.

"The company of God" is also a collective of individuals working toward a shared purpose. The expression and reality behind it, however, point to a greater purpose and different set of realities than those associated with the more visible companies of this world. As a surrogate expression for the kingdom of God on earth, "the company of God" is the subject of what follows. Both the expression itself and the realities behind it are worth considering as a central concept for innovation theology.

The premise this essay explores is simply this: while often unseen, too often ignored and very different from companies of this world, the company of God "operates" in, through and among various worldly companies with which we are all familiar. The company of God may not choose to operate in every earthly company. But the notion that God might be interested and involved in these companies and their innovating efforts is neither unreasonable nor necessarily a new idea. And if there is any truth to this premise, then company leaders may want to consider how the innovating efforts of their companies align with the purpose and presence of the company of God.

This premise does not imply that the operations and innovations of the company of God depend upon our awareness. The company of God is there whether we see it or not. It has been quietly operating for quite some time. Likewise, it is prudent to remember that while the phrase "company of God" reminds us of God's presence, purpose and activity, it also implies the distinct possibility that others God chooses to involve in God's company—other individuals and companies—may not be ones we would choose. It's God's company after all, not ours.

As a way of describing God's involvement in change, the expression does not preempt divine interest in matters related to the salvation of an individual's soul. God's corporate interests do not obviate an interest in personal matters. God's interest and involvement in such company matters may actually envelope such individual concerns.

But first we should get a bit more comfortable with the expression itself and then take a closer look at the realities behind it before we consider the relevance for innovation theology.

THE EXPRESSION

As a surrogate for the kingdom of God on earth, "the company of God" may simply be easier on the ears. Kingdoms are unfamiliar to those fully enculturated in democratic societies. Democratic forms of government were not the political norm when Jesus used the phrase "kingdom of God." Neither were companies as much a part of the societal landscape then as they are now. Many, if not most of us, are simply more familiar with companies than kingdoms. Many of us have worked for one or more. A few of us have owned one, in whole or in part. Very few of us, however, have ever been subjects of a monarch, with interesting and obvious exceptions.

Currently our societal landscapes are saturated with companies. Their influence is considerable. Companies cross borders of many kinds, national, geographic and categorical. Not all of them are commercial organizations nor are all of them global. Many have other than economic purposes. Others root themselves deeply in local contexts. But whether global or local, economic or social ventures, every company will contend with change, sooner or later. And theologically speaking, sooner or later every company will either align with the company of God or not.

Not all companies are the same of course. Companies come in a wide variety of shapes and sizes, engage in a diverse spectrum of activities and represent a plethora of purposes. What *is* common among companies, however, is the association of individuals each working for a common or shared purpose. Common purpose is there, regardless of the separate and distinct agendas that each individual may have, such as a paycheck, contributions to a cause, or the gratification of deploying one's skills and expertise. What is common among kingdoms, however, is not so much the cause as the monarch.

The vocabulary of kingdoms—sovereignty, reign and realm—resonates with the imposition of order, the conservation of power and the location of authority. The vocabulary of companies on the other hand, resonates more closely with the adaptation and innovation required by change. "Company" may be unconventional, but it is not necessarily unorthodox or even heretical. It is not that "company" is more modern and "kingdom" is old fashioned. Rather, "company" may simply be more useful for the purposes of innovation theology. The freedom, activity and presence of God sound more applicable to innovation than sovereignty, reign and realm of God.

To be fair, "company" and "kingdom" have positive and negative associations earned from their long and varied histories. Neither maintains any immunity from nefarious examples of each. History is as replete with clueless kings and oppressive kingdoms as it is with corrupt companies and ventures that produce no value.

Unlike kingdoms, companies are defined and described in a variety of ways, including agency, ownership, capabilities, resources and interactions with the market and broader economy.[2] Relationships and transactions all play significant roles but differ according to perspective, interest and theory. For example, an accountant's perspective might describe a company as what is listed on its balance sheet: assets, liabilities, and the net equity left over. An investor might describe a company as a collection of tangible and intangible assets, with a current flow of operations (and cash) as well as a potential for growth. A systems thinker might describe a company as a dynamic system comprised of an evolving sequence of past, present and prospective interactions with its ecosystem of clients, customers, owners, suppliers, markets and competitors. A leader and manager might describe the company in terms of its organizational purpose, people, practices and what it produces. A legal perspective might define a company as a fictitious person with all the rights of a real person along with a legal limit to the personal liability of owners.

Each of these perspectives may be interesting for innovation theology to explore at some point. However, when it comes to the notion of ownership—that which underlies the legal doctrine of limited liability—theology has a distinctly different point of view.

Admittedly the "company of God" is a metaphor and, as with most metaphors, truth happens where the metaphor breaks down especially in regards to ownership or "controlling interest." With this metaphor there are at least two places where the metaphor breaks to reveal a bit of truth.

The first break in the metaphor has to do with the legal doctrine of limited liability. It's an idea that has to do with limiting the risk of owners. Whether small or large, independent or dependent divisions of a larger corporation, most companies enjoy the privilege and legal right to limit the liability of their owners or shareholders.

This legal invention doesn't appear to be the case for the company of God. Quite the contrary, the company of God has no need for such a limit. It is quite possible that the company of God carries no liability, at least to its major shareholder. It may be, for God, just equity.

2. Various points of view on the "theory of the firm" can be found on *Wikipedia*, one of the earliest of which at least in modern times was the transaction cost theory of Ronald Coase.

The second break in the metaphor is perhaps more of a prophetic critique of common corporate practice. This is the inclination of many company founders to plot their exit strategy. An exit strategy[3] has to do with the sale of the business or, more delicately put, the transfer of ownership. Typically "exit strategy" assumes a transaction wherein owners of the company give up their full or partial ownership in exchange for cash. When a company is formed with an exit strategy, it reflects a fundamentally different mind-set on the part of the owners from a mind-set of owners who do not anticipate such a transaction.[4]

For God and God's company there is no exit strategy, no longer any final liquidity event.[5] The end is not a transaction or a removal of owner's equity. There seems to be a succession plan, to be sure, but in the company of God success may be viewed less a result and more an event in a succession of events. In other words, unlike many other companies, the company of God appears to be in business for keeps. This has direct bearing on innovating.

Initiating an entrepreneurial start up or innovation effort with at least one eye on the exit is inherently disingenuous. Creating new value for others while simultaneously planning the escape route, or starting a company with the objective of selling out discredits the effort and distorts the purpose of a company—to create and serve a customer with the value.[6] Plotting the exit strategy, especially *during* the entrance, does little to engender confidence necessary to catalyze a willingness of others to commit.

Exit strategies unavoidably reveal transactional mind-sets where what owners get is the significant, if not primary, concern. Entrance (or innovation) strategies, on the other hand, tend to come from relational mind-sets, where the purpose of the company is not only to create new value for others but to create customers and serve them. In commercial organizations these two mind-sets—the transactional and the relational—must be maintained in some kind of balance to be sure. But the balance

---

3. "Exit strategy" is also an expression used in military strategy understood as an explicit plan to minimize losses of lives and material. (See *Wikipedia*, s.v. "exit strategy.")

4. Erickson, *Raising the Bar*, 2–27. Gary recounts his eleventh hour, near "death" experience with an exit strategy he ultimately chose not to take.

5. God's commitment to Noah (and to us) is that there will not be another "liquidity" event (Gen 8:20–22).

6. Drucker, *Management*, 61.

must inexorably tip toward the relational and generous when creating value for another. Transactional and exit strategies retard the generosity, trust and forgiveness required for sustained relationships. Something is missing when our only rationale for investing is simply what we will get in return.

Isn't there another rationale for investing in innovation? Might it be for the chance to leave the social spaces, physical places and people who inhabit them a little better than we found them? This is the kind of question an innovation theology asks, a question that may not otherwise even surface without a theological perspective, and perhaps without the company of God.

Responding to change is dangerous when done alone. So is innovating. It is also unnecessary.

Responding to change *with* the counsel of others is prudent, even when we may seemingly be the only one affected. Counsel from a wise and trusted other is typically a good idea. "Fools think their own way is right, but the wise listen to advice."[7] Keeping our own counsel increases the likelihood that what we imagine to be a response is really a reaction. Alone we are more vulnerable to all manner of self-justification. Such justifications are not as easily forthcoming with the counsel of another.

Responding to change *in* the company of others is a bit more complex. Whether family members, coworkers, fellow volunteers or members in common cause, responding to change with others presents a host of other things to consider. Responding to change in the company of others inescapably involves social realities, whether our present company chooses to resist, embrace, adapt or create new value. With social realities come both political and moral ones. And when the company with whom we are responding is a commercial concern it will necessarily involve economic realities as well. But being a part and member of that company—regardless of the company—implies obligation along with affiliation. It does not absolve us of our individual responsibilities

Responding to change *in the company of God*, however, may be another matter entirely. Surprisingly, it may bring us a whole new set of resources, perspectives and even colleagues. Perhaps these have been there all along and we just didn't see them. But when in the company of God, this new set is brought near, expanded potential is freshly awakened. Some call this hope. Others call it encouragement. But whatever we

7. Prov 12:15; also 11:14; 15:22.

call it, responding to change in the company of God brings confidence to otherwise daunting, complex and uncertain contexts of change.

Responding in the company of God does not imply that we are no longer in the company of others. Quite the opposite is the case. All the various social, moral, political and economic realities remain. In the company of God, however, we have the advantage of a plumb line to direct and guide choices that affect the bottom line. In the company of God we also are more likely to experience the presence, purpose and animating power of God who can do for us what we cannot do for ourselves.

Using "the company of God" as a surrogate for the kingdom of God on earth doesn't lessen or resolve the ambiguities left to us in the words "company" or "kingdom." Both exhibit many of the same ambiguities carried by other words used to describe the ways humans associate with each other. Organizations, ventures, initiatives, communities, institutions, enterprises, businesses, the list could go on. All share with "company," however, the notion of human beings associating with each other for some shared purpose, however well or poorly defined.

We might be able to locate and even describe a specific company but *defining* what every company actually is in a standard way may be an impossible task. The impossibility of defining "company" in a consistent and meaningful way may itself be worth noting. But the expression "the company of God" differentiates the interests and orientation of this company from those of others.

Discerning the differences is both necessary and useful, particularly if we are aware of the influence God's plumb line[8] has on our bottom lines. It is only our tendency to compartmentalize the religious from the political, the spiritual from the material, and matters of the soul from matters of the household and societal economy, that prevents us from seeing clearly the purposes and presence of this company of God. Using the phrase "company of God" may point to a significantly different company compared to other companies. But it is still a company.

As a surrogate expression for the kingdom of God on earth, "the company of God" is merely a metaphor. But metaphors bring new insights, broader understandings, and extensions of scope and significance. They can create new space to explore implications that may otherwise go unexplored and unexamined. Such is the intent here. For the metaphor to be effective, however, it should be grounded in the realities it intends

8. Amos 7:7–8.

to broaden, extend and deepen.[9] To better understand the nature of these realities, therefore, we must first be clear about the meaning of "the kingdom of God."

THE KINGDOM OF GOD

The preponderance of biblical occurrences of the phrase "the kingdom of God"[10] occur in the New Testament,[11] primarily in the gospels of Matthew, Mark and Luke. The phrase represents the over-arching and central message of Jesus before and after the resurrection. Regarding this there is widespread agreement among New Testament scholars.

What the phrase actually means, however, garners considerably less consensus among the same scholars. Is it a vision for the future, a present reality, or both? Is it a spiritual phenomenon that transforms the lives of individuals, a socioeconomic dynamic that radically reorders society, or both? Is it a gift that is received, a territory that is entered, or both? Can we describe it only by saying what it is not, or only approximate its meaning through parables with elusive and ambiguous interpretations? Must we accept that it will remain a mystery, at least in part, acknowledging it is not for us to know its times or manifestations?[12] And if it must remain a mystery, then are we for whom it is a mystery, somehow locked out of the kingdom regardless of how much we seek it?

Many of us who pray the way Jesus taught us to pray make an assumption about the kingdom of God. This assumption, often subconsciously held, shows up in the first request of the Lord's Prayer: "Thy kingdom come, thy will be done."[13] The tacit assumption becomes more explicit in what comes next: "on earth as it is in heaven." The assumption is that there is a gap between heaven and earth, between the will of God and the realities of our experience. The good news is that this gap can be closed, and in fact, *is being* closed, no matter what the evidence otherwise

9. Perrin, *Rediscovering the Teachings of Jesus*, 87n1.

10. "Kingdom of God" is also understood as "kingdom of heaven" (especially in Matthew's gospel) and "reign of God."

11. Though the phrase and/or concept is not absent in the Hebrew Scriptures. Selman, "Kingdom of God in the Old Testament," 161–83.

12. Matt 24:36, 42; 25:13; Mark 13:32–37; Acts 1:6.

13. Matt 6:5–15, esp. v. 10. "Kingdom" and "will" are likely synonymous, at least in the prayer's expression, given the parallelism that saturates prophetic oracles and the Psalms.

seems to suggest. In closing the gap the prayer asks for heavenly realities to shape earthly realities, not the other way around.

This is such a familiar prayer to us that we can often miss the implications. If we pause, however, to consider that for which we are praying, it strikes me that it is perhaps one of the boldest prayers we could pray. It is essentially asking for heaven to manifest itself on earth.

This is an impossible task for humans but not an impossible one for God. It has been said of prayer that it doesn't change God so much as it changes us.[14] Perhaps the question for each of us is whether we see ourselves working for the kingdom of God or for some other kingdom, including perhaps our own? Or is our only question what must I do to guarantee a reservation for myself in the kingdom of God not on this earth but in heaven, not in this time but in the next?[15]

The good but challenging news about the kingdom of God is that to hold a reservation for the kingdom in a next life we must participate in the kingdom of God in this life. Regardless of what you and I might anticipate in the next life, this life still requires our time and attention with all its very worldly, messy, imperfect, uncertain and complex circumstances. Here and now God is still active and engaged and "on earth as it is in heaven" is where the company of God operates. Its purpose is to close the gap between heaven and earth.

Much of the debate among scholars regarding the meaning of the kingdom of God has historically centered around its timing. The kingdom of God is thought of as a past memory, a present reality or a future hope. There is plenty of biblical evidence for each of the three. Holding all three simultaneously, however, is difficult to say the least. When the past dominates our understanding of the concept, the kingdom of God points to the restoration of ancient traditions. When the future dominates, the kingdom of God suggests a future hope for individual salvation, societal justice or both. When the present presides, however, the kingdom of God suggests the presence and activity of God—God's current interests, engagements and interventions in the affairs of humankind.

It is this last one—the kingdom of God in the present—that likely holds the most interest for innovation theology. Why? Responding to change is something that happens in the here and now. When that

14. "I pray because I can't help myself. I pray because I'm helpless. I pray because the need flows out of me all the time—waking and sleeping. It doesn't change God—it changes me" (C. S. Lewis, as quoted in the film *Shadowlands*).

15. Matt 19:16–30; Mark 10:17–31; Luke 18:18–30.

response intends to create new value for others it may be realized in the future but the effort it requires is in the present. Innovating may have a mind for the future and certainly an appreciation of the past, but its activity is centered in the here and now.

The kingdom of God *on earth* carries an inherent interest in closing the gap between heaven and earth. Innovating is similarly interested, or at least should be. As a result, innovation theology as an applied theology will likely have more interest in the present, "at hand" and "among you" aspects of the kingdom of God, if only because innovating happens in the present tense.

If we bring forward only those biblical references to the kingdom of God that are not explicitly oriented to the future, only those situated more clearly in the present, what we find are several attributes that not only have to do with the company of God, but hold guidance and direction relevant to innovating.

THE KINGDOM ON EARTH

A thorough and complete exegesis of all these "present oriented"[16] references is beyond the scope of this essay and likely the competence of the author. Indeed, the present orientation of the kingdom of God can confound even the best. Consider when Jesus was asked by the Pharisees about when the kingdom of God was coming, he answered, "The kingdom of God is not coming with things that can be observed; nor will they say, 'Look, here it is!' or 'There it is!' For, in fact, the kingdom of God is among you."[17] Clearly, the kingdom of God in the now is not self-evident to all.

However, these present oriented references point directly to a few distinguishing characteristics, which when combined, make this kingdom different from any and all other human kingdoms. These characteristics include the present kingdom's bias for *persons in need, forgiveness extended, local commitment, participation more than outcomes,* and *serving not status.* These are the who, how, where and why of the kingdom of God on earth. Take a brief look at each of these.

---

16. Some of the kingdom of God references are oriented to the future, others to the present. To see the difference, compare the parable (and Jesus' explanation) of the sower and the seeds (Matt 13:1–9 explained in 13:18–23) and the parable of the weeds among the wheat (Matt 13:24–30 explained in 13:36–43).

17. Luke 17:20–21.

Persons in need. In the Beatitudes[18]—arguably a diagnostic for the kingdom of God on earth—Jesus says that the kingdom of God belongs to the poor in spirit and to those who are persecuted for righteousness' sake. Because these two Beatitudes are the first and last in the set of eight, we can reasonably infer the kingdom of God belongs to those named in the other six—those who mourn, the meek, those who hunger and thirst for righteousness, the merciful, the pure in heart and the peacemakers.

All of these are persons in need. In fact, it may be appropriate to infer that the kingdom of God on earth is not only *for* persons in need but *among* persons in need. Those who have been transformed by loss or longing can be more acutely aware of their own powerlessness. As a result, they are better positioned to see and understand the new value that can be created for others, particularly others in need. Isn't this experience-born empathy what distinguishes sacrificial love (*agape*) from other kinds of love?[19]

This inference aligns with Jesus' designation of those to whom he thought he was especially sent[20]—the poor, the captives, the blind, and the oppressed. Likewise, when the disciples of John the Baptist come to Jesus to ask him, "Are you the one who is to come or are we to wait for another?" Jesus replies, "Go and tell John what you have seen and heard: the blind receive their sight, the lame walk, the lepers are cleansed, the deaf hear, the dead are raised, (and) the poor have good news brought to them."[21]

The kingdom of God on earth has a bias for persons in need, the marginalized, poor and oppressed; the lost and those who have lost.

Forgiveness extended. Peter asks how often forgiveness should be extended.[22] Jesus famously replies, "Not even seven times, but seventy times seven." Then Jesus compares the kingdom of God to a king who wished to settle accounts with his slaves to explain this forgiveness strategy.[23]

In the parable the king shows compassion and forgives the one who owes a considerable sum but cannot repay it. The king's forgiveness comes only after the debtor acknowledges the dire consequences of his inability to repay the debt. This debtor, however, turns right around and demands

18. Matt 5:3–10.

19. Lewis, *Four Loves*.

20. Luke 4:18–19. As Jesus is quoting Isa 61:1–2, the list of certain persons in Isaiah is similar: the oppressed, the brokenhearted, captives, prisoners and all who mourn.

21. Luke 7:21–22.

22. Matt 18:21–22.

23. Matt 18:23–35.

payment from another who owes him considerably less. The contradiction did not escape the notice of others. They bring this to the attention of the king, who calls the forgiven one back in to face the music and fess up.

The parable unambiguously points to an essential characteristic of the kingdom of God on earth—extending to others the forgiveness we have received ourselves. Of course, such forgiveness is hardly extensible without having first received it our selves. But extending forgiveness becomes a challenge when we have either amnesia about the forgiveness we have experienced or transactional proclivities to settle accounts and "reconcile" perhaps even more than the books. Such amnesia causes us to think of ourselves as end points where forgiveness rests, rather than the channels where forgiveness flows. "The kingdom of God is known in terms of the experience of the forgiveness of sins; the only proper response to that experience is a preparedness in turn to forgive."[24]

The kingdom of God on earth has a bias for forgiveness extended.

Local commitment. Jesus' explanation of the parable of the sower and the seeds refers the kingdom of God.[25] Jesus compares the content of the message of the kingdom of God to the seed that is sown on different soils. When sown on the hard, well-trod path, the seed finds no soil at all. It is not understood. When sown in rocky soil, the seed may be received with joy, but it cannot take root. When trouble comes, as it inevitably will, the joy is short lived and what has sprouted falls away. When the seed is sown among thorns—the cares of the world and the lure of wealth—the seed is choked out and it yields nothing. It is only in the good soil—soil wherein the seed can take root—that the seed is able to bear fruit and yield, even exponentially. Seeds are irrelevant unless and until they find soil in which to commit themselves. Local commitment. "Think globally, act locally" may have gotten it right.

The parables of the mustard seed, the yeast, the treasure in the field, and the pearl of great price[26] also speak of this local commitment as part and parcel of the kingdom of God. What each of these parables suggests is that the potential of the kingdom of God, however it is imagined, is irrelevant if it is not planted, if there is no "un-hedged" commitment to it.

The kingdom of God on earth has a bias for local commitment, where time, attention and devotion are planted and roots are established.

---

24. Perrin, *Rediscovering the Teachings of Jesus*, 126.

25. Matt 13:19.

26. Matt 13:31–32 (mustard seed); 33 (yeast); 44 (treasure); and 45 (pearls).

Participation more than outcomes. In the instruction set Jesus lays out to the seventy[27] Jesus makes it clear that regardless of the outcomes the seventy are to say at the end of their efforts, "The kingdom of God has come near to you." This declaration is to be expressed whether their efforts are received or not. The outcome of their efforts matters, certainly. But the outcome is not the responsibility of the seventy.

Letting go of the outcomes is also inferred in Jesus' counsel to the disciples not to worry—not to strive for what they are to eat or drink—even for the most basic necessities of life. "For it is the nations of the world that strive after all these things, and your Father knows that you need them. Instead, strive for God's kingdom, and these things will be given to you as well."[28] Our part in the kingdom of God on earth is not to worry about the outcomes. Rather, it's about working for the kingdom's purposes.

Perhaps nowhere else is this participation-more-than-outcome emphasis clearer than in the parable Jesus tells about the day laborers.[29] Though hired at different intervals and therefore working different lengths of time, the landowner chooses to pay them all the same amount. Our common sense of fairness is offended by this parable. Yet the parable concludes with the reminder of the absolute freedom of the landowner to do what he chooses with what belongs to him. The chance to participate in the work of the kingdom of God on earth is more important than whatever rewards or results happen come to those who participate.

The kingdom of God on earth has a bias for our participation more than our worry with outcomes.

Serving not status. In a revealing little narrative recorded in the Gospel of Matthew the mother of James and John approaches Jesus to ask for a favor.[30] The favor turns out to be more than a little favor. "Declare that these two sons of mine will sit, one at your right hand and one at your left, in your kingdom." Jesus responds by saying that she has no idea what she is asking, and after a brief exchange, says that such a favor is not his to grant.

This interchange would at first appear to be one of those future oriented references regarding the kingdom of God. But when the other disciples got wind of the mother's request, Jesus took the opportunity to bring it all back to the present, diverting the maternal interest in the

27. Luke 10:1–12.

28. Luke 12:30–31.

29. Matt 20:1–16.

30. Matt 20:20–28.

future and turning the quest for status upside down. "Whoever wishes to be great among you must be your servant, and whoever wishes to be first among you must be your slave; just as the Son of Man came not to be served but to serve."

This interest in serving not status often catches us by surprise. It seems at first counterintuitive, as it did for the disciples who when invited to "come and inherit the kingdom prepared for you from the foundation of the world"[31] asked, "Lord, when was it that we saw you hungry and gave you food, or thirsty and gave you something to drink? And when was it that we saw you a stranger and welcomed you, or naked and gave you clothing? And when was it that we saw you sick or in prison and visited you?" Jesus answers, "As you did it to the least of these, you did it to me."

The kingdom of God on earth clearly has a bias for service not status.

These characteristics of the kingdom of God on earth direct and guide us to what it means to respond to change and to innovate in the company of God. When we are more focused on persons in need than the innovativeness of our solutions, more ready to extend the forgiveness we have received, more willing to commit ourselves locally than achieve scalability, more concerned about the quality of our participation than the quantity of our rewards, and more interested in serving than status, then we may be "not far from the kingdom of God." Could it be that one reason so many innovating efforts end in failure and wasted effort stems from these efforts being otherwise directed?

A word of caution is due here, though. In all our well-intentioned serving, experience-born empathy, local commitment, forgiveness extended and participation, we can so easily forget the fact that God plays the lead. God's leadership is so often missed, partly because God is among us as one who serves while we are looking for God's leadership as one who rules. Isn't God the One whose understanding is unfathomably detailed,[32] who knows needs even before we ask?[33] Isn't it God who animates the growth, who initiates the forgiveness, who takes special care for persons in need, who commits locally before we do? Isn't it God who looks after the outcomes, in part, so that we might be freed to concentrate on the inputs?

---

31. Matt 25:31–46.

32. Ps 139.

33. Matt 6:8.

If these are the distinguishing realities of the kingdom of God on earth—God's engaged, active presence—they do not necessarily make the expression "the company of God" the *only* surrogate. These realities, however, provide direction for the task of innovation theology, to which we now turn our attention.

RELEVANCE FOR INNOVATION THEOLOGY

If the expression "company of God" finds acceptance, its utility will not likely be found in any reform of theology, per se. Rather, the value of the expression may more likely reside in its inherent prophetic challenge for companies and their leaders to carefully consider where and why innovations are needed.

Aligning our innovating efforts with the purposes of God's company gets us closer to doing what we are designed to do—work toward closing the gap between heaven and earth. It also promises a purposefulness, satisfaction and sense of fulfillment that is not possible nor as authentic or satisfying from any other "returns" for which we may otherwise invest ourselves. However, aligning ourselves with the company of God in order to increase the probability of success in innovating is highly susceptible to self-justification and all manner of self-delusion. It's also adolescent theology.

Historically, companies have proven more responsive to change than any other organizational form. Companies are more adaptive and malleable. Companies have proven certainly more responsive than kingdoms. Castles are the legacy of monarchs and their reigns. Old forts with massive defenses still stand despite the fact that there is no longer anything against which to defend. They have become museums. The nature and character of such adaptive capability, and God's interest in it, will likely prove of significant interest to innovation theology, largely because adaptive capability represents greater potential for responding to change and may be the most important capability a company intending to innovate can have.[34]

An early example of this adaptive capability was in the company of Francesco di Marco Datini. Datini was born in Prato, Italy, in 1335. After starting his company under the banner "For God and Profit" in Avignon, he returned to Prato where he set up over three hundred different partnerships operating in a variety of different businesses, from retail

34. Teece, "Dynamic Capabilities," 509–33.

shops to textiles and jewelry and even banking. Datini was convinced that being *en campagnie* (in company) with others just made better business sense than operating alone. Datini became known as "The Merchant of Prato," a recognized success largely based on his ability to "keep things as loose and flexible as possible."[35]

Datini knew then what many have emulated since. Companies carry greater responsive and adaptive potential. In fact, the influence, effectiveness and adaptability of companies led John Micklethwait and Adrian Wooldridge to observe:

> Hegel predicted that the basic unit of modern society would be the state, Marx that it would be the commune, Lenin and Hitler that it would be the political party. Before that, a succession of saints and sages claimed the same for the parish church, the feudal manor, and the monarchy. . . . They all have been proved wrong. The most important organization in the world is the company: the basis of the prosperity of the West and the best hope for the future of the rest of the world.[36]

Perhaps this applies even more so to the company of God.

Before we get carried away with the potential of companies, however, we should consider the company's relationship with the state. Companies have seemingly always had uneasy relations with nation states, from which these companies obtain their rights to exist and operate. The unease between the two might be due in part to the greater willingness and ability of companies to adapt and respond to change than their slower, more plodding peers among institutions with ruling and regulating authority. That God might choose to use both—the responsive, adaptive company and the regulatory, governing institution—for the purposes of God's company is certainly well within the scope of God's choice. Nor is such a choice without biblical precedent.

One of the more remarkable passages of scripture is Isaiah's short oracle of eight verses that names Cyrus as God's own *anointed*.[37] Not only is Cyrus not an Israelite. He is not even from traceable descendents of Abraham. He's a completely secular figure, a Persian King. None of this prevents God from commissioning Cyrus to be an instrument of the company of

---

35. Micklethwait and Wooldridge, *Company*, 11.

36. Ibid., xv.

37. *Anointed* means "messiah," or in the New Testament, "Christ."

God. And just to be sure there is no doubt about who does the anointing, God uses the first person pronoun no less than fourteen times:

> ... whose right hand I have grasped ...
>
> I will go before you ...
>
> I will break in pieces the doors of bronze
>
> I will give you the treasures of darkness
>
> ... so that you may know that it is I, ... who calls you by name ...
>
> I surname you, though you do not know me,
>
> I am the Lord ...
>
> I arm you, though you do not know me ...
>
> I am the Lord, and there is no other.
>
> I form light and create darkness,
>
> I make weal and create woe;
>
> I the Lord do all these things.
>
> ... I the Lord have create it.[38]

Another remarkable passage points to the same divine operation. It is also outside the conventional boundaries to which we typically confine the company of God. It is Jesus' recognition of faith on the part of the Roman centurion. Like Cyrus, here is another, a complete outsider, of whom Jesus was amazed and said, "I tell you, not even in Israel have I found such faith."[39]

We typically want to contain and limit the purposes of God. But Scripture, Jesus and God will not let us. God always looks well beyond the beloved community.[40] Why should we imagine that God might refrain from using secular companies—whether sprawling global corporations, mid-size organizations or even small, family companies—to use as instruments of God's purpose, if God so chooses?

The company of God, descriptively at least, reflects the freedom of God. This freedom includes the freedom to reconfigure, adapt and form relationships with whomever and whatever God so chooses. The company of God is quite capable of making acquisitions of other companies, even without the awareness of the acquired. If the acquired company is positioned to serve the purposes of the company of God, who are we to

---

38. Isa 45:1–8; see also Childs, *Isaiah*, 353–54; and Brueggemann, *Isaiah*, 2:75–76.

39. Luke 7:1–10; Matt 8:5–13.

40. Brueggemann, *Isaiah*, 2:76.

say that the acquired must consciously agree, much less even be aware of the divine acquisition?

Who and what is acquired—individuals, other companies and organizations, even nations—can be transformed in the process for the purposes of the company of God. Such acquisitions, or divestments, are the choice of the Acquirer more than the choice of the acquired. In fact, if it were possible for the acquired to control or orchestrate the acquisition we would likely have the dangerous situation where those who believe they are acting on behalf of God risk self-justification, not to mention self-righteousness. Self-assurance that one is operating in the company of God may itself be a sign of the opposite.

This adaptive, adoptive and even acquisitive freedom of God's company—arguably a derivative aspect of God's sovereignty—suggests a concept of ownership very different from what we normally think of as ownership. God's ownership (inferred from his authorship[41] as the creator) and our conceptions of ownership rooted as they are in John Locke's notion of the natural right of property are quite different. This makes it a bit difficult to wrap our minds around the practical implications of God's ownership,[42] in contrast to the ownership of company assets, tangible or intangible.[43]

However, this much can be said. God's ownership is more a matter of the free and purposeful intention of the Author to do with as God chooses, than it is about proprietary "rights" of the Divine. I suspect that God is not too concerned with God's rights. We may choose to transfer and assign ownership rights to others with what we believe (mistakenly or not) that we own. But I don't believe that God gives up, assigns or transfers God's ownership "rights" (or responsibilities) to others. Stewardship is the *delegation* of management responsibility, not ownership.

Notwithstanding the fall, God's original intention seemed to be to put us in the garden to "till it and to keep it,"[44] not own it. As Gerhard

41. While "authorship" may be similar to ownership there are some significant differences that may be worth exploring for innovation theology, given the importance of intellectual property (i.e., inventorship with patents and authorship with copyrights) for so many companies.

42. Exod 19:5; Ps 24:1; 95:5; Ezek 18:4.

43. Given that 75 percent or more of market capitalization of publically traded companies is now based on intangible assets vs. tangible or "book value," the intellectual property these assets represent and their influence on innovating is worth exploring theologically, though beyond the scope of this essay (see Blair, *Unseen Wealth*.)

44. Gen 2:15.

von Rad put it: "That [mankind] was transferred to the garden to guard it indicates that he was called to a state of service and had to prove himself in a realm that was not his own possession."[45]

The concept of a company carries a strong preference for a sense-and-respond orientation compared to the command-and-control orientation associated with "kingdom." And while a command-and-control mind-set may be appropriate and even necessary for managing and running existing operations, it is disastrous for responding to change and innovating.

Companies that respond to change and innovate faster and better than their peers have done so in large measure due to their capability to sense-and-respond. "Throughout its history, the company has shown an equally remarkable ability to evolve: indeed, that has been the secret of its success."[46] More than any other institution or organization, companies have learned to respond to change and innovate faster and better. This does not imply that all companies have learned to do this. Those that have not tend to be short lived. Neither does it imply that their greater responsiveness to change means the company will achieve a longer life than its peers who suffer from learning disabilities.[47] Rather, it is simply implying that there are no other socioeconomic architectures better suited to responding to change and innovating than the company.[48] Kingdoms are simply slower to respond and adapt.

"Company" doesn't *necessarily* imply this sense-and-respond mind-set. There are plenty of declining companies who have lost their way regardless of their relative or current state of profitability. Many of these are well along the path of decline, having lost a sense of their own entrepreneurial vocation, or having allowed their core competences to drift into core rigidities.[49] To be fair, neither "company" nor "kingdom" is likely the perfect metaphorical carrier of the purpose and presence of God. But "company" certainly holds a more relevant frame for

45. Rad, *Genesis*, 80.

46. Micklethwait and Wooldridge, *Company*, 181.

47. Geus, *Living Company*, vii.

48. Some might suggest that the "network" represents a viable alternative social architecture. However, networks have neither the internal system of accountabilities (see Micklethwait and Wooldridge, *Company*, 184), nor the focus of purposeful action that companies do.

49. Leonard-Barton, "Core Capabilities," 111–25.

responding to change and innovating because of this stronger association with sense-and-respond.

Most adaptive systems, those that sense-and-respond, are able to do so effectively because they have a center point that enables them to maintain their balance, like the keel of a sailboat. The ability to sense-and-respond stems from the ability to sense and make sense of what is going on amid the winds of change blowing through the immediate environment, and comes from having a sufficiently strong and coherent sense of purpose or direction. In the case of a sailboat headed upwind, the skipper knows when to change tacks partly because he knows where he is headed *and* where the wind is coming from.

The keel in a company is its purpose or reason for being. "A reason for being expresses essential organizational purpose. It states what the organization exists to do, as opposed to what it must do to exist."[50] The command-and-control of kingdoms tends to rely on planning and assumes a much higher degree of control than either reality or change actually affords. "Planned responses do not work,"[51] especially in highly uncertain and unpredictable environments. More important than planning is "the ability to transform apparent noise into meaning faster than apparent noise" is received.

> Sense-and-respond organizations leverage this insight into a generic way of fostering adaptive sense-making and action. The particulars of what is sensed and of how it is interpreted are role-specific [and purpose-specific] and depend on the amount of adaptability required.[52]

The way to turn noise into signal and signal into meaning is to be clear on what one's purpose is, as an individual or an organization. In the company of God this purpose is clear, despite our propensity to muddle it up. That the company of God has no exit strategy does not imply that it has no strategy or purpose at all. Its strategy, if we can infer it from Jesus' own understanding of his purpose, is the same as the strategy of the kingdom of God on earth:

> The spirit of the Lord God is upon me,
> because the Lord has anointed me; he has sent me

50. Haeckel, *Adaptive Enterprise*, 114.

51. Ibid., xvii.

52. Ibid., xviii, brackets mine.

to bring good news to the oppressed,

to bind up the broken-hearted,

to proclaim liberty to the captives, and release to the prisoners;

to proclaim the year of the Lord's favor, and the day of vengeance of our God;

to comfort all who mourn.[53]

With such a clear sense of purpose, any individual or organization is freed to sense what is happening in the environment, make sense and respond in a way that is true to that purpose *and* the (new) sense it can make of its environment. In such sense-and-respond mind-sets there is a greater bias for what is voluntary, compared to what is compelled or coerced, for what is done out of a generous spirit compared to a transactional one, for what is born out of trust than specified in legal contracts, and for risks worth taking more than liabilities worth limiting.

Saying that the company of God is more sense-and-respond oriented than command-and-control oriented might suggest a God that is more interested in responsiveness than in stability or consistency. Depending upon one's reading of the Old Testament saga of God's dealings with the people of Israel, this could be a reasonable conclusion. The God of the Old Testament is anything but monochromatic and monosyllabic, much less static.

CONCLUSION

Why consider a surrogate for the kingdom of God on earth? Why not stick with the phrase as it is? After all, it's a phrase that saturates the gospels of Matthew, Mark and Luke, and shows up in some noteworthy places in the rest of the New Testament. The answer is quite simple and pragmatic. "The company of God" resonates better with contexts of responding to change and innovating.

The prophet Samuel was particularly sensitive to this, despite being overruled by God. In that debate between Samuel and God about the whole king and kingdom idea,[54] Samuel was clearly of the opinion that it was a bad idea. Samuel thought it was better to not overthink or over-organize.

---

53. Isa 61:1–2; see also Luke 4:18–19, wherein Jesus adds "recovery of sight to the blind."

54. 1 Sam 8–16.

Besides, the people wanted a king because their neighbors all seemed to have one.

Perhaps Samuel might have preferred the alternative of a company, had it been available to his imagination. At least it might have avoided the risk associated with so many sovereigns. Or perhaps Samuel's parting counsel is as relevant to companies today as it was to the fledgling young kingdom then:

> If you will fear the Lord and serve him and heed his voice and not rebel against the commandment of the Lord, and if both you and the king who reigns over you will follow the Lord your God, it will be well; but if you will not heed the voice of the Lord, but rebel against the commandment of the Lord, then the hand of the Lord will be against you and your king.[55]

Being invited into an innovating, responsive and global company with one sustaining purpose, an eternal, ongoing purpose that is greater than any other company's purpose, is really good news. We should get to know more about this company and its purpose of closing the gap between heaven and earth.

Certainly more about the company of God can and should be explored in succeeding conversations about innovation theology. And whether the phrase sticks or we return to the workable but slightly longer "the kingdom of God on earth," the exploration of its purpose will be especially important for directing and guiding society in its response to change and where and why innovations are needed.

For now, however, it may be enough to at least point to where the phrase "the company of God" represents its counterpart in the biblical vocabulary. More importantly it likely suggests how being a participant *in* this company, "in Christ" to use Paul's phrase, might help close the gaps between heaven and earth for all of us, and help us avoid the various idols, illusions and delusions of the kingdoms and companies of mankind.

---

55. 1 Sam 12:14–16.

CONVERSATION STARTERS

1. Might the five biases of the company of God (the kingdom of God on earth) be relevant to the clarification of where innovations are needed now and why?

2. How can biblical theology encourage earthly companies to find their alignment with the company of God?

12

Church as Servant Subsidiary

Like a sheep before its shearers is silent . . .[1]

MY MOTHER AND HERS were among the first to teach me about matters of faith. Much of their early lessons came by way of nursery rhymes and short little sayings. Choreographed hand movements accompanied a few of them. One of these taught me about church. The lessons still lingers. It goes like this:

> *Put both hands together by inserting, from the outside in, your right hand's fingers in between those of your left hand.*
> "This is the church."
> *Then, keeping fingers interlaced, free the index fingers of each hand so that both come to touch teach other.*
> "This is the steeple."
> *Keep all fingers interlaced. Turn both hands open, with palms facing up. Wiggle your fingers.*
> "Open the doors and see all the people."

This was my first introduction to ecclesiology. It has likely influenced my thinking more than I am aware. However, the pairing of the verbal declaration "this is the church" with the physical binding of my hands, left an imprint of the union in communion, of an uncomfortable binding, relieved only with a steeple formed by two fingers, and a final

1. Isa 53:7.

release, when I open my palms upward. The tactile experience shaped my cognitive understanding of this spiritual community called church.

Rhymes and hand movements may leave impressions about the nature of the church. But when change arrives, more than rhymes and hands are needed to discern whether the church has a role to play and even something to contribute in response.

As you might imagine, the following essay proposes the church does indeed have a role to play and much to contribute. Its role and contribution come from the enduring[2] position and purpose of the church as a servant subsidiary of the company of God.[3] The servant role and subsidiary position however does not preclude the church from taking provisional postures, particularly where responding to change and innovating are the immediate concerns.

The modest focus of this essay does not offer a comprehensive ecclesiology with the more classical concerns of "one, holy, catholic and apostolic." This in no way intends to ignore or deny the importance of these more traditional attributes and doctrines. Rather, the intent is simply to describe the role and contribution of the church in contexts of change and responses to it. *Position*, *purpose* and *postures* seem more useful vocabulary to describe the church in these contexts. In times of change the church can find itself "out of position," drifting away from its purpose, and assuming postures counter to its purpose and overextending its position.

That the church can lose its way from time to time does not make it unique or differentiate it from other organizations and individuals. Chances of losing one's way simply increase in times of change. The unfamiliar presents uncertainties about whether and how to respond. Muddled thinking and multitasking add to the likelihood of equivocation. Even long-standing organizations and institutions are vulnerable to "mission-creep" or "strategy-drift" where proximate goals and penultimate concerns occlude the light that shines from what is primary and ultimate. Responding to change can disconnect us from our higher or ultimate purpose.

The church is not immune to this vulnerability at the level of a local congregation or a regional or global assembly. Over the past two

2. Niebuhr, *Christ and Culture*, 1. Niebuhr called culture the enduring problem for the church. This adjective seems fitting for the church's purpose as well.

3. By the "company of God" is meant the kingdom of God on earth (see the essay, "This Company Has No Exit Strategy").

thousand years, the church has succumbed to this vulnerability likely more often than the church would want to admit. But despite those lapses, the church has survived and in many cases thrives, not so much as a result of its own doing but, as it often confesses, because God is doing what the church cannot do for itself.

That the church has an enduring position which is subsidiary, an enduring purpose which is to serve, and can take on provisional postures to adapt to changes in its immediate context, is the primary thesis of this essay. This applies whether we are thinking of the church as a local congregation or a denomination-wide assembly or specific tradition within the larger communion of saints. What follows looks more closely at the church's subsidiary position, its servant purpose and its freedom to take relevant but temporary postures to fulfill its purpose.

The church's enduring position, enduring purpose and provisional postures are wonderfully guided by the Apostle Paul's metaphor to describe the church as the *body* of Christ. The thesis draws upon the body metaphor and even how Paul applies it, before speaking to a provisional posture for the church, at least in North America.

THE BODY (OF CHRIST)

Various scriptural images are used to describe the church, including the "household of God," the "pillar and bulwark of the truth,"[4] and even "the bride," though this latter image is only indirectly implied. None, however, are as clear, potent and useful as Paul's image and metaphor of the body of Christ.[5] The familiarity of the human body to all of us is one reason this metaphor has proven so lasting.

Paul used the body metaphor to address the disunity emerging in the congregation at Corinth. Paul's original intent was to persuade the congregation there that unity amid diversity was essential and possible. As a descriptive metaphor for the church, the body is well suited to speak to what is practically required to achieve and maintain the interdependence that enables unity amid diversity.

With his use of the body metaphor, those who advocate "design" or "systems thinking" might consider Paul one of their own. In systems thinking, diverse and individual parts of a whole must to work together

4. 1 Tim 3:15.

5. Rom 12:4–8; 1 Cor 12:12–28a; Eph 1:22–23; 5:23.

for the whole to work. Each part must have some proficiency in its own area of specialization. Each member must also have some sense of the whole to modulate its own tendencies to either under- or over-perform. In other words, each individual member must be attentive to what makes for the good of the whole, even to the point where and when the individual subordinates his own interests.

Also in systems thinking, peripheral awareness of parts for the whole is enabled by "interfaces," to use the more clinical term. Each part of a system has system interfaces necessarily residing *in between* other members. The function of an interface is to subordinate or reconcile the parochial interests of the individual member to the interests of other members and to the interests of the whole.

Paul's application of the body metaphor punctures the cognitive habit of assigning more importance to one part or member over another. "On the contrary," Paul says, "the members of the body that seem to be weaker are indispensable, and those members of the body that we think less honorable we clothe with greater honor, and our less respectable members are treated with greater respect; whereas our more respectable members do not need this."[6]

Paul is offering us a very practical vision of a highly integrated whole. Subjection to each other is the basis of the integration. It is the very thing that enables the integrity of the whole. It clearly implies how individual members are to treat each other, not only with respect and tolerance, but actually to be "subject" to each other. Without this willingness to be "subject to," we are left with a disintegrating and disabling disunity, a divisiveness that erodes the whole.

Paul even used the body metaphor to bolster his advice to husbands and wives to be "to be subject to one another."[7] Paul's counsel to put our selves in subjection to another is a more organic expression than the antiseptic "interface." But both describe the same principle. In his application of the metaphor Paul captures the essence of the church's position itself. Being "subject to" describes what governs the interrelationships of the individual members to each other, the whole to the head, and pinpoints the position of the church relative to the kingdom of God on earth. Members are to be subject to one another and the church subject to the company of God.

6. 1 Cor 12:22–24.

7. Eph 5:21.

Unity, integrity, integration are all implied in the metaphor of the body. But there is one other aspect of this metaphor Paul would not want us to overlook: that Christ is the head of this body. A headless body is a corpse, without life, without purpose or intent. Paul's body metaphor does not neglect the head who is Christ.[8] Purpose is incarnate in the head and essential in the context of uncertainty, ambiguity, and complexity that change presents.

The implication for the church is clear. The church is always "subject" and "subordinate to" its "head"—the Crucified Anointed One. And as that Anointed One was himself sent by God for the purpose of proclaiming the good news of the kingdom of God,[9] so the church's purpose will be always be subject and subordinate to the purpose of this proclamation.

The metaphor closely couples the body's anatomical and structural characteristics to its purpose. In short, Paul's body metaphor helps us understand the church's enduring position and enduring purpose. The metaphor also provides potent guidance for the church in understanding what postures it may choose to take in the context of its immediate circumstances and environment, particularly when that context is saturated with change.

Consider how the human body is designed to move, and move without changing identity. Our bodies enable us to take up different positions, as for example, moving from one corner of the room to another, or one building to another. Likewise, our bodies enable us to reconfigure themselves in different postures—sitting, kneeling, leaning forward or leaning back. With our posture we both show and express intention, attention, and even devotion. The metaphor of the body is rich with implications, if not inspired with meaning, particularly in the context of change and responses to it.

Though Paul did not use the metaphor in this context, there is nothing to suggest that he would object. Even the Greek word for church—*ekklesia*—has much to recommend its application in the context of responding to change. *Ekklesia* is a compound word, comprised of *kaleto* (to be called) and the prefix *ek* (out). When one is called, response is what is expected. Responsiveness and response-ability is built in to the word itself. With the prefix *ek* (out), the word indicates an assembly that itself is "to be called

8. Col 1:18, 24; Eph 5:23.

9. Luke 4:18, 43.

out." The word is saturated with the implications of response-ability and movement.

Paul was not the only one to draw attention to the body. The Gospel of John shares Paul's attention to the body, in particular the body's ability to adjust its posture. Remember Jesus kneeling in front of the woman caught in the act of adultery?[10] Jesus deliberately changes his posture twice in the course of this interaction. The gospel writer deliberately draws our attention to it. In fact, posture change becomes a part of the interaction itself. Jesus is the one who changes his posture, bending down and then straightens up, twice, while the woman being judged remains standing the whole time.

Drawing attention to this posture change is not intended to imply a conformance to this world, like when a chameleon changes its colors as a defensive move to blend in.[11] Instead, the ability and freedom to adjust posture is a capability that the church may underutilize, perhaps in the mistaken notion that to maintain faithfulness to an enduring position and purpose, it must also hold the same posture.

But before we propose such a posture, it is prudent to center ourselves on the church's enduring position and purpose.

ENDURING POSITION

The enduring position of the church is subsidiary. The church is not the company of God—the kingdom of God on earth. Rather, it is a subsidiary of this company, subordinate to the kingdom of God on earth, not synonymous with it.

The church is certainly supportive of and in service to the company of God. But it is not the company itself. In fact, the church may be one among other subsidiaries as well. Whether there are such subsidiaries, and why, is entirely up to God to decide.

Unfortunately the church has mistakenly imagined itself to *be* the company of God from time to time. It has lost sight of its subordinate

---

10. John 8:1–11.

11. Though we often cite Paul's statement in Rom 12:2—"be not conformed to this world"—Paul also declares, "Some proclaim Christ from envy and rivalry, but others from goodwill. These proclaim Christ out of love, . . . others proclaim Christ out of selfish ambition, not sincerely. . . . What does it matter? Just this, that Christ is proclaimed in every way, whether out of false motives or true; and in that I rejoice" (Phil 1:15–18).

position. Such lapses have led to disastrous consequences. Some of the more glaring examples might include the crusades, the abuses of the Inquisition, the overzealousness of the Scottish founder of the Presbyterian Church, John Knox, and even the more recent albeit diffused efforts of the so-called "Christian right" to fight power with power.[12] Though well-intentioned perhaps, the failure to understand the subsidiary and subordinate position of the church often compliments the dangerous assumption that the church and the company of God are identical.

The following analogy illustrates what a subsidiary and subordinate position means. Many companies, particularly those with regular operations, will make the distinction between "line" and "staff."[13] Line functions are those that directly and immediately advance the outcomes of an organization's efforts like producing, packaging and distributing the products it makes and even selling what it makes to customers. Staff functions are those that indirectly support the line functions with specialized expertise or advisory support, like accounting, public relations, employee benefits and legal advice. The generally recognized rule of thumb for staff positions is that their authority is limited to areas where they have specialized functional expertise *and* a company-wide standard of uniformity is important. With respect to the church and the company of God, the former is "staff" and the latter is "line."

Despite this rule of thumb, conflicts often arise between line and staff. Leaders on the line may be unreceptive to advice from staff. Often staff can lose sight of their position and overreach their authority, insisting those on the line follow their advice. Sometimes it's both. Adhering to Paul's admonition "be subject to one another" is challenging enough between peers, but when organizational power is uneven, it can be especially difficult.

This distinction was at times difficult for the disciples to understand. Consider the fact that on more than one occasion Jesus found himself having to correct the misunderstanding and misguided aspirations of his disciples, corrections that took the form of both words and deeds.

First, there's the example just after Peter confessed what others were thinking but too afraid to say, "You are the Anointed One, the Son of the

---

12. Hunter, *To Change the World*, 99–100.

13. The designations "line" and "staff" likely came out of military contexts and are far from recent (e.g., David was "staff" to Saul and his brothers who were on the "line" in the battle with the Philistines; 1 Sam 17.)

living God."[14] Jesus then tells Peter and the other disciples the dark news of what is about to happen—that he "must go to Jerusalem and undergo great suffering at the hands of the elders and chief priest and scribes and be killed, and on the third day be raised."[15] But Peter, likely full of himself after making such a bold affirmation, rebukes Jesus, saying, "God forbid it. This must never happen to you." Here Jesus corrects him in a strikingly sharp way: "Get behind me, Satan! You are a stumbling block to me; for you are setting your mind not on divine things but on human things."

Then there is the example of Jesus critiquing the public's elevated esteem for the scribes and the Pharisees, and the way the scribes and Pharisees themselves played to it. "They love to have the place of honor at banquets and the best seats in the synagogues, and to be greeted with respect in the marketplaces and to have people call them rabbi."[16] But Jesus says to his disciples that will not be so with them. No titles. No "rabbi." No "teacher." "You are all students." And then to drive the point home he concludes with the phrase repeated several times elsewhere: "the greatest among you will be your servant."

Then, there is the enacted example of Jesus washing his disciples feet.[17] Here, so there is no misunderstanding, Jesus makes it very explicit what he has done. "You call me Teacher and Lord—and you are right, for that is what I am. So if I, your Lord and Teacher, have washed your feet, you also ought to wash one another's feet. For I have set you an example that you also should do as I have done to you. Very truly, I tell you, servants are not greater than their master, nor are messengers greater than the one who sent them."

These examples remind us that the subsidiary position is not always well understood, especially by those in the subsidiary position. A chronic temptation and tendency toward exceptionalism gets in the way. Followers often become inflated or intoxicated with the admiration from those who mistakenly identify the message of truth and good news with the messengers who deliver it.

This was not a new problem with Jesus and his disciples. In fact it was explicitly foreshadowed in Isaiah's prophesy[18] to the people of Israel in

14. Matt 16:13–20.

15. Matt 16:21–23.

16. Matt 23:1–12.

17. John 13:1–20.

18. The servant songs of Isaiah (42:1–9; 49:1–12; 50:4–9; 52:13—53:12).

exile, a position not unlike the position the church occupies today in North America. By identifying Israel as God's servant, Isaiah spoke a surprising and challenging truth. "Although the designation 'servant' is traditional, it is anything but 'natural' in the midst of exilic despair," Walter Brueggemann points out. "In exile, Israel tended to be more self-preoccupied and self-absorbed with its own destiny. In this utterance, however, YHWH changes the subject and summons grieving Israel out beyond its own self-preoccupation to other work."[19]

In these biblical examples and even more contemporary ones,[20] this tendency of followers to overreach, arises, at least in part, from amnesia about subsidiary position. "It cannot be the church's commission to form the world after its own image. Every direct intervention by the church in economics, politics and culture has up to now been subject to the suspicion that it was serving the church's own interests; and this suspicion is hard to destroy. For this reason the church ought not to claim any direct power in secular matters."[21]

Hans Kung makes this subsidiary position of the church very clear:

> It is impossible to speak of Christian society or even of the Church as being "God's kingdom on earth." . . . There can be no question of identity, . . . [nor any] question of continuity, . . . for the reign of God is not the product of an organic development, of a process of maturation or interpenetration, but of a wholly new and unprepared perfecting action of God. Man's part is the way of readiness and openness, obedience and watchfulness, faith and repentance. So far from stressing identity, we should be concerned to stress the basic difference between the church and the reign of God. To apply to the Church what is said in the New Testament about the reign of God will inevitably lead to an intolerable glorification of the church.[22]

In the midst of much change, even turbulent change, I believe we can be confident in saying that the enduring position of the church, regardless of the church's past tendencies to get out of position, is as a subsidiary of the company of God. This position implies responsiveness, localness and the in-between-ness of being "subject to," not only to one

19. Brueggemann, *Isaiah*, 2:42.

20. Hunter, *To Change the World*, 111–31.

21. Moltmann, *Church in the Power of the Holy Spirit*, 167.

22. Kung, *Church*, 92.

another and the head of the church, but to the enduring purpose of the company of God.

ENDURING PURPOSE

Closely coupled with its enduring, subsidiary position is the church's enduring purpose: to serve the company of God. The forms of such service may be many and varied, based in part on local conditions, challenges and circumstances.[23] Indeed, these forms may change from one era to the next. However, the single purpose of the church endures: to serve the company of God. It is in this sense that the church is in the world, but not of it.

Any servant to a greater or higher purpose fits, supports and serves the purposes to which the servant remains subordinate. The church is no exception. The church is not an end in and of itself, but a means. In this very means-ends distinction ambiguity and confusion often arises. With the church it is an ambiguity that bubbles up from different understandings about the purpose of the company of God and the even broader, less time dependent, purpose of the kingdom of God.

Despite Paul's pleas to be "of one mind,"[24] there has seldom been universal agreement about the single purpose of the church or a common articulation of it. People have understood the purpose of the church in a variety of different ways and voiced it with an even greater variety of expressions. These understandings seemingly stretch across a continuum between the Great Commission and the Great Commandment.

At the Great Commission end of the continuum is a purpose often understood as the conversion of individual souls wherein spiritual redemption for the individual believer is the experience sought and discipleship the result that ensues. "Go therefore and make disciples of all nations, baptizing them in the name of the Father and of the Son and of the Holy Spirit, and teach them to obey everything that I have

---

23. The universal church is present in each local congregation. Despite the diversity and variety of local forms of the church, each local church carries the "DNA" of the whole, at least in intent. World Council of Churches Faith and Order Paper 198 (2005), D. "The Church as Communion of Local Churches," 64–66.

24. 1 Cor 1:10.

commanded you."[25] However, even the Great Commission is a *command-ment* of Jesus.[26]

On the Great Commandment end of the continuum is a purpose for the church that is more along the lines of the "increase of the love of God and love of neighbor."[27] The Great Commandment, at least as the dialogue between Jesus and the scribe portrays it in Mark's gospel, is actually a pair of commandments:

> "Hear, O Israel: the Lord our God, the Lord is one; your shall love the Lord your God with all your heart, and with all your soul, and with all your mind, and with all your strength." The second is this, "You shall love your neighbor as yourself." There is no other commandment greater than these.[28]

After seeing that the inquiring scribe agreed, Jesus says this: "You are not far from the kingdom of God." Hans Kung expresses the commandment side of the continuum this way:

> The church exists in the world. But it can lay no exclusive claim to certainty of salvation *vis-a-vis* the world nor to spiritual authority. What it wants is quite different: to give selfless and unpretentious service to the salvation of the world. To be truly catholic the Church must think of itself not as synonymous with the world, nor yet on the other hand as an exclusive society of those already saved, but as an open community of people dedicated to serve and work for the salvation of all, of the whole of mankind.[29]

The salvation of the whole of mankind, of course, is the primary interest and purpose of the company of God. Or to express this purpose cryptically, the purpose of the company of God is to close the gap between heaven and earth in heaven's favor.

To understand the purpose of the church we must first understand the purpose of the company which it serves—the company of God. The purpose of any subsidiary will necessarily be subordinate to, but aligned

---

25. Matt 28:16–20.

26. This suggests that our continuum is likely more theoretical and rhetorical than actual.

27. Niebuhr, *Purpose of the Church and Its Ministry*, 27–38.

28. Mark 12:28–34. Matthew's version (22:34–40) shows the same pairing between the *Shema* (Deut 6:4–5)—the love of God—and the love of neighbor (Lev 19:18).

29. Kung, *Church*, 319.

with, the purposes of the host. In the previous essay[30] this question of the nature and purpose of the company of God was addressed. We need not repeat it here, except to say that the kingdom of God is greater than the company of God (the kingdom of God on earth).

The purpose of the kingdom of God will necessarily show up in the company of God, and subsequently the church as the subsidiary to the company of God. At some point, however, a clear expression of the purpose of the church needs to be made. Such expression will provide solid footing for the church to maintain sufficient balance required to take on a relevant posture in response to changes in its current and immediate context. Innovation theology likely will benefit from such an expression, one way or the other.

PROVISIONAL POSTURES

As a body (of Christ) each congregation strives to remain faithful to its enduring position and purpose. But in the process, might it become so accustomed to a fixed posture that it grows stiff, even rigid? In attempting to be faithful to an enduring position and purpose, does it mistakenly assume its posture should remain the same also? Or can the church maintain alignment with its enduring position and purpose while flexing its posture? Jesus did this with the woman caught in the act of adultery, bending down and straightening up as and when it was called for.

By posture, think of the Paul's body metaphor and the near universal experience of what happens to the body when a single posture is held for too long. For example, as I compose this very paragraph on a laptop, my attention to the pixilated text on the display becomes so fixated I end up holding the same posture for too long. Stiffness sets in. When the tension in my neck and shoulders talks back to me I notice and adjust. I return to good posture, straightening my back and shoulders. Relief doesn't last long before I must do so again.

This returning to good posture hints at the church's choice to return. Rather than slouching toward Bethlehem[31] God seems to call the church as God called Israel before, to recover its proper posture, particularly when it periodically becomes temporarily conformed to this world. Isaiah suggests that there may be more to this return than we might imagine.

30. See ch. 11, "This Company Has No Exit Strategy."

31. Yeats, "Second Coming."

In returning and rest you shall be *saved*,
in quietness and rest is your strength.[32]

Sadly this invitation to return is immediately followed by, "But you would not."[33]

"All too easily the church can become a prisoner of the image it has made for itself at one particular period in history."[34] This is not to deny that the church has an enduring position. Neither does this deny that the church has an enduring purpose to serve in acts and words, bearing witness to the presence and purpose of the company of God. Rather, it is to say that this enduring position and purpose "is only revealed in change; its identity exists only in variability, its continuity only in changing circumstances, its permanence only in varying outward appearances. In short, the 'essence' of the church is not a matter of metaphysical stasis, but exists only in constantly changing historical 'forms.'"[35] These forms constitute what might be called provisional postures.

While the subsidiary position and the servant purpose of the church endure, the church is *in* a worldly context that is anything but static. The posture it takes should be responsive to the perceived presence and purpose of the company of God.

As the intention of God manifests itself in change, and as the call of God invites us through change to respond, the purpose of the church is to bear witness to the presence and purpose of the company of God in both the change and response. This purpose is essential to innovators, if they seek meaning before money, intrinsic value before extrinsic returns and are interested in creating new value for others that matters. It is a purpose embodied more appropriately without judgment or contempt, but in a spirit to encourage innovators to consider the presence and purpose of the company of God. If innovators want to create new value for others, their desire will be better served when it is more aligned with the presence and purpose of the company of God.

This implies that the church may be better positioned and purposed than it might otherwise realize. For the church to simply ask of any considered response to change whether, where and why innovations are needed may be a start. Or possibly the church might need only ask (not

32. Isa 30:15.

33. Isa 30:16.

34. Kung, *Church*, 4.

35. Ibid.

answer) how possible answers align with the interests of the company of God. Answers to such questions as these might make it more explicit whether extracted values are rooted in intrinsic value, whether the transactions envisioned are building relationships or merely exploiting them, whether what is pursued is money or meaning, and whether the response to change is merely about the accumulation of wealth or about a more substantive, redemptive or reconciling reality.

In this limited purpose of making the call and will of God more explicit to innovators, better choices can be made, by both individuals and organizations, regarding where innovations are needed and why. Answers to these questions will no longer be left to some "invisible hand" of the market, nor to the variable imaginations of entrepreneurs and inventors who may otherwise ignore the interests, presence and purpose of the company of God. Possible answers of course require prayerful discernment within a community of members who are subject to one another and to the Founder[36] of the company of God.

If there is any truth in the preceding paragraph then it may imply that the church should not be conservative, preservative, or progressive in orientation to change or in attitude toward responses to change, or in judgments about innovations. Rather it should be willing to go to the leading edge, even the bleeding edge, to serve the interests of the company of God, knowing that company's purpose is for the whole, not just a part. Its posture should always be provisional primarily because its context is always changing.

This is what Richard Niebuhr famously called the "enduring problem of the church": culture.

ENDURING CONTEXT

Referring to culture as a "problem" actually exacerbates the problem. When something is called a "problem" it frames the situation in such a way as to imply that there is a solution. When Christ or the church is juxtaposed to culture, it is difficult to avoid the implication that the former holds the solution and the latter is the problem. But is culture really a problem to solve? Is culture not simply a way of describing the context we live in?

36. Called in the Letter to the Hebrews the pioneer and perfecter of the faith (Heb 12:1–2).

"Culture" is one of those words that attract more connotations than it can possibly contain. Niebuhr himself recognized this and took some pains to define it carefully as "the 'artificial, secondary environment' which man superimposes on the natural. It comprises language, habits, ideas, beliefs, customs, social organization, inherited artifacts, technical processes, and values."[37] Niebuhr went on to highlight the chief characteristics of culture as saturated with human achievement and values. The virtues of culture are viewed as typically good for society, realized in temporal and material embodiments and worth sustaining because of their goodness.[38]

So what's the "problem"? Isn't culture simply the context in which the church lives and moves and has its being? Isn't culture simply the same context in which change invites innovations almost as inexorably as stimulus calls for response? Wouldn't it be more appropriate to look at culture as our given *context* rather than a "problem"? In fact, isn't the church itself inextricably enmeshed in culture, indeed, a part of culture?

To be fair, Niebuhr chose "Christ" rather than "church" to set up the juxtaposition in *Christ and Culture*. But even Niebuhr acknowledges that the meanings evoked by "Christ," "Christianity" or "church" in the minds of believers and unbelievers alike, are difficult to keep separate.[39]

Instead of the world or culture being a "problem" for the church and its parent company of God, this world and culture is the enduring context—the territory in which the company of God operates. It is in this context that God sends invitations, enveloped in change, to respond and even to seriously consider in those responses the creation of new value for others. It is in this context that the company of God has likely already begun to respond, with or without the church. So what we consider "our" innovations arising out of our creativity and cleverness may need to be reconsidered, if not wholly revised. The imperative that consistently accompanies the good news that the kingdom of God is near is repent: change your way of knowing, thinking and responding.

Regardless of whether a congregation chooses to separate itself from its external culture, see and celebrate the best in that culture, work to correct and redeem the culture, endure the culture or even attempt to transform

---

37. Niebuhr, *Christ and Culture*, 32. Here Niebuhr cites Bronislaw Malinowski's "Culture," in *Encyclopedia of Social Sciences*, 4:621.

38. Ibid., 32–39.

39. Ibid., 12.

the culture, the church might first consider its subsidiary position and servant purpose to avoid the overreaching mistakes made in the past.

Niebuhr himself likely saw this tendency of the church to over-reach. Five years after he published *Christ and Culture*, he observed, "Whether the term Church or the term Christianity is used, there is an internal contradiction in a theology and a Christian educational system that regards the work of the Church as the final activity to be considered."[40] The contradiction is a common one arising from the substitution of proximate for ultimate goals, or the confusion of the relative for the absolute; in other words, when the church mistakenly imagines itself to *be* the company of God.

As Christians we cannot escape living in a changing culture. This is where we live and are called to respond. As individual Christians, however, we are not alone in our response. We are members of churches and therefore subject to one another, to the Lord and subordinate to the presence and purpose of the company of God.[41] But this subjection and subordination does not imply that the last reality with which we are concerned is the servant subsidiary of the company of God. The summary commandment is not to love Christianity or the church with all your heart, soul, mind and strength, though this is what some may see in the way the church or Christianity is exalted. Such exaltations of the church or Christianity lead to responses that do not reconcile one with the other, whether neighbors or enemies. It leads rather to direct competition with rival religions or worldviews, to convert rather than reconcile, or even worse.

So, what is the church to do now, particularly in North American where many assume the church has lost its voice, relevance or both?

POSTURES PROPOSED FOR TODAY

The remainder of this essay proposes provisional postures for the church[42] today, especially in the context of change and innovation. The postures proposed here address a cultural context in which innovations are clothed with insights from science, technology, engineering and math

---

40. Ibid., 40–47.

41. Can anyone really be a Christian without being a member of a church, even a local congregation?

42. In particular, the North American mainline and Evangelical Protestant churches.

(STEM). The provisional postures proposed for the church are at least three: *pastoral space, prophetic sign* and *personal sacrifice*.

Such spaces, signs and sacrifices will likely vary in their relevance to local conditions and circumstance. But the three may better reflect the enduring position and purpose of the church in our current culture, at least better than assuming the broader culture is a problem with only five alternative strategies or solutions.[43] Each of these three are inspired and shaped by the Servant Songs in Isaiah[44] as embodied in the life, teaching, death and resurrection of Jesus.

Pastoral Space

Change, reactions to it and even innovating[45] can take away both our breath and sense of place. *Pastoral space* intends to connote what many congregations are already doing, though some perhaps in too limited a degree. Often without awareness of its significance in contexts of change, congregations are consciously creating safe, nurturing "breathing space" for people displaced, burdened, fatigued and victimized by change. "Breathing space" intends to offer not only a place to catch our breath, but also the breath of the Living God.

Pastoral space should be one of a local congregation's existing "core competencies,"[46] and a deployable capability and capacity. Physically and socially, congregations are well equipped to provide sanctuary for those displaced by change. The "equipment" can be found not only in its physical buildings. It can be formed by the fellowship (*koine*) of the congregation. It can also be found in the narrative roots of the church's deep past. Experiences of captivity, exodus, wandering in the wilderness and exile are all well represented in the narratives and poetry of the Old Testament, the foundation for the New. In short, the church is already in a position to take this posture of solidarity with those who have not yet begun to recover from what they may perceive as the victimization of change.

---

43. The five alternative strategies or solutions outlined by Niebuhr in *Christ and Culture* being "against," "of," "above," "in paradox with," and "transforming" culture.

44. Isa 42:1–9 (First Servant Song); 49:1–12 (Second Servant Song); 50:4–9 (Third Servant Song); 52:13–53:12 (Fourth Servant Song).

45. The church might easily realize that innovation itself can be part of the cause for displacement, burdens, fatigue and victimization.

46. Prahalad and Hamel, "Core Competence of the Corporation."

The spaces[47] are physical, social, narrative and, of course, spiritual, all of which may be necessary for individuals and organizations to recover from the despair of the victim narrative and find hope in being freed from it. The church has an abundance of resources already oriented to these kinds of spaces—well-suited to speak to victims of change, those who have not only lost their place in their world but who are refugees of change, literally and figuratively.

The church—both as local congregation and denominational aggregates—can and should look to Isaiah's Servant Songs for direction and guidance for cultivating pastoral space for others. Guidance can be found in the first Servant Song[48] where the servant is introduced as one who "will not cry or lift up his voice, or make it heard on the street."

This may require restraint from some churches and individuals within them. However, the guidance goes on to suggest gentleness: "A bruised reed he will not break, and a dimly burning wick he will not quench; he will faithfully bring forth justice."

According to Walter Brueggemann, God is inviting Israel, even in its exile, to

> practice vulnerability and to be attentive to others who are vulnerable, "bruised reeds and dim wicks." Israel's way of relationship is thus drastically contrasted with the way of Babylon (or any other worldly power), which is to break such reeds and snuff out such wicks. Israel is to pursue a different way in the world—to refuse the modes of power mostly taken for grated.[49]

The servant's task is to bring forth justice, but to do so "unobtrusively," especially in relations with those who are fragile and suffering.

Instead of forceful, self-righteous anger expressed "on the street" in the name of justice, Isaiah reminds us who the servant serves, the One "who gives breath to the people upon [the earth], and spirit to those who walk in it."

Pastoral spaces are those where people catch their breath and breathe deeply. These spaces are places where people discover their salvation and strength simply "in returning and rest" and in "quietness and trust."[50]

47. Nonaka and Konno, "Concept of 'Ba.'" Nonaka and Konno connect space ("ba") with the knowledge-creation foundation of innovating.

48. Isa 42:1–9.

49. Childs, *Isaiah*, 324.

50. Isa 30:15.

Such spaces are increasingly rare, precious and important in the midst of the pace of living that leave people hurried, frantic, and breathless.

The Second Servant Song[51] goes on to speak of deeper and broader dimensions to this pastoral space. The deeper dimension resides in a more intimate knowledge of the One who formed the servant "in the womb; to bring Jacob back to him [the Lord], and so that Israel might be gathered to him." The broader dimension reminds us that this space is not just for members of the church, not simply a parochial pasture intended for Christians. Rather,

> It is too light a thing that you should be my servant
>
> to raise up the tribes of Jacob and restore the survivors of Israel;
>
> I will give you as a light to the nations,
>
> that my salvation may reach to the end of the earth.

This Song gives us the image of what makes the space "pastoral" with an entry to the space that is accessible:

> They shall feed along the ways,
>
> on all the bare heights shall be their pasture;
>
> they shall not hunger or thirst,
>
> neither scorching wind nor sun shall strike them down,
>
> for he who has pity on them will lead them,
>
> and by springs of water will guide them.
>
> And I will turn all my mountains into a road,
>
> and my highways shall be raised up.

The Third Servant Song[52] touches on the intent of pastoral space to "sustain the weary with a word," while the Fourth Song[53] expresses the contrition of those who see the difference between being in this space and apart from it: "All we like sheep have gone astray; we have all turned to our own way, and the Lord has laid on him the iniquity of us all."

The truth of the Servant Songs

> cannot be reduced to a rational formula. It must remain poetry that glides over rational reservation. We are not told how hurt and guilt can be reassigned and redeployed from one to another. We are not told how the suffering of one makes healing possible

51. Isa 49:1–12.

52. Isa 50:4–9.

53. Isa 52:13—53:12.

for another. But it is so here [in this pastoral space]: "we" have thus been healed and made whole. We are here in this pastorally delicate transaction that is at the core of salvific faith.[54]

What makes the space pastoral in fact is that one life can be vulnerable enough to permit restoration of another.

Prophetic Sign

Prophetic sign is a second provisional posture of the church. As a *sign* this posture could be embodied in a truth-filled act. It could also be an image, like Amos' fourth vision of the plumb line, an image that unmistakably calls for alignment with the purposes of the One who holds the line. As a sign it is silent, but carries an unambiguous clarity in meaning, penetrating the heart and conscience as much as the mind. As *prophetic*, the sign calls for repentance in those for whom the message is intended.[55]

As a prophetic sign the plumb line of Amos is particularly well suited for contexts of responding to change and innovation. The image alone speaks to the anxious uncertainties and ambivalent variabilities victors of change exploit. Those who the world regards as victors in response to change and innovation are often those whose success is based on riding the waves of change to their own advantage. Their rides are on the surface and only for as long as the wave lasts. The plumb line pierces this surface and penetrates the temporary wave with a deeper, more permanent truth. Plumb lines are vertical. They intersect the horizontal equivocations and obfuscating ambiguities that so often accompany change and innovating. They represent another dimension of reality made straight by moral gravity and the lofty grip of God.

God, "standing beside a wall built with a plumb line and holding a plumb line in his hand," asks Amos what he sees. Is God more interested in having us see our purpose and position than he is in having us see him? Is God more interested in having us participate in the "building up," as the Apostle Paul describes it,[56] aligned with the purposes and presence of the company of God? Does this posture invite us to ask of innovators

---

54. Brueggemann, *Isaiah*, 2:146.

55. The prophetic message always includes the messenger as a recipient of the message as well. Authentic prophets are also subject to the judgment (and hope) of the message they carry.

56. 1 Cor 8:1: Knowledge puffs up, love builds up.

and so-called change masters[57] how their plans and efforts align with the plumb line that God is holding?

For a church to be an embodiment of a prophetic sign does not imply that it becomes an angry advocate for justice, though justice is never far from its intent. Making straight and plumb what is built may be more to the point. It also implies that any success a congregation has must be compared not to the world's standards of institutional growth or the reach of its influence on the culture, but on how well it is aligned with the purpose and presence of the company of God.

Likewise, the church, as a servant subsidiary of the company of God, is also tasked with bearing witness to what it sees, not what it holds. God, not the church, is holding the plumb line. The sign is intended to penetrate superficial and exploitative efforts by simply asking[58] if the contemplated response to change is aligned with the purposes and presence of the company of God.

Bearing witness to the plumb line will go a long way to answering the question where innovations are truly needed and why. Bearing witness to the plumb line should also help innovators make meaning before they try to make money, to look for intrinsic value before extracting transactional value and to view investments with a spirit of generosity rather than the cold cognition of calculations.

The Servant Songs light the path for the church to see its way to this prophetic posture. The first Servant Song is saturated with the classical characteristics we associate with the prophetic: the task of "bringing forth" and "establishing" justice, the foreshadow of Isaiah's "opening the eyes of the blind" and "setting the prisoners free" with which Jesus identified himself[59] and even the validation of a true from a false prophet: "See, the former things have come to pass, and new things I now declare."

Perhaps the most striking prophetic chord struck in the first Song and struck again in the second is the sign itself. This sign is not an image like the plumb line. It is an embodiment. "I have given *you* as a covenant to the people." The servant Israel is given as "a covenant to the people"— to the people of the whole earth.

The implication for the church is clear. The church itself is called to *be* the prophetic sign of the covenant God desires and makes with all

57. Kanter, *Change Masters*, 13.

58. Not telling but asking.

59. Isa 61:1–2; Luke 4:18.

people. The church carries in its body the covenant that God has made with all people. The church is intended to embody this covenant.

This embodiment resonates with Jeremiah's new covenant, "not like the covenant that God made with the ancestors of Israel and the house of Judah" but one that God "will put *within* them" and "write on their hearts." No longer shall they teach one another, or say to each other, 'Know the Lord,' for they shall all know me, from the least of them to the greatest."[60]

Prophetic persistence in the face of resistance is carried in the third Song, continuing what the first two began. But the embodiment of the prophetic sign reaches it deepest and most piercing expression in the Fourth Song. Here the Servant is clearly a person more than an anthropomorphic sign or embodied covenant. The sign is pure sign, with no speech but plenty of voice:

> He was oppressed, and he was afflicted,
> yet he did not open his mouth;
> like a lamb that is led to the slaughter,
> and like a sheep that before its shearers is silent,
> so he did not open his mouth.

The servant as the prophetic sign is anything but physically attractive. The servant's appearance appeals to no one.

> He had no form or majesty that we should look at him,
> nothing in his appearance that we should desire him.
> he was despised and rejected by others;
> A man of suffering and acquainted with infirmity;
> And as one from who others hide their faces,
> he was despised, and we held him of no account.

But despite the physical revulsion, there is a strange attraction:

> Just as there were many who were astonished at him—
> so marred was his appearance, beyond human semblance,
> and his form beyond that of mortals—
> so he shall startle many nations;
> kings shall shut their mouths because of him.

60. Jer 31:31–34.

And then the highest praise for any prophetic sign is made—that the prophetic sign communicates without needing the accompaniment of written or spoke words; "for that which had not been told them they shall see, and that which they had not heard they shall contemplate."

Innovations that are truly new go well beyond the words we have in stock to describe or name them. And innovations that are both truly new and deeply valuable go well beyond explanations. The explanations are supplanted by recognition of this strange attraction that can be seen with the eyes of the mind and heart.

The prophetic sign is no longer just in the person of the servant— ultimately the suffering servant incarnate in Jesus. The sign is carried in the act of the servant's suffering, the self sacrificial act "which becomes an offering for sin" and "through which [or shall we say through *whom*?] the will of the Lord shall prosper."

"Prospering" is simply the succeeding purpose and presence of the company of God. In the "pouring out himself to death" the prophetic sign brings up the emptying (*kenosis*) of Jesus[61] and leads us to another possible provisional posture.

Personal Sacrifice

Responding to change and innovating require personal sacrifice. Those who choose to lean in rather than back from personal sacrifice, experience a joy that comes from giving up what was once precious but may now no longer be. In the giving up—in the sacrifice itself—something changes in the one who sacrifices, personally.

Where pastoral space puts victims of change front and center, and prophetic sign challenges those who take full credit for being victors in change, *personal sacrifice* speaks to the free generosity of volunteers, who choose to give their time, attention and devotion, and in many cases, themselves.

Personal sacrifice is not to be confused with ritual sacrifice. Nor is it a personal sacrifice if the relinquishment does not really matter that much to the one making the sacrifice. The prophet Amos was but the first in a long line of other prophets to sound this note about superficial

---

61. Phil 2:7.

sacrifice.[62] Instead, "the sacrifice acceptable to God is a broken spirit, a broken and contrite heart, O God, you will not despise."[63]

The church's role in this is to encourage personal sacrifice of itself and of its members for the company of God. This is part and parcel of what it means to be a servant subsidiary. At the very least this means a purposeful saying "no" to our own desires in favor of the purpose of the company of God. The church's role here is to be an example, and imitator of Christ, in sacrificing its time, attention and devotion. And as an imitator of Christ, the church invites its individual members—people who are strapped for time, often suffering from attention deficits and unsure what devotion should look like—to give their time, attention and devotion for a different kind of treasure.

As the Servant Songs make clear and in a progressive manner, personal sacrifice and the suffering that accompanies it may be the most challenging of the proposed provisional postures for the church. And yet, it is not impossible. Some congregations have deep reservoirs of grace, from years of personal and direct experience in being victims of change, even oppressed by victors of change. Yet, these congregations are still willing to volunteer for the company of God.

One such church is located in Charleston, South Carolina—the Emmanuel African Episcopal Methodist Church. This congregation was able to differentiate between ultimate and proximate goals amid great personal loss. They were able to create pastoral space, embody prophetic sign and respond to the call of personal sacrifice. Here's the report from the *Los Angeles Times*:

> In an extraordinary emotional display of raw pain and grace, the relatives of those slain in a shooting at a historic black church confronted suspected killer Dylann Roof in court on Friday. Through tears, some reached for forgiveness.
>
> "We welcomed you Wednesday night in our Bible study with open arms," said Felecia Sanders, who survived the attack at the Emanuel African Methodist Episcopal Church by feigning death, but whose son, Tywanza, died. "You have killed some of the most beautiful people that I know. Every fiber in my body hurts . . . and I'll never be the same. Tywanza was my son, but Tywanza was my hero," she said. "May God have mercy on you."

62. Amos 5:21–24.

63. Ps 51:17.

Anthony Thompson, the grandson of victim Myra Thompson, told Roof, "I forgive you, my family forgives you. We would like you to take this opportunity to repent. Do that and you'll be better off than you are right now."[64]

Be subject to one another.

What I first heard in a rhyme and felt in the choreography of my hands, endures in a new expression of words: that the church can be *a space* created for communion, *a sign* that points to a reality above and *a threshold* to attract others because of the life and love of the people already there. Just as our bodies are designed to move, adjust and adapt, so the body of Christ should, can and must respond, adapt and adjust to change.

The position and purpose of the church may endure, but the postures taken are always provisional and temporary. For now, in the context of change and innovation, the servant subsidiary of the company of God just may be to embody pastoral space, prophetic sign and personal sacrifice.

64. Tanfani and Serrano, "Families of Charleston."

CONVERSATION STARTERS

1. How might the church reclaim its relevance in restless, irritable and discontented contexts of change in this world?

2. What forms of nonverbal witness might the church find most fruitful and faithful in offering pastoral space, prophetic sign and personal sacrifice?

3. Should the church avoid making common denominational position statements and instead take up quiet but clear positions? Should the church focus on local, bottom-up adaptations through the local congregational presence?

13

Innovating with Company Assets
Scripture and Spirit

For the letter kills, but the Spirit gives life.[1]

ASSETS RESTRAIN WHAT A company does in the present and constrain what it might do in the future. Assets do the same for individuals as well. Some might even go so far as to say assets *define* organizations, and unfortunately sometimes also, individuals.

Being defined by assets may overstate their influence. But whether shaped or defined, assets and attitudes about them affect how we respond to change and our willingness to innovate. Generally, organizations and individuals are *less* likely to innovate when they view their assets as fixed. Viewed as fixed, assets become things to preserve, protect and maintain in their current configuration. Seeing assets as fixed can block lines of sight on change and atrophy readiness to respond.

In contrast, organizations and individuals are *more* likely to innovate when they are willing to combine assets in new ways. Such readiness and willingness correlates with the freedom to see, accept and make sense of change on its own terms instead of maintaining an anxious concern to extend the life of the asset.

The willingness to recombine and reconfigure also applies to assets in the company of God. In fact, if biblical theology has something

1. 2 Cor 3:6.

substantive to contribute to innovation, the substance will be found in new combinations of the two assets unique to the company of God: Scripture and the Holy Spirit. Likewise, theology's attitudes toward these assets will prove to be either stumbling or building blocks to what theology can contribute.

What follows explores how these two assets combine and what difference the combinations make to innovating. Before proceeding, however, a brief primer on assets is in order, as is a closer look at the nature of each of these two core assets of the company of God and our attitudes toward them.

ASSETS

Accountants define an asset as "a resource controlled by an entity as a result of past events and from which future economic benefits are expected to flow."[2] Accounting principles classify assets into two types: tangible or intangible.

Tangible assets include both current and fixed assets, where current assets are cash, receivables, short-term investments and inventory. Fixed assets include property, plant and equipment, land, buildings, furniture, computers, etc. *Intangible assets* have no physical substance, are not easy to evaluate and include such things as patents, copyrights, trademarks and even something called goodwill.

If Scripture were listed as an asset of the company of God it would likely be regarded as tangible and fixed. Despite variations in the earliest manuscripts, the sixty-six "books" of the Bible have remained the same for hundreds of years, relatively speaking.[3] Depending on our understanding of the clause "controlled by an entity," Scriptures certainly qualify as "a resource resulting from past events and from which future benefits are expected to flow."

---

2. See the International Financial Reporting Standards's annually updated definition of "asset" (ifrs.org). See also *Wikipedia*, s.v. "asset."

3. Official declarations (*de jure*) of "complete" canons were not made until the Council of Trent (1546) for Roman Catholicism, the Thirty-Nine Articles (1563) for the Church of England, the *Westminster Confession of Faith* (1647) for denominations of the Reformed Tradition, and the Synod of Jerusalem for the Greek Orthodox (1672). As early as the 4th century, however, a relatively stable set of books was used and regarded in common practice (*de facto*) as Scripture.

If the Holy Spirit were listed as an asset, it would likely be regarded as an intangible one. It is without physical substance and hard to evaluate, much less describe. Many can readily tell when the Holy Spirit is present not only by the "fruits of the Spirit" but by the energy we feel and the outcomes we see. It is perhaps no coincidence that the Holy Spirit is so often expressed in the Hebrew with the word *ruah*, which translates as both "wind" and "breath." We can feel its effects though we cannot see its substance. The workings or movements of the Holy Spirit, however are an intangible asset that we don't control.

Assets are typically aggregated on balance sheets that list assets and the values assigned to them. However, balance sheets merely *list* assets and the values assigned to them. By themselves neither balance sheets nor assets *do* anything. Assets must be animated if real value is to be created and delivered. What animates assets is not what but who—people working together with them and with each other.

Companies are more than assets on balance sheets of course. Likewise, the company of God is not limited to its two unique assets. But it is certainly shaped by them, especially by their various combinations in response to change.

Why the interest in assets?

A company's ability to *produce* value comes from how well it combines its assets. But when a company *creates* new value for others, a new combination of assets is required. Such new combinations may well include the addition of other assets as well.

The French economist J. B. Say—the one who coined the term "entrepreneur"—spoke to the necessity of new combinations of assets in his description of the entrepreneurial act. The entrepreneur is one who sees an asset in what others regard as merely a material or even waste.[4] J. B. Say's original observation is worth remembering, especially in light of how "entrepreneur" and its derivatives are so often misused today. It also reminds us that any new combination of assets is likely to first combine an intangible asset with tangible ones.

Attitudes about assets may be as significant as the assets themselves and their combinations. Attitudes affect the willingness to consider new combinations. Willingness to reconfigure, recombine and redeploy one's assets is increasingly recognized as the single most important capability

---

4. Drucker, *Innovation and Entrepreneurship*, 21, 27, 33.

a company can have for innovating.[5] A company's readiness to alter and adapt its familiar and proven routines may be even more important than its timely inventions for innovating. Organizational theorist David Teece calls this attitude and ability "dynamic capability."

The lack of "dynamic capability" can be seen in the mind-sets of incumbent organizations. The reluctance of incumbents to reconfigure their assets makes it more difficult to innovate. This reluctance is understandable, perhaps. After all, "if it ain't broke, don't fix it." Success can reinforce a fixation on keeping assets in their current combination. But change itself, along with the activity of rivals with less to lose, provide nagging reminders to incumbents that new combinations are possible and often preferable.

Willingness to consider new combinations of assets resonates with a concept core to biblical theology. The Greek word for it is *metanoia*— itself a combination of two Greek roots, *meta* (change) and *noia* (knowing). Literally it means to change our way of knowing or thinking. The English word for *metanoia* is repentance. This is basic to biblical theology and applies not only to organizations and individuals, but to the company of God as well.

Willingness to change our way of thinking opens us to new combinations of the two assets of the company of God. When the intangible and current asset of the Holy Spirit combines with the tangible and fixed asset of Scripture, the meaning in Scripture is revealed and the Holy Spirit breathes (new) life into the sense we can make of our changing current contexts, and the value we may create as a result.

COMPANY ASSETS RECONSIDERED

If theology is to make practical contributions to innovating it will need its own dynamic or adaptive capability. Theology will need the willingness and ability to combine its two primary assets in new ways. An initial step in this direction may require a little *metanoia*—a rethinking of just what these two assets are and are not. As a result, a brief look at the nature of these two assets is warranted, beginning with Scripture.

What we call the Bible looks and feels like a book, at first. In fact, many call it the "Good Book." A Bible is meant to be read, however, and when its pages are opened and read, it becomes apparent that it is more

5. Teece, "Explicating Dynamic Capabilities," 1319–50.

of a library than a single book. The variety of its literary forms is as broad as its historical contexts are many and long. Reading the range of its contents requires a different kind of engagement than what a novel or magazine article demands of a reader.

There are at least two ways to engage with the Bible's contents. One is to *read it from the side*. When reading the Bible from the side, readers take the position of a spectator. The other way is to read it *from underneath*, or to *be read by it*. This is to engage with its contents as *Scripture*. At the moment the reader becomes the one being read, the content becomes scriptural. In a functional and practical sense this is what is meant when we call Scripture the "Word of God." We are in effect affirming and claiming our own (and others') previous experiences of having been read by it.

When Scripture reads us, its first expressions *describe* our current context before *prescribing* what we are to do. This is especially significant for current contexts where change occurs and we are called to make sense of it. When we read the Bible as literature, history or an ancient compendium of interesting wisdom, readers can easily "presume to stand above the text, outside the circle of tradition and from this detached vantage point adjudicate the truth and error"[6] of Scripture's fixed and past perspective. When we read the Bible not as literature but as Scripture then the reader "stands within the received tradition, and, fully conscious of his own time-conditionality" is able to discern, in the company of God, where the Holy Spirit is leading.[7] The experience of being read and interpreted by Scripture is not possible without the Holy Spirit. Scriptures "do not serve as a frozen deposit of tradition or doctrine, but a living vehicle through which the will of God is perceived."[8]

As with most assets, Scripture didn't just appear out of the blue. It was centuries in the making. In that process there were plenty of *transcription* issues; poor handwriting, scribal "notes in the margins" and even the scarcity of what to write on, all contributed to these transcription challenges. Some of these transcriptions issues became preserved. With the advent of the printing press many became fixed.

Beyond transcription issues, there are always *translation* issues. When moving from one language to another there is always a gap between original intent and context and what readers receive in their

---

6. Childs, *New Testament as Canon*, 51.

7. Ibid., 51–52.

8. Ibid., 40.

current context.[9] That these are important issues for biblical scholarship goes without saying.

However, when we regard these collections of the written (and likely first oral) word as Scripture, we are in effect claiming that the realities and meaning the writing points to are authoritative. The authoritativeness is not carried by the print or ink-inscribed symbols on a page, or now, pixilated on a display screen. Rather, the authority comes from the experienced relevance these writings have to our current lives and contexts.

Regardless of who actually wrote the words the first time and regardless of who then transcribed and translated the words, when we say "God authored these writings," we are saying that what is written, more than any other volume or collection of writings, reads us, interprets us, and helps us make more and better sense of our lives, including changes we cannot make sense of as well without these writings. It's the relevance of Scripture to the current contexts of our lives that validates its authority more than anything else. Ultimately Scripture is not authoritative or relevant because of *claims* that it is so. It is authoritative and relevant because of and in the experience of those who find it so. This is the nature of this asset—how and why Scripture works—as scripture.

This is a closed loop, so to speak. The Word (of God) as read, understood and embodied by the believing and confessing reader is validated in the reader's experience of being read—well-read. This is what the confessing community continues to confess, acknowledge or, if you will, admit.

What do we know of the other asset, the Holy Spirit?

We know less about the nature and substance of the Holy Spirit than we do about its movements and effects. This fits with an intangible asset. What we do know, however, is that the expression "filled with" frequently accompanies references to the Holy Spirit in the New Testament. "Filled with" implies a space not already filled; like a container with sufficient spare volume. The Holy Spirit is not the container, of course, but what is filling its receptive capacity.

Franciscan Richard Rohr describes this dynamic in his book *Falling Upward*. Rohr observes that many of us, by the time we reach our fifties, wake up to a startling truth. After years of investing in building the outer containers of our lives—careers, identities and lifestyles—we discover the

9. These gaps may be the most obvious spaces where the ongoing inspiration of the Holy Spirit comes in.

container is empty.[10] Most refuse to accept the truth, and quickly return to the empty shell of the *status quo*, even with the knowledge that it is empty. Only a few, Rohr estimates, are truly willing to accept the emptiness and begin to seek something meaningful to fill their lives.

However, when these few begin to find the content that "fills in" new meaning to their lives the old container no longer works. Just as Jesus said, "Neither is new wine put into old wineskins; otherwise, the skins burst, and the wine is spilled, and the skins are destroyed; but new wine is put into fresh wineskins, and so both are preserved."[11]

Despite the intangible nature of the Holy Spirit, Jesus left us a clue to its character when he promised his disciples not to leave them orphaned. That Jesus gives us this clue when saying good-bye is fitting. Jesus sees his disciples anticipating the void left in the aftermath of his departure. As a result, Jesus promises to fill it. "I will ask the Father and he will give you another Advocate, to be with you forever."[12] This Advocate (or Helper, or Counselor or Comforter) is the Holy Spirit. Jesus describes the counselor as the "spirit of truth"—a spirit and a truth that the world does not understand.[13] This is the paraclete (*paraclesis*).

Despite the complexities, ambiguities and nuances in translations of the Greek word *paraclesis*, the variety of translations all point to a consistent characteristic. The Holy Spirit is inherently *collaborative*. The Holy Spirit works *with* us—comes up alongside us—as did the resurrected Jesus with the two on the road to Emmaus. The Holy Spirit does not take over but leaves room for cooperation and collaboration among and between those the Spirit fills.

When we are in the company of God we will find ourselves in the Spirit; the Spirit among us, perhaps even more than *in* us. It is a shared, communal and collaborative space created by this one who "comes up alongside" us, who, instead of telling us what to do and how to do it, instead of *prescribing* an answer or solution, encourages, helps, advocates.

10. Rohr, *Falling Upward*, xiii, 1–15.

11. Matt 9:17.

12. John 14:15–17, 25. Here Jesus describes the Holy Spirit as the "advocate" or "helper" using the Greek work *paraclatos* (or the paraclete)—not the "defender of the disciples before God but their counsel in relation to the world" (*TDNT*, s.v. "Holy Spirit"). The image reminds us of the resurrected Jesus who comes up alongside Cleopas and the other on the road to Emmaus and opens their minds to the truth they could not see in the Scriptures on their own. See Luke 24:27, 32.

13. Haenchen, *John 2*, 126.

The Holy Spirit does not do for us what we can do for ourselves, but does do what we cannot do for ourselves. This is the unscripted Spirit—an inherently collaborative participant who has our best interests at heart, but does not take the responsibility or choice away from us.

These are the characteristics of each of these two assets, briefly described. But what about their combinations?

The late Brevard Childs described Scripture as the "indispensable ground for all Christian theological reflection."[14] "Indispensable ground" is always affected by the atmosphere above it. This atmosphere is influenced, led and even filled with the Holy Spirit. To think of Scripture and the Holy Spirit as two independently functioning assets is not only inappropriate. It is self-limiting. When combined, however, these two assets can empower theology to make significant contributions to how we respond to change and innovate. These two already do so in the company of God. Fresh insights for making sense of change and compelling clarifications for where innovations are needed and why come from these combinations.

When taken separately, however, each asset can become something *we* try to control, crippling responsiveness to change and our ability to adapt. For example, scriptural prescriptions applied directly end up as "forced fits." Personal claims of inspiration from the Holy Spirit risk presumption, as in "God told me to . . . " Taking either asset separately, we end up assessing Scripture from the side and the Holy Spirit as ours to own and direct.

In the company of God, however, these assets are neither fully fixed nor in our control. It is, after all, not our company, but the company of God. When we regard Scripture as a fixed asset it is more apt to remain stuck in the past, captive to incumbent scribes who hold the Word in a kind of "technologized" bondage.[15] Scriptural texts start to overshadow—block rather than shed light on—current contexts. Likewise, when the Holy Spirit is viewed separately, there remains the uncontained risk of all sorts of ideological corruption and self-justification, without the "grounding" found in Scripture.

The power of the two assets and the value they create is in their combination. "These two vehicles of revelation—Word and Spirit—are neither to be identified, nor are they to be separated and played one against the

14. Childs, *New Testament as Canon*, 546.

15. Ong, *Orality and Literacy*, 80–82, 172–74.

other."[16] However, together they hold deep and untapped potential for responding to change and for innovating. Combined they can make significant contributions to making sense of change and the creation of new value for others.

DESCRIPTION BEFORE PRESCRIPTION

Consider how our orientation to assets affects our acceptance of change and our response to it. Two questions naturally arise when significant change confronts organizations or individuals. One tends to receive more attention than the other.

"What are we going to do?" is typically the first question. Sometimes it is accompanied by a more despairing, sky-is-falling kind of question "What's going to happen to us (me) now?" Sufficient confidence within an organizational setting usually allows cooler heads to prevail, thus avoiding more apocalyptic concerns. But regardless of cerebral temperature levels, "what should we do?" is the question that garners the first and most attention. And while it's absolutely necessary to answer, the answers are *prescriptive*. Organizations call the resulting prescriptions "strategies."

"What do we believe is going on now?" is the other question. This one often garners less attention and is frequently treated as a secondary consideration. The ensuing answers are *descriptive*. Organizations call these "situation assessments," "future scenarios," or simply "forecasts." Descriptive answers attempt to make sense of the changes going now and consider where those changes might be leading. They intend to diagnose and describe, not prescribe.

Description should always be the horse and prescription the cart, especially in responding to change, making sense of it and innovating. It is always preferable to ask and answer the descriptive before tackling the prescriptive. But as we all know, carts have a way of getting in front of horses. The prescriptive often overshadows the descriptive. When perceived urgency to get to a prescribed solution overshadows a deliberative description of the current and future environment, we risk reacting to change rather than responding. In the process we inadvertently give away our freedom, and indeed, our ability to respond.

Cart-before-horse thinking is nothing new. When the new realities of the Spirit bewildered those gathered at Pentecost, Peter raised his voice

16. Childs, *Biblical Theology of the Old and New Testaments*, 86.

over the hubbub of the perplexed to make sense of it all. And when they heard what Peter said "they were cut to the heart" and immediately asked Peter and the other apostles, "What should we do?"[17] The first word out of Peter's mouth in response was "repent"—change your way of thinking. The same first word is in Jesus' summary of his own ministry: "repent for the kingdom of God is at hand." It was the same first word in the message and mission of John the Baptist, and arguably the prophetic tradition before him.

Making sense of change and innovating also requires a change in our way of thinking (*metanoia*) centered first and foremost in fresh descriptions of the change and its context. Many will attempt to ignore change, or express contempt for it altogether. Those with an entrepreneurial mind-set, however, will seek and see something different in the very same set of facts and conditions. Readiness to redescribe and reassess *before* prescribing is necessary before we can identify where new value is needed and why. This caused Peter Drucker to characterize innovation as primarily a descriptive skill, "a diagnostic discipline."[18]

Drucker went on to emphasize that while there are always a few innovations that themselves create change, most are in response to change. As a result, making new sense of change is the essential skill of entrepreneurs and innovators. With this skill entrepreneurs look for the "symptoms" of change and faint signals of the *sources* of opportunity in those signals. Drucker identified seven sources, and even ranked them in order of reliability:

1. the unexpected,

2. incongruity,[19]

3. a process need,

4. change in industry or market structure,

5. changes in demographics,

6. changes in perception, mood and meaning, and finally

7. new knowledge, both scientific and nonscientific.

17. Acts 2. It is noteworthy that in the full Acts 2 passage, "What does this mean?" (Acts 2:12) preceded the "What should we do?" question (Acts 2:37).

18. Drucker, *Innovation and Entrepreneurship*, 35.

19. Ibid. Drucker defines incongruity as the difference "between reality as it actually is and as it should be" which sounds very close to how we might define "injustice" or unjust conditions.

Such a list of recognizable sources of innovations invites further[20] theological search for corollaries in the scriptural cannon with which to frame and describe current contexts of change. For example, biblical corollaries to these sources might be represented by past acts of God that point to where the company of God is present and active now.

Two of Drucker's more reliable sources—incongruities and changes in the industry or market structure—may resonate with different eras within the biblical saga of the people of Israel. Israel's captivity under the oppression of Pharaoh; the succession of structural changes unleashed by the liberating intervention of the exodus event; wandering in the wilderness to occupying the promised land; the division of the kingdom into Judah in the south and Israel in the north; the exile and return: each of these structural changes and the narratives associated with them hold rich descriptions for understanding our present and changing circumstances and contexts and potential sources of innovation. Making sense of current dynamics and locating where new value can be discovered may be guided by the experience of bondage, wilderness wandering, exile and return. Biblical theology for innovation will need to identify more of these corollaries along with criteria for their application to current contexts and changes.

Scripture holds both descriptions of past changes and prescriptions in the responses that ensued. Some were aligned with the company of God. Some were not. Regardless of alignment, however, both the descriptions and prescriptions recorded in Scripture have become a prime source of guidance and direction for the believing community for centuries. This is what makes Scripture the authoritative and practical source for all matters, including matters of "faith and life."[21] These scriptural descriptions should also prove relevant for making sense of, and responding to, change today. This is one of the benefits of being in the company of God.

Even with Scripture, however, prescriptive urgency can overshadow descriptive insight. When we look to Scripture only for an answer to "what are we to do now?" we risk ignoring the descriptive in Scripture, descriptions that bring penetrating insight and foresight to our ability to make sense of change. "What would Jesus do?" (WWJD) may be a worthy prescriptive question to have in mind as we search the Scriptures for an answer. But this question, when asked alone, assumes we have already

---

20. Such a further search is warranted but beyond the limited scope of this essay.

21. *Westminster Confession of Faith*, ch. 1, "Of the Holy Scripture," vi.

come to an appropriate assessment of the current context for which we are injecting Jesus.

On the one hand, when we look to Scripture only as a source of *prescriptions* it becomes difficult to avoid a "should" mind-set. Normative behavior becomes the only thing that counts. When norms are all that matters, change will neither be understood nor accepted and creating new value for others will neither be new nor of much value. It is analogous to prescribing without a diagnosis. Prescriptive "shoulds" inevitably lead to heavy-handed persuasion and coercion.

On the other hand, when Scripture is viewed as a source of *descriptions*, empathy, acceptance and understanding come more easily. Curiosity and compassion is encouraged. Descriptive thinking tends to invite shared curiosity and empathic understanding, which, if done "where two or three are gathered," can lead to consensus rather than a coerced compromise.

This seems to be the case for both Testaments, Old and New.

Descriptive "scripts" in the Old Testament might come from longer narrative passages that extend beyond short texts. These passages contain patterns in the relationship and interactions between God and the people of Israel. These longer passages provide frames through which to understand our current contexts. The broader narratives of the Egyptian bondage or the liberation from it (exodus), the wilderness wandering, the entrance into the promise land, the exile and the return from exile, these are but a few examples. Old Testament prophetic archetypes, metaphors and poetic images should also be explored for possible descriptions through which theology brings deeper understanding of change in our current contexts.

Such descriptive frames will evoke questions that before were not even considered. For example, blind belief in the promise of global economic development can seduce policy makers into justifying oppressive labor conditions, not unlike what happened to the people of Israel under Pharaoh.[22] Should innovations honor human community *before* economic opportunity? Or consider another example. Has digital connectivity made us captive in a virtual kingdom of our own making? Or are we now "in exile" in the way we "connect" rather than authentically communicate? Are we losing our ability to empathize and both feel and

22. Marglin, *Dismal Science*, 223–44.

express compassion?[23] If so, might innovations Sherry Turkle refers to as *realtechnik*[24] return us from this exile to a more authentic social reality unmediated by digital interfaces, robotics and pixilated simulations?

Places to look for descriptive "scripts" in the New Testament might include teachings, parables and the accounts of interactions with Jesus. For example, ability to describe and discern change in the present context did not escape Jesus.[25] No more striking example of how the resurrected Jesus used Scripture to describe changes taking place can be found than what he did on the road to Emmaus. Here the resurrected Jesus comes up alongside Cleopas and the other, trudging away from Jerusalem, both of them dejected at the implications of the events that had just happened.[26] These two were sad because of their misunderstanding of the change that had just taken place. But Jesus—unrecognized by either of them—said to them, "Oh, how foolish you are, and how slow of heart to believe all that the prophets have declared. Was it not necessary that the Messiah should suffer these things and then enter into his glory?" Then Luke tells us, "beginning with Moses and all the prophets, he interpreted to them the things about himself in all the scriptures." After, he was revealed to them in the breaking of the bread. Then these two said to each other, "Were not our hearts burning within us while he was talking to us on the road, while he was opening the scriptures to us?"

Or in John's gospel when Jesus is speaking to his critics and says, "You search the Scriptures because you think that in them you have eternal life; and it is they that testify on my behalf. Yet you refuse to come to me to have life."[27]

Even the central event in Paul's life—his dramatic conversion on the road to Damascus[28] changed him from following prescriptions to persecute, and instead turned him toward proclamations of the new reality *described* by the life, death and resurrection of Jesus. It left him with "something like scales" falling from his eyes so that he could see again. But this time he could see in a completely new light. His way of describing what was changing around him was based on a completely new sense

---

23. Turkle, *Alone Together*, 56, 72, 107, 172, 293; Turkle, *Reclaiming Conversation*, 3–17.

24. Turkle, *Alone Together*, 294.

25. Matt 16:1–4.

26. Luke 24:13–35.

27. John 5:39–40.

28. Acts 9:1–25.

of his own immediate context and his role in it. Paul had a new way of making sense to the nations, kings and even the people of Israel.

Prescriptive use of Scripture may be a scribal bias. It may be one reason theology has ignored innovation and innovating has remained ignorant of theology's potential contribution. This is both ironic and tragic, given how necessary descriptive capability is to innovators and entrepreneurs and how present and pertinent it is to theology's primary source book.

Theology has at its fingertips a great wealth of penetrating diagnostics in Scripture for identifying and understanding change, particularly for current contexts wherein the company of God proves to be present, active and effective. Bringing these diagnostic descriptions into the dialogue among investors, sponsors, entrepreneurs and intrapreneurs should contribute much to answer where innovations are needed and why, and to do so more substantively. Such theological descriptions should also keep values grounded and balanced, particularly when understandings of value tends to delaminate[29] when viewed only from economic or ethical perspectives.

Scripts in Scripture are essential to understand what in change is important to pay attention to. These scripts *describe* what God has done in the past in change and in response to change. These scripts indicate what is important to the company of God. They do not necessary prescribe what is the intention of God now.[30]

The presence and movement of the company of God manifests itself in the changing dynamics of our current context, sometimes quickly or, sometimes slowly. Sometimes the signs are in the change, sometimes in the resistance to it. But current context is always unscripted. It is always now, enfolding. It requires us to pay attention and bring the past text into the current context.

TEXTS AND CONTEXTS

We read texts, but we live in contexts. Texts linger and remain, while our current contexts change. This by no means suggests that the fixed text

29. See ch. 8, "Make Meaning *Before* Money," for a more complete understanding of delaminated value.

30. The quixotic quest for the repeatable formula is a common desire among administrative managers more than experienced innovators, and perhaps appropriate for imitation, not for innovation.

remains in the past. Quite the opposite is the case. When Scripture reads us it becomes the compass with which we can navigate in the present. When we are in the company of God we are more apt to be read by the text of Scripture. In the process we are more able to make sense of what is changing in our current contexts. In the company of God, Scripture proves to be such a compass, particularly when the change we experience removes most of what is obvious and familiar and requires us to traverse through what we cannot see or understand.

Approaching Scripture as a navigational aid takes us only so far, however. A compass orients. It does not direct, describe or prescribe. At the very least, Scripture can reorient us. This is perhaps a first step in making sense of change and navigating a response. But reorientation is essential for innovating. Current contexts are always unscripted and changing, and these are the primary stimulus for innovation. Creating new value for others requires us to pay attention to both context and changes in it. This is where the opportunity for new value shows itself.

Value is perhaps more important than any other aspect of innovation. It is more important than whether the innovation is regarded as creative or not, or even how "new" it is thought to be. If an innovation does not carry value, it remains stillborn—an interesting idea, but just an idea.[31] The nature and character of this value is inseparable from the context in which the value is realized and for which the value is conceived and embodied. In short, for innovating and for value, context is just about everything.

The point here is that scriptural text and current context are inseparable. We cannot have one without the other, nor can one engage with the other without the Holy Spirit. If the text becomes all that matters, the current context will be either poorly understood or ignored. When theology gets overly focused on the ancient text more than the current context, little will be offered for creating new value for others. Exclusive focus on the scriptural text will overshadow making any sense of current contexts. Efforts will become all about interpreting Scripture more than making sense of change, as if these are separable. A myopic zeal for interpreting relatively fixed biblical texts can easily lead the interpreter to ignore individuals and organizations trying to make sense of their lives in their dynamic current contexts. In a word, it ends up making theology irrelevant.

31. And of course, there is no way of assessing whether the value is there for the other without actually giving it a go.

"Text" itself as a word comes from the Latin verb *texto* which means "I weave" and from which we derive textiles and texture. To extract a text from its context is a bit like pulling a thread out from the woven fabric of which it is a part. A text divorced from its context is functionally no longer what it used to be. The context, weave and fabric are diminished as well. With all the focus on the text, little room is left for the "a-textual" Holy Spirit.

Paul speaks to this very issue in his second letter to the church at Corinth when he asks rhetorically whether there is need for a letter of recommendation. "Surely we do not need, as some do, letters of recommendation to you or from you, do we? You yourselves are our letter, written on our hearts, to be known and read by all; and you show that you are a letter of Christ, prepared by us, written not with ink but with the Spirit of the Living God, not on tablets of stone but on tablets of human hearts."[32]

This may simply be speaking to the centuries-old evolution of what Walter Ong called the "technologizing" of the spoken and heard word.[33] Writing and print, and now the digitized and wirelessly connected transmissions of mediated messages, has so saturated our lives and behavior that simple, unmediated oral conversations may be becoming increasingly rare. Texting is now a verb!

When Scripture remains unread on pages bound together in the form of a book sitting on the shelf, it is a lifeless object. However, when the book is opened and the text read in conversations "where two or more are gathered" there is a breath than resonates in spoken words and subsequent hearings. Dead texts are resurrected, given new life in vocalization. The revelation and creation of new sense and new value is nourished from the "sounded" word in a current context. May this be a filling with the Holy Spirit and grounded in the Word? May this indicate that God is at work?

CONVERSIONS IN CONVERSATIONS

When we try to make sense of changes in our current context and look for where new value for others might be possible, and where we find pertinent passages of Scripture to bring descriptive value to our current

32. 2 Cor 3:1–3.

33. Ong, *Orality and Literacy*, 80–82.

context, something fresh and enlivening happens. Energy is released at the very least. Often direction is clarified.

These conversations also involve the tangible and intangible assets of the company of God. This happens best in face-to-face conversations and often leads to more conversations that need to be had.

In these conversations multidirectional, micro-conversions are going on. Some believe these kinds of conversions-in-conversations are the core of the innovating process.[34] Ikujiro Nonaka and Hirotaka Takeuchi categorize these conversions as socializing, externalizing and internalizing processes where true learning begins and substantive innovating is nourished.

Socializations occur when the tacitly held beliefs and knowledge of one affect the tacitly held beliefs and knowledge of another. Externalizations occur when the tacit becomes text and thereby codified for dissemination and use by others. Internalizations occur when the texts and scripts of practice become a part of the tacit understanding of the ones who follow it. These conversions sound similar to the conversions of text-to-spirit-filled vocalizations stimulated by combinations of Scripture and the Holy Spirit.

Enabling these socializing, externalizing and internalizing conversions are simply conversations. Paul's "aside" in the letter of Romans—"faith comes from what is heard, and what is heard comes through the word of God"[35]—may be more pertinent than peripheral to our largely and increasingly "textualized" culture.

Conversions in such conversations are of more than passing interest. This holds true for both theology and innovating. For theology's interest the observations of Ong are worth considering:[36]

> God is thought of always as "speaking" to human beings, not as writing to them. The orality of the mindset in the Biblical text, even in its epistolary sections, is overwhelming. The Hebrew *dabar*, which means word, means also event and thus refers directly to the spoken word. Jesus, the Word of God, left nothing in writing, though he could read and write (Luke 4:16).

34. Nonaka and Takeuchi, *Knowledge-Creating Company*, 56: "The key to knowledge creation lies in the mobilization and conversion of tacit knowledge." Tacit knowledge is typically most effectively expressed and shared among practitioners in oral, face-to-face conversations.

35. Rom 10:17.

36. Ong, *Orality and Literacy*, 74.

The observations of innovators shared through live conversations are the best and perhaps only way to reach a common understanding of new value. In these conversations innovators are not only generating ideas. They are experiencing tacit-to-tacit, tacit-to-explicit and explicit-to-tacit conversions of knowledge. In the process they nurture the creation of new value for others. As a result, new knowledge is created and innovations are born.[37] This applies as much to problem solving as it does to problem setting.

Innovators and entrepreneurs must not only make sense of a situation that initially, and for a time, makes no sense. They must also initiate and even act on tentative hypotheses regarding what problem is worth solving. In short, responding to change and innovating is about authoring as well as interpreting.[38] Change seldom presents itself in a nice neat package, much less as a well-defined problem. Change evolves, sometimes quickly, sometimes slowly, but rarely in an organized or orderly fashion. Pieces go missing. Holes appear in our perceptions and the emerging situation is uncertain if not ambiguous.

Both problem solving and problem setting are best accomplished in a collaborative and iterative manner, most effectively in oral, face-to-face conversations. Knowledge workers of all stripes and across most every domain are increasingly recognizing that while the solving of problems often requires technical expertise, the setting or framing of problems is not itself a technical problem.

> When we set the problem, we select what we will treat as the "things" of the situation, we set the boundaries of our attention to it, and we impose upon it a coherence which allows us to say what is wrong and in what directions the situation needs to be changed. Problem setting is a process in which, interactively, we name the things to which we will attend and frame the context in which we will attend to them.[39]

This is precisely where theology has much to contribute to innovating—in the *setting* of problems. Given the combination of its two primary assets, theology has a significant opportunity to bring to problem-setting both its interpretative and sense-making capabilities. While theology may not contribute much to the technical aspects of problem-solving, it

---

37. Nonaka and Takeuchi, *Knowledge-Creating Company*, 6.

38. Weick, *Sensemaking in Organizations*, 9, 14.

39. Schon, *Reflective Practitioner*, 40.

has much to offer both framing and filling the contexts from which new values for others emerges.

Too often this theological capability and capacity is severely limited to prescriptive critique of our current context by theologians and non-theologians alike. Sadly, theology is thereby relegated only to acts of reflecting upon what the Bible says and then applying the resulting interpretation of the text in the form of a prescriptive remedy, normative judgment or sanctioned permission. However, those who have been equipped with theologically informed interpretative skills could readily apply these same skills to the sense-making tasks of current and changing contexts. This requires not so much the learning of a new skill as redirecting acquired competences to the descriptive task with the combined assets of Scripture and Spirit. The potential benefits reside not only in helping clarify where innovations are needed and why. Benefits also include improving our understanding of what is intrinsic and substantive in change rather than superficial and extrinsic.

Scripture provides an abundant reservoir of patterns, insights, values and meanings that are useful today for making sense of the changing contexts of our lives and for recognizing value at deep and sustainable layers of what matters. Scripture, when read and brought to life in the conversations and practices of a community of faith can be that compass for identifying where the company of God is moving and what trajectory it is taking now.

Several years ago I was lucky enough to participate in an in-depth examination of what many considered at the time the most advanced innovating system in the world. This was the Toyota Development System.[40] One of the more striking principles of that system's practice is the deep respect for two seemingly opposite practices. On the one hand, Toyota demonstrates an obsessive desire to avoid the waste of relearning by relentlessly codifying and disseminating what they have already learned. On the other hand there is an equally obsessive bias for face-to-face conversations—for both problem framing and problem-solving. In a way, Toyota is developing their own "scripture" in writing down what they do not need to relearn, while simultaneously pursuing, through unscripted conversations, where innovations are needed and why.

---

40. Not to be confused with the more widely understood Toyota Production System. Though there are some interesting parallels, the systems serve different purposes and exhibit some significantly different practices.

MAKING SPACE FOR DE-SCRIPTING
AND DE-SCRIBING

Proclivity to *prescribe* can easily discredit theology's descriptive relevance. This proclivity may be more of temptation of practitioners than theology *per se*. "The Bible says" is a familiar preface, not unlike the more secular, "Research shows." What is sure to follow either is an implicit or explicit prescription, or at the very least, a justification for the point the speaker wants her listeners to get. Prescriptions can be targeted to individuals, organizations and societal institutions alike. However neither a fixed text nor a prescriptive intent create much enduring value for those on the receiving end. No one likes to be a target.

Institutions with an interest in theology, and theology's potential contribution to innovation[41] might do well to take a page out of Toyota's playbook, or better yet, a page from theology's own Master. Following the lead of Jesus in his response to the woman caught in the act,[42] his intervention creates a new space for her to choose a new way of living. He gives her the space to be responsible and so gives her the ability to respond, no longer as a victim, nor victor, but as a volunteer in her own life and perhaps in the lives of others.

In this passage—a story more than a "text"—which unfolds through a series of interactions with very detailed descriptions, Jesus neither condemns nor condones. Rather, he creates a space for the woman, whose life he literally saves from stoning. He creates new value, and not only for her.

Clearly Jesus had a different mind-set than the scribes and the Pharisees—those who were so ready to prescribe, judge and condemn. Jesus demonstrates a firm grasp of the immediate context and situation. He embodies in himself, as evidenced by his response, a complete and coherent assessment of this highly charged and changing context. Jesus doesn't react but instead takes a long pause, bending down and writing with his finger in the ground, before straightening up and saying to the scribes and Pharisees, "Let anyone among you who is without sin be the first to throw a stone at her." Not only does he create space for the woman. He creates a new space for those who were so ready to judge and condemn, a space in

---

41. Theology's contribution to innovation may make a greater impact than theologically informed attempts to influence or shape culture. Culture is comprised of artifacts and outcomes. Innovation (and art) is the input.

42. John 8:3–11.

which the contemptuous turned and went away, one by one, starting with the elders. The space for grace Jesus created left both the woman and her accusers changed.

But as is often the case with the Gospel of John, the passage continues[43] with Jesus defending his own "testimony"—a word itself that means a considered description of the facts or the truth of a situation, not a prescription. Jesus even says "my testimony is valid because I know where I have come from and where I am going," in contrast to the scribes and Pharisees who do not. Jesus then says, "You judge by human standards; I judge no one."

Jesus did not "take a position" in the way we normally think about position-taking. He has not prescribed what the woman should now do. Instead, he has come up alongside her, intervening between her and her accusers. In the process he avoids prescribing anything and instead, knowing where he was coming from and where he was going, he could be confident, even amid the fierce resistance of incumbent tradition and traditionalists, to bring the "light of life" to the woman and the world, not the darkness of dead texts, law, judgment and condemnation.

If theology were to give up its scribal penchants for prescribing solutions and passing judgment, and constrain itself to participating in the description of current contexts where change shows up, then innovators and entrepreneurs might see in theology the potent diagnostic resource that it is. With a theological perspective, the interests, purpose and presence of the company of God might be made more explicit, giving innovators and entrepreneurs better insight into the new value they are attempting to create for others.

CONCLUSION

When current conditions of our present context are stable and unchanged, looking for prescriptive answers to follow may make some sense. Imitating the success of others who have "been there, done that" appears to be a reasonable route to go in such circumstances.

However, when current conditions are unstable and changing, prescription is not what we need, at least at first. What is needed, rather, are descriptions to use for making sense before we rush to follow anyone or anything. Imitation may be easier. But in changing and uncertain

43. John 8:12.

contexts imitations may be irrelevant, if not dangerous. In change, imitation is doing the same thing and expecting different results. Many call this insanity.

Biblical theology has much to contribute here, likely more to the innovators and innovating than to the innovations. But any such contribution will not likely come from biblical theology taking a conventional role of prescribing. Rather, theology's contribution is more likely to come in describing contexts to the end that innovations become even more substantive, sustainable and rooted in intrinsic value for others. Neither are biblical theology's contributions likely without open conversations that weave text and context, words printed and words spoken, in the illumined and potent way that the Holy Spirit freely releases the truth that makes us free, both those who speak it as well as those who hear it.

Taken and used together, the two assets of the company of God can help make sense of change, help make our choices wiser and even help discern the context in which real substantive value can be created for others. If and when we keep our collaborative discernments of the current context balanced and grounded in the past patterns of God's Word, we just may be able to see together the emergence of God's work and will today.

Like a fixed and tangible asset, Scripture provides us with a reliable compass to navigate the unfamiliar and uncertain that seems to accompany change. It can help us describe what in change is more important to pay attention to than not. It can even point to where innovating may be needed and why, especially when the context itself doesn't speak very clearly on its own.

Like an intangible asset the Holy Spirit proves to be a potent companion—a helper or advocate—for making sense of change and reminding us whose company we are in and what is of more interest to God's company compared to the interests of other companies. It reassures us that we are not alone in our attempts to make sense of change and in our attempts to create new value for others. In fact, rather than being victimized by change, the Holy Spirit reveals to us how and where we are being called by change to respond in ways aligned with the purposes and interest of the company of God.

When both assets are deployed together, however, the advantages of being in the company of God become more fully present and available.

However temporary, partial or imperfect may be the sense we make of change, or the response we choose to take, or the innovations we conceive and embody, God will do for us what we cannot do for ourselves, but God may not necessarily do for us what God would like us to do ourselves, together, with and for each other.

What is likely to matter to the company of God may be contained in Scripture, but it is not confined to Scripture. More is always revealed through our unscripted responses to change in the company of God. Or as Isaiah reminds us of what God said, and likely is still saying:

> Do not remember the former things,
> Or consider the things of old.
> I am about to do a new thing:
> Now it springs forth, do you not perceive it?[44]

---

44. Isa 43:18–19a.

CONVERSATION STARTERS

1. Is "descriptive witness" sufficient for biblical theology to make its contribution to innovating, or must it also provide a "prescriptive witness" as well?

2. Are there passages of Scripture more primary than others for accepting change, making sense of it and innovating in response to it?

3. Does biblical theology necessarily close its heart and mind to the continued free movement of God's Spirit in claiming a "closed canon"? Or is an "open canon" more supportive and relevant to the contributions innovation theology can make to the purposes of the company of God? Is this really an either/or?

Postscript

Next Steps

A SINGLE NOTION AND affirmation undergirds the preceding essays: God is both interested and invested in innovation. To express this in a more imperative manner: the One for whom all things are possible continues to invite us to co-create new value for others in the company of God.

If there is any truth to this, the theologically interested might want to consider engaging in conversations with the entrepreneurially active. Such conversations might take the modest purpose to explore and chart the largely unexplored territory of innovation theology. In this wilderness there will likely be some wandering, a little whining, but also a lot of wondering, all of which promises more substantive and sustainable innovation.

Specifically, institutions of theological education might want to become sponsors and hosts of such conversations. As hosts, invitations will need to be sent out to others beyond the institution's familiar boundaries. Those on the invitation list will necessarily include innovators, economists, technologists and others who are entrepreneurial inclined, though themselves theologically curious. Identifying these participants may take some effort, but may also be easier than we might at first imagine. Those already engaged in charting where theology intersects with the dynamics of contemporary culture, the marketplace and leadership may be the most likely participants from sponsors and hosts.

Given the other things on the short list of priorities for schools of theology these days, innovation theology may not make it to the top on its own. However, responding to change with the aim of creating new value for others may be refreshingly relevant to the existing items already atop those lists; items like social and economic justice, the stewardship of creation, truth and reconciliation, or the recovery of individuals and organizations who have lost their way, even the growing numbers who check the box "none" (or "done") for religious affiliation. In fact, innovating may be more relevant than we typically think to what it means to till and keep[1] the garden God has given us, or to being our brother's and sister's keeper.[2]

Based on the simple affirmation, these essays offer a non-obvious but bold proposal: that biblical theology has something both meaningful and practical to contribute to innovating. Whether this proposal achieves any success or not, the occurrence, character and content of conversations regarding innovation theology will bear witness. Time will tell.

In the meantime, change keeps changing, and God—a living, loving and unbelievably patient God—keeps inviting us through change to respond. We can react or we can respond. This choice seems constant.

If we choose to respond rather than react, then we have another choice to make—whether our response will aim to create new value for others in the company of God, or seek refuge and extend for as long as possible what appears to be familiar, safe and even secure, in our own company. Innovation theology can and should help us to see, make sense of, believe and even make the right choice.

1. Gen 2:15.
2. Gen 4:9.

Bibliography

Ackoff, Russell L. *Differences That Make a Difference*. Axminster, UK: Triarchy, 2010.

———. "From Data to Wisdom." *Journal of Applied Systems Analysis* 16 (1989) 59–70.

———. *Re-Creating the Corporation: A Design of Organizations for the 21st Century*. New York: Oxford University Press, 1999.

Ackoff, Russell L., and Fred E. Emery. *On Purposeful Systems: An Interdisciplinary Analysis of Individual and Social Behavior as a System of Purposeful Events*. New Brunswick: Transaction, 1972.

Aeppel, Timothy. "Why Is Productivity Slowing Down?" *Wall Street Journal*, January 28, 2013.

Australian Public Service Commission. "Tackling Wicked Problems: A Public Policy Perspective." October 25, 2007.

Blair, Margaret. *Unseen Wealth: Report of the Brookings Task Force on Intangibles*. Washington, DC: Brookings Institution Press, 2001.

Blomberg, Craig L. *Neither Poverty Nor Riches: A Biblical Theology of Possessions*. Downers Grove: InterVarsity, 1999.

Bouderi, Robert. *Engines of Tomorrow: How the World's Best Companies Are Using Their Research Labs to Win the Future*. New York: Simon & Schuster, 2000.

Bovon, Francois. *Luke 2: A Commentary on the Gospel of Luke 9:51—19:27*. Translated by Donald S. Deer. Minneapolis: Fortress, 2013.

Brown, Leslie, ed. *The New Shorter Oxford English Dictionary*. 2 vols. Oxford: Clarendon, 1993.

Brown, Stuart. *Play: How It Shapes the Brain, Opens the Imagination, and Invigorates the Soul*. With Christopher Vaughan. New York: Penguin, 2009.

Brueggemann, Walter. *Isaiah*. 2 vols. Louisville: Westminster John Knox, 1998.

———. *The Practice of Prophetic Imagination: Preaching an Emancipating Word*. Minneapolis: Fortress, 2012.

———. *The Prophetic Imagination*. Minneapolis: Fortress, 2001.

———. *Reality, Grief, Hope: Three Urgent Prophetic Tasks*. Grand Rapids: Eerdmans, 2014.

———. *Remember You Are Dust*. Eugene: Wipf & Stock, 2012.

Buechner, Frederick. *Telling the Truth: Gospel as Tragedy, Comedy and Fairy Tale*. New York: Harper & Row, 1977.

Calvin, Jean. *The Institutes of the Christian Religion*. Edited by John T. McNeill. Translated by Ford Lewis Battles. 2 vols. Philadelphia: Westminster, 1975.

Cameron, Doug, and Julian E. Barnes. "Pentagon Presses Contractors to Innovate." *Wall Street Journal*, November 20, 2014. http://online.wsj.com/articles/pentagon-to-defense-contractors-innovate-1416527136.

Carr, Herbert Wildon. *Henri Bergson: The Philosopher of Change*. London: Elibron Classics, 2004.

Chase, Alston. *In a Dark Wood: The Fight over the Forests and the Myths of Nature*. New Brunswick, NJ: Transaction, 2001.

Cheverton, Richard. *The Maverick Way: Profiting from the Power of the Corporate Misfit*. Costa Mesa, CA: Maverickway.com, 2000.

Childs, Brevard S. *Biblical Theology of the Old and New Testaments: Theological Reflection on the Christian Bible*. Minneapolis: Fortress, 2011. First published 1992.

———. *Isaiah*. Louisville: Westminster John Knox, 2001.

———. *The New Testament as Canon: An Introduction*. Philadelphia: Fortress, 1984.

Christensen, Clayton M. *The Innovator's Dilemma: When New Technologies Cause Great Firms to Fail*. Boston: Harvard Business School Press, 1997.

Christensen, Clayton M., and Michael E. Raynor. *The Innovator's Solution: Creating and Sustaining Successful Growth*. Boston: Harvard Business School Press, 2003.

Christensen, Clayton M., and Derek van Bever. "The Capitalist's Dilemma." *Harvard Business Review*, June 2014. https://hbr.org/2014/06/the-capitalists-dilemma.

Collins, Jim. *How the Mighty Fall and Why Some Companies Never Give In*. New York: HarperCollins, 2009.

Cox, Harvey. *The Future of Faith*. New York: HarperCollins, 2009.

Csikszentmihalyi, Mihaly. *Creativity: The Psychology of Discovery and Invention*. New York: HarperCollins, 1996.

Daly, Herman E. *Beyond Growth: The Economics of Sustainable Development*. Boston: Beacon, 1996.

———. *Steady-State Economics*. 2nd ed. Washington, DC: Island, 1991.

Daly, Herman E., and John B. Cobb. *For the Common Good: Redirecting the Economy toward Community, the Environment and a Sustainable Future*. Boston: Beacon, 1994. First published 1989.

Davenport, Thomas H., and John C. Beck. *The Attention Economy: Understanding the New Currency of Business*. Boston: Harvard Business School Press, 2001.

Denning, Steve. "The Surprising Reasons Why American Lost Its Ability to Compete." *Forbes.com*, March 10, 2013. http://www.forbes.com/sites/stevedenning/2013/03/10/the-surprising-reasons-why-america-lost-its-ability-to-compete.

Drucker, Peter. *The Ecological Vision: Reflections on the American Condition*. New Brunswick: Transaction, 2001.

———. *Innovation and Entrepreneurship: Practice and Principles*. New York: Harper & Row, 1985.

———. *Management: Tasks, Responsibilities and Practices*. New York: Harper & Row, 1974.

Dukas, Helen, and Banesh Hoffmann, eds. *Albert Einstein, the Human Side: New Glimpses from His Archives*. Princeton: Princeton University Press, 1979.

Dweck, Carol S. *Mindset: The New Psychology of Success*. New York: Ballantine, 2006.

Erickson, Gary. *Raising the Bar: Integrity and Passion in Life and Business*. San Francisco: Jossey-Bass, 2004.

Foster, Richard. *Innovation: The Attacker's Advantage*. New York: Summit, 1986.

Frankl, Viktor E. *Man's Search for Meaning*. New York: Washington Square, 1984.

Friedman, Edwin H. *A Failure of Nerve: Leadership in the Age of the Quick Fix*. New York: Seabury, 2007. First published 1999.

———. *Generation to Generation: Family Process in Church and Synagogue*. New York: Guilford, 1985.

Geus, Arie de. *The Living Company: Habits for Survival in a Turbulent Business Environment*. Boston: Harvard Business School Press, 1997.

Gilding, Paul. *The Great Disruption: Why the Climate Crisis Will Bring On the End of Shopping and the Birth of a New World*. New York: Bloomsbury, 2011.

Goodchild, Philip. *Theology of Money*. Durham: Duke University Press, 2009.

Gordon, William J. J. *Synectics: The Development of Creative Capacity*. New York: Collier, 1968. First published 1961.

Haeckel, Stephan H. *Adaptive Enterprise*. Boston: Harvard Business School Press, 1999.

Haenchen, Ernst. *John 2: A Commentary on the Gospel of John Chapters 7–21*. Translated by R. W. Funk. Philadelphia: Fortress, 1984.

Hock, Dee. *The Birth of the Chaordic Age*. San Francisco: Berrett-Koehler, 1999.

Horden, William. "Idolatry." In *A Dictionary of Christian Theology*, edited by Alan Richardson, . Philadelphia: Westminster, 1969.

Hunter, James Davison. *To Change the World: The Irony, Tragedy, and Possibility of Christianity in the Late Modern World*. Oxford: Oxford University Press, 2010.

Hyde, Lewis. *The Gift: How the Creative Spirit Transforms the World*. Edinburgh: Canongate, 2007. First published 1983.

Ip, Greg. "The Dangers of Deflation: The Pendulum Swings to the Pit." October 25, 2014. https://gregip.wordpress.com/2014/11/17/the-dangers-of-deflation-the-pendulum-swings-to-the-pit.

Isaacson, Walter. *Einstein: His Life and Universe*. New York: Simon & Schuster, 2007.

Jackson, Tim. *Prosperity Without Growth: Economics for a Finite Planet*. London: Earthscan, 2011.

James, William. *The Varieties of Religious Experience: A Study in Human Nature*. New York: Random House, 2002.

Johansson, Fran. *The Medici Effect: Breakthrough Insights at the Intersection of Ideas, Concepts, and Cultures*. Boston: Harvard Business School Press, 2004.

Jung, Carl G. *Synchronicity*. Princeton: Princeton University Press, 2011. First published 1960.

Kahneman, Daniel. *Thinking, Fast and Slow*. New York: Farrar, Straus and Giroux, 2011.

Kanter, Rosabeth Moss. *The Change Masters: Innovation for Productivity in the American Corporation*. New York: Simon and Schuster, 1983.

Kittel, Gerhard, and Gerhard Friedrich, eds. *Theological Dictionary of the New Testament*. Edited and translated by Geoffrey W. Bromiley. 10 vols. Grand Rapids: Eerdmans, 1964.

Krishnamurti, Jiddu. *The Impossible Question*. http://www.jkrishnamurti.com/krishnamurti-teachings/view-text.php?s=books&tid=9&chid=57009.

Kung, Hans. *The Church*. New York: Sheed and Ward, 1967.

Leonard-Barton, Dorothy. "Core Capabilities and Core Rigidities: A Paradox in Managing New Product Development." Special issue, *Strategic Management Journal* 13 (1992).

Lester, Ricard K., and Michael J. Piore. *Innovation: The Missing Dimension*. Cambridge: Harvard University Press, 2004.

Lewis, C. S. *The Four Loves*. New York: Harcourt, Brace, 1960.

———. *Mere Christianity*. New York: HarperCollins, 2001. First published 1952.

Luther, Martin. *Saemmtliche Schriften*. Edited by Ed Walch. Translated by Erika Bullman Flores. St. Louis: Condordia, 1880–1910.

Magnuson, Stew. "Military 'Swimming in Sensors and Drowning in Data.'" National Defense, January 2010. http://www.nationaldefensemagazine.org/archive/2010/January/Pages/Military'SwimmingInSensorsandDrowninginData'.aspx.

Marglin, Stephen A. *The Dismal Science: How Thinking Like an Economist Undermines Community*. Cambridge: Harvard University Press, 2010.

McIntyre, Marilyn. *Caring for Words in the Culture of Lies*. Grand Rapids: Eerdmans, 2009.

Meadows, Donella. *Thinking in Systems: A Primer*. White River Junction, VT: Sustainability Institute, 2008.

Mele, Nicco. *The End of Big: How the Digital Revolution Makes David the New Goliath*. New York: St. Martin's, 2014.

Mehrabian, Albert. *Non-verbal Communication*. Chicago: Aldine-Atherton, 1972.

Micklethwait, John, and Adrian Wooldridge. *The Company: A Short History of a Revolutionary Idea*. New York: Random House, 2005.

Moltmann, Jurgen. *The Church in the Power of the Holy Spirit: A Contribution to Messianic Ecclesiology*. New York: Harper & Row, 1977.

Moore, Geoffrey A. *Crossing the Chasm*. New York: HarperBusiness, 1991.

Morath, Eric. "Treasury Secretary Lew Warns of Lower Potential Economic Growth: Congressional Budget Office Projects Average Growth Rate of Just 2.1% Going Forward." *Wall Street Journal*, June 11, 2014.

Morgan, James M., and Jeffrey K. Liker. *The Toyota Product Development System: Integrated People, Process, and Technology*. New York: Productivity, 2006.

Moser, Paul K. *The Elusive God: Reorienting Religious Epistemology*. Cambridge: Cambridge University Press, 2008.

Nicholson, William. *Shadowlands*. New York: Penguin, 1990.

Niebuhr, Reinhold. *Moral Man and Immoral Society: A Study in Ethics and Politics*. New York: Scribner, 1960. First published 1932.

Niebuhr, H. Richard, *Christ and Culture*. New York: Harper & Row, 1951.

———. *The Meaning of Revelation*. New York: Macmillan, 1941.

———. *The Purpose of the Church and Its Ministry*. New York: Harper & Row, 1956.

Nisbett, Richard E. *The Geography of Thought: How Asians and Westerners Think Differently . . . and Why*. New York: Free, 2003.

Nonaka, Ikujiro, and Noboru Konno. "The Concept of Ba: Building a Foundation for Knowledge Creation." *California Management Review* 40 (1998) 40–54.

Nonaka, Ikujiro, and Hirotaka Takeuchi. *The Knowledge-Creating Company: How Japanese Companies Create the Dynamics of Innovation*. New York: Oxford University Press, 1995.

Ong, Walter J. *Orality and Literacy: The Technologizing of the Word*. London: Routledge, 2002. First published 1982.

Packard, David. *The HP Way: How Bill Hewlett and I Built Our Company*. New York: HarperCollins, 1995.

Paley, William. *Natural Theology or Evidences of the Existence and Attributes of the Deity*. London, 1802.

Palmisano, Sam. "Managing Investors." Interview by the *Harvard Business Review*, June 2014. https://hbr.org/2014/06/managing-investors.

Perrin, Norman. *Rediscovering the Teachings of Jesus*. New York: Harper & Row, 1967.

Piattelli-Palmarini, Massimo. *Inevitable Illusions: How Mistakes of Reason Rules Our Minds*. New York: Wiley, 1994.

Powell, Esta. "Catharsis in Psychology and Beyond: A Historic Overview." www.primal-page.com/cathar.htm.

Prahalad, C. K., and Gary Hamel. "The Core Competence of the Corporation." *Harvard Business Review*, May–June 1990.

Rad, Gerhard von. *Genesis: A Commentary*. Philadelphia: Westminster, 1972.

Ries, Eric. *The Lean Start-Up: How Today's Entrepreneurs Use Continuous Innovation to Create Radically Successful Businesses*. New York: Crown, 2011.

Rittel, H. W. J., and M. M. Webber. "Dilemmas in a General Theory of Planning." *Policy Sciences*, June 1973.

Rohr, Richard. *Falling Upward: A Spirituality for the Two Halves of Life*. San Francisco: Jossey-Bass, 2011.

Rubenfire, Adam. "CEO's Partly Sunny Economic Outlook." *Wall Street Journal*, July 23, 2014.

Scharmer, C. Otto. *Theory U: Leading from the Future as It Emerges*. San Francisco: Berrett-Koehler, 2009.

Schumpeter, Joseph. *Capitalism, Socialism and Democracy*. New York: Harper, 1942.

Scheff, Thomas J. *Catharsis in Healing, Ritual, and Drama*. Berkeley: University of California Press, 1979.

Schein, Edgar H. "Anxiety of Learning: An Interview with Edgar H. Schein." *Harvard Business Review*, March 2, 2002.

Schon, Donald A. *The Reflective Practitioner: How Professionals Think in Action*. New York: Basic, 1983.

Schwartz, Peter. *The Art of the Long View: Paths to Strategic Insight for Yourself and Your Company*. New York: Doubleday, 1991.

Selman, M. J. "The Kingdom of God in the Old Testament." *Tyndale Bulletin* 40 (1989) 161–83.

Senge, Peter, et al. *Presence: Exploring Profound Change in People, Organizations, and Society*. New York: Random House, 2004.

Skidelsky, Robert, and Edward Skidelsky. *How Much Is Enough: Money and the Good Life*. New York: Other, 2012.

Smith, Adam. *The Glasgow Edition of the Works and Correspondence of Adam Smith*. Edited by R. H. Cambell and A. S. Skinner. Oxford: Clarendon, 1976.

———. *The Theory of Moral Sentiments*. New York: Penguin, 2009. First published 1759.

———. *The Wealth of Nations*. New York: Modern Library, 2000. First published 1776.

Solomon, Andrew. Interview by Terry Gross. "For Sandy Hook Killer's Father, Tragedy Outweighs Love for His Son." Fresh Air, National Public Radio, March 13, 2014.

———. "The Reckoning: The Father of the Sandy Hook Killer Searches for Answers." *New Yorker*, March 17, 2014.

Suzuki, Shunryu. *Zen Mind, Beginner's Mind*. Boston: Shambhala, 2006.

Taleb, Nassim. *The Black Swan: The Impact of the Highly Improbable*. New York: Random House, 2007.

Tanfani, Joseph, and Richard A. Serrano. "Families of Charleston 9 Forgive Shooting Suspect in Court." *Los Angeles Times*, June 19, 2015.

Taylor, Jill Bolte. *My Stroke of Insight: A Brain Scientist's Personal Journey*. New York: Viking, 2008. Material used as basis for TED Talk, February 2008.

335

Teece, David. "Explicating Dynamic Capabilities: The Nature and Microfoundations of (Sustainable) Enterprise Performance." *Strategic Management Journal* 28 (2007) 1319–50.

Teece, David J., et al. "Dynamic Capabilities and Strategic Management." *Strategic Management Journal* 18 (1997) 509–33.

Tillich, Paul. *Systematic Theology.* Vol. 1. Chicago: University of Chicago Press, 1971.

Turkle, Sherry. *Alone Together: Why We Expect More from Technology and Less from Each Other.* New York: Basic, 2011.

———. *Reclaiming Conversations: The Power of Talk in a Digital Age.* New York: Penguin, 2015.

Utterback, James M. *Mastering the Dynamics of Innovation: How Companies Can Seize Opportunities in the Face of Technological Change.* Boston: Harvard Business School Press, 1994.

Vincent, Lanny. "Innovation Midwives: Sustaining Innovation Streams in Established Companies." *Research-Technology Management*, January–February 2005.

———. *Prisoners of Hope: How Engineers and Others Get Lift for Innovating.* Indianapolis: Westbow, 2011.

Warren, Rick. *The Purpose Driven Life: What on Earth Am I Here For?* Grand Rapids: Zondervan, 2002.

Weick, Karl E. *Sensemaking in Organizations.* Thousand Oaks, CA: SAGE, 1995.

Wilson, Frank R. *The Hand: How Its Use Shapes the Brain, Language and Human Culture.* New York: Vintage, 1999.

Wink, Walter. *The Human Being: Jesus and the Enigma of the Son of the Man.* Minneapolis: Fortress, 2002.

Wladawsky-Berger, Irving. "Some Advice on How to Jump Start Entrepreneurship and Job Creation." *CIO Journal / Wall Street Journal*, November 7, 2014.

World Council of Churches. "The Nature and Mission of the Church: A Stage on the Way to a Common Statement" (2005). Faith and Order Paper 198.

Yeats, W. B. "The Second Coming." In *The Norton Anthology of Modern Poetry*, edited by Richard Ellmann and Robert O'Clair. New York: Norton, 1973.

Zeleny, M. "Management Support Systems: Towards Integrated Knowledge Management." *Human Systems Management* 7 (1987) 59–70.

Subject Index

aligning ourselves with, 269
anxiety about identity put to rest,
248
in business for keeps, 259
carrying no liability, 258
church as not, 283
as collective working toward a
shared purpose, 256
connecting dots in, 175
conversations involving tangible
and intangible assets of, 320
current projects no longer just our
projects, 169
doing for us what we cannot do for
ourselves, 139
every company aligning with, 257
framing the hierarchy with and by
the purposes of God, 162
having no exit strategy, 255–76
helping close the gaps between
heaven and earth, 276
innovating in, 25, 27, 146
innovations improving the
probability of success, 54
invitation to innovate in and with,
145
inviting to voluntarily join, 208
as "line," 284
making acquisitions of other
companies, 271–72
making sense in, 158–59
making sense without, 154
metrics of, 21
not limited to its two unique assets,
306
ongoing and larger narrative of,
159
"operating" in, through and among
worldly companies, 256
providing an identity, 168–69
purpose of, 288–89
reflecting the freedom of God, 271
relevance for innovation theology,
269–75
responding to change and
innovating, 275
as a surrogate for the kingdom of
God on earth, 130, 256–61

willingness to recombine and
reconfigure assets in, 304–5
compass, Scripture as, 318
competence, 238, 238n31, 239, 242
competition, infecting the dominant
imagination, 110
complex systems, coincidences in, 206
compliance, shaping the presence and
posture of the invited, 136
complicated change contexts, 83
computer, characterizing how we
make-sense, 160
Comte, Auguste, 100
"Concept of 'Ba'" (Nonaka and
Konno), 295n47
conceptual boundary, forming for
God, 72
conditions, imposing on Nature, 207
conflicts
of interest, 117, 140
in process of finding form and
substance, 122
Confucius, 170
congregations, creating "breathing
space," 294
connecting the dots, 69, 167, 175,
182–84
connections
crossing boundaries, 188–89
enabled by metaphors, 211
between innovation and theology,
67–69
shaping the character of the sense
we make, 212
strength of, 183
connective tissue, healing of, 106
connectivity, 181
Connolly, John, 152
connotations, of "value" in English,
176–77
conscience, 200, 203
consequences
if innovation has nothing to do
with God, 53
for those who decline an invitation,
145
conservation mind-set, 125
considered response, 133

343

Scripture Index

OLD TESTAMENT